365 Meditations
for Mothers
by Mothers

365 Meditations for Mothers by Mothers

Sally D. Sharpe, Editor

Hilda Davis-Carroll, LeNoir H. Culbertson,
Clare Golson Doyle, Mary Ritzman Ebinger,
Leanne Ciampa Hadley, Rebecca Laird,
Laura Leigh Parker, Sheron C. Patterson,
Lillian C. Smith, Stephanie Thompson,
Kathleen F. Turner, Ginny Underwood

DIMENSIONS
FOR LIVING
NASHVILLE

This book is printed on recycled, acid-free, elemental-chlorine–free paper.

Library of Congress Catloging-in-Publication Data

365 meditations for mothers by mothers / Sally D. Sharpe, editor; writers, Hilda Davis-Carroll ... [et al.].
    p. cm.
    ISBN 978-0-687-49255-8 (pbk. : alk. paper)
    1. Mothers—Prayers and devotions—English.   2. Christian women—Prayers and devotions—English.   3. Devotional calendars.   I. Sharpe, Sally D., 1964-   I. Davis-Carroll, Hilda.   III. Title: Three hundrd sixty-five meditations for mothers by mothers.
    BV4529.18.A165 2007
    242'.6431—dc22

2007012772

Contents

Introduction

A Mother's Love

Mother's Day was fast approaching, and this would be my first year to celebrate the holiday as a bona fide honoree. Six months earlier I had become a mother for the very first time, and Mother's Day would never be the same again. Still, as wonderful as it would be to officially be initiated into the ranks of mothers everywhere, my thoughts were fixed on my own mother. You see, since the birth of my daughter, an incredible realization had flooded my mind and heart, and Mother's Day was the perfect time to share my revelation.

I called the florist and ordered a special arrangement to be delivered to Mom's doorstep. We lived several hours apart, and I would not be able to deliver the gift in person. It was just as well, because I didn't want anything to detract from the message itself. When the kind lady on the other end of the phone asked how the card should read, I dictated these words: "Now I know how much you love me."

I had always known that my mother loved me very much. She had "told" me so in a thousand different ways. Yet only after experiencing a mother's love in my own heart could I begin to comprehend the depth of my mother's love for me.

Helen Steiner Rice expresses the incomprehensible nature and beautiful mystery of a mother's love in her poem "A Mother's Love." She concludes that a mother's love is "another wondrous evidence of God's tender guiding hand."

A mother's love *is* evidence of God's hand. In fact, you might say that God's "fingerprints" are all over our hearts. After all, it is God who gives us this capacity to love our children—whether or not they are ours by birth—with such tenderness, devotion, and ... well ... *fierceness.* And as we love them according to our God-given design, it is God who whispers to us, "Now you know how much I love you ... *yet so much more.*"

Oh, how we need to hear God's whispers! We mothers—who tend to give and give and give until we're running on empty—need to know that we're loved more deeply than we can imagine. We need to be reminded that God is crazy about us—no matter what. Yet the endless demands and distractions of a mother's busy life—both pleasant and unpleasant—threaten to dull our spiritual ears.

Twelve Christian writers who know firsthand the joys and the pains that come with a mother's love have come together in this book to help you listen day by day for God's whispers of love and encouragement. Though they write in a variety of styles and draw from a multitude of experiences, they have a common purpose: to remind you that you are deeply and unconditionally loved, and that it is God who will replenish your mother's love and equip you to be the mother you were created to be.

Whether you are a biological mother, an adoptive mother, a stepmother, or a foster mother; whether you have one child or several; whether your children are learning to crawl or are about to fly from the nest—you will find that these devotions "ring true" because they are written by other Christian mothers who have experienced some of the common joys and challenges of motherhood. Whatever the ages or stages of your children, you will find practical and biblical encouragement and guidance for the daily tasks of mothering.

I invite you to begin using the book at any time of the year, making your way through the months until you've completed a year's cycle. It is my hope that, in the process, your spirit will be renewed and your batteries recharged as you learn to listen for the whispers of God's love.

Sally D. Sharpe, Editor

About the Writers

Hilda Davis-Carroll (JULY) is Director of the Faith-based Health Initiative for the Tennessee Department of Health. This job allows her to bring together her passion for teaching about wholeness and her love for the faith community. She is married to Dr. Kevin Carroll, Head of the Department of Music at Paine College. She has a daughter, Erin Ashley Grimes, whose growing into adulthood motivates her meditations.

LeNoir H. Culbertson (FEBRUARY) lives in Clarksville, Tennessee, where she serves as Senior Pastor of Madison Street United Methodist Church. Her husband, Barry, has served as a chaplain at Vanderbilt University Medical Center for the past twenty-five years. They are parents of two college-aged sons.

Clare Golson Doyle (NOVEMBER) lives in Shelbyville, Tennessee, where her husband, Lloyd, is pastor of First United Methodist Church. Clare is a full-time mother to Elizabeth, age thirteen, and Allen, age ten, and a freelance writer. She is a soccer mom, a band booster, and a regular volunteer in church activities for children and youth. In addition to contributing to *365 Meditations for Teens* and, with her husband, *365 Meditations for Couples,* she also has written Sunday school curriculum for various age levels.

Mary Ritzman Ebinger (AUGUST) has three children and three grandchildren. She is a certified counselor and enjoys leading marriage enrichment retreats with her husband based on their book *Do-It-Yourself Marriage Enrichment.* Together they have contributed to *365 Meditations for Couples* and *365 Meditations for Families.* Through the years she has been actively involved in both foreign and domestic missions work. She lives in Gaithersburg, Maryland.

Leanne Ciampa Hadley (DECEMBER) is an elder in The United Methodist Church and has spent the past twenty-five years specializing in the spiritual lives of children. She is the founder and president of First Steps Spirituality Center, dedicated to providing spiritual support to hurting children and teens at no cost, located in Colorado Springs. She lives with her husband and two teenage sons and enjoys hiking in the mountains and growing flowers.

Rebecca Laird (MARCH) is the mother of two teenage daughters. She currently serves as Associate Pastor for Spiritual Development at the Central Presbyterian Church of Summit, New Jersey. The author of several books and hundreds of articles, she most recently coedited *Spiritual Direction: Wisdom for the Long Walk of Faith* by Henri Nouwen.

Laura Leigh Parker (APRIL) is the wife of Richard and the mother of David, Matthew, Mark, and Daniel. She has a background in elementary education and now homeschools her three oldest children. She loves her church where she teaches fifth-grade Sunday school. Bible study, gardening, reading, and having tea with friends are some of her joys.

Sheron C. Patterson (JANUARY) is a wife and mother of two teenage sons. Over the past twenty years she has served as Senior Pastor of numerous churches in Dallas, Texas. Additionally, Sheron is the author of numerous books on healthy relationships, the cohost of a nationally syndicated radio program, and a relationships expert for local and national television.

Lillian C. Smith (JUNE) is a wife and mother of two young sons. Currently serving as Director of Connectional Ministries, Eastern Pennsylvania Conference of The United Methodist Church, she formerly served as first Associate General Secretary, Division on Ministries with Young People, General Board of Discipleship. In addition to contributing to *365 Meditations for Women by Women*, she has written Sunday school curriculum for youth. She lives in Pennsylvania with her family.

Stephanie Thompson (OCTOBER) currently serves as coordinator and pastoral counselor for a faith-based HIV/AIDS prevention and care organization in Nashville, Tennessee. She has more than sixteen years of experience serving as a social worker and supervisor, substance abuse counselor, and group developer/facilitator. She founded Sharing Our Strength and SEASONED Women, which are groups designed to address the psycho-spiritual needs of women in recovery from various addictions. She also served as codeveloper of the eight-week women's health and HIV prevention education curriculum SACRED Women. Stephanie has three daughters and four grandchildren.

Kathleen F. Turner (SEPTEMBER) is a writer whose articles have appeared in such periodicals as *Guideposts*, *The Upper Room*, and *Virtue* magazine. She is also a contributor to *365 Meditations for Mothers of Young Children* and *365 Daily Meditations for Women*. Kathy works as an administrative assistant and is an active member of Toastmasters. She and her husband, Darrell, have led a couple-to-couple Bible study at their church. They have two daughters and make their home in Fort Wayne, Indiana.

Ginny Underwood (MAY) is executive director of programs and strategic initiatives for United Methodist Communications. Her work focuses on telling multimedia stories about people making a difference, highlighting social justice issues confronting our culture and giving voice to those who are often unheard. She is married to John Underwood. They are the parents of Avery and Alyssa, the source of many of her meditations. She is also a member of the Comanche tribe of Oklahoma.

January

Bumps in the Road

SHERON C. PATTERSON

JANUARY 1   EXPECT BUMPS IN THE ROAD

We are afflicted in every way, but not crushed.
(2 Corinthians 4:8 NRSV)

Being a mom is a blessing that we cherish every day, yet in the midst of it all there are trials and tribulations—some minor and some major. I call them bumps in the road. We encounter them with our children, our spouse, our friends, or even ourselves. Sometimes upon impact the bumps seem insurmountable. There is pain and confusion. I believe that such hard times come to make us strong and to help us rely on the power of God.

The best way to approach bumps in the road is to expect them and, more important, expect to get over them. Remembering how God helped me over previous bumps serves as my fuel for the next one. The encouraging words of Paul also embolden me to press on.

This month I will share some of the bumps in my road. They are real and candid. I pray that they touch your situation and equip you to effectively handle the problems along your pathway, too.

Dear God, I can truly say thank you for my trials; they have brought me closer to you. It is amazing what we have accomplished together. Amen.

JANUARY 2   A VALUABLE INHERITANCE

I am reminded of your sincere faith, a faith that dwelt first in your grandmother Lois and your mother Eunice and now, I am sure, dwells in you.   *(2 Timothy 1:5 RSV)*

Writing your last will and testament can seem morbid, but it brings the important issues to the surface. As my husband and I discussed our wills, our thoughts turned to our sons and what we wanted to leave for them. We listed tangible items such as possessions and monetary amounts. These are needed for daily survival.

Then we reflected on spiritually important items such as faith in God and belief in God's Word. These are intangible spiritual inheritances. The New Testament writer Paul glowingly described the spiritual inheritance of his young apprentice, Timothy. Thanks to Timothy's mother and grandmother, Lois and Eunice, he became a great leader in the church.

As moms, we owe our children a spiritual inheritance. It does not necessarily have to come after we are gone. Every day we have the opportunity to pass on the Christian faith by our actions.

Dear God, allow my life to be a living lesson on faith to daily help my children grow closer to you. Show up in me and shine brightly for them. Amen.

JANUARY 3   WHAT'S FOR DINNER?

"Look at the birds of the air; they neither sow nor reap nor gather into barns, and yet your heavenly Father feeds them."
(Matthew 6:26 NRSV)

The demands of putting dinner on the table every evening are monumental to me. There do not seem to be enough hours in a day to complete the items on my list. Between working, driving the kids to and from school, squeezing in exercise class, and running errands, food preparation is my least favorite chore. Yet like clockwork my family asks the ubiquitous question: "Hey, Mom, what's for dinner?" In response, I want to scream, because I don't have a clue. Other times I want to run away from all of the responsibility because I feel overwhelmed.

In the midst of this frenzy, God comforts me by turning my thoughts to the birds. They are busy with bird survival, and God helps them get it all done. They do not panic or worry. If we can just think and act like the birds, we can be victorious in so many areas of our lives.

Dear God, often I feel at my wits end, alone and overwhelmed. In these times, I need you to break into the chaos and calm me with your love and support. Amen.

JANUARY 4   PUPPY LOVE

Love is patient and kind; love is not jealous or boastful; it is not arrogant or rude. **(1 Corinthians 13:4 RSV)**

Puppy love is an exhilarating experience. You remember—it's the initial encounter with romance that comes with butterflies in the stomach and dreamy eyes. It is that fleeting, juvenile love that overtakes many young people.

Chris is in the midst of this, and I must confess, it is fun to watch. He went on his first date today. It was not really a date—he and his friend were dropped off at a nearby movie theater by their parents and brought back to separate homes afterward—but he was excited anyway. Even though this is nothing serious, I do want Chris to know of God's blueprint for love, which is a lasting type of love. Otherwise, he may be drawn into the false imitations of love presented in our society.

We moms have a responsibility to show our children what real love is all about by the way they see us interact with others.

Dear God, make me a loving mother whose actions teach my children what your love is all about. When I am not feeling very loving or loveable, rescue me from myself and fill me with your love. Amen.

JANUARY 5   BEING A GOOD FRIEND

A friend loves at all times.   **(Proverbs 17:17 NASB)**

An interesting after-school event occurred today. Robby's best friend, Brad, was looking dejected and lonely as he played video games alone in the den. Robby was nowhere to be found. He became bored with his buddy and abandoned him to take a nap. Robby did not understand the need to show himself friendly to his buddy even if he was tired or busy.

There is value in being a good friend to others. There is a link between how we treat others and how they treat us. The writer of Proverbs emphasized the importance of consistently and constantly treating those we are close to with love and care. These words cause me to take a look at the ways I treat my friends and strive always to be loving.

Dear God, I want to be a loving friend at all times, but I realize that I need your help to move my needs and wants out of the way. Focus me on being a blessing to others. Amen.

JANUARY 6   GRANDPARENTS LOVE THEM, TOO

Grandchildren are the crown of the aged. (Proverbs 17:6 NRSV)

This may not make sense, but sometimes I feel like my parents love my sons more than they love me. This is probably an irrational fear, but my folks seem to have more time, money, and laughter for the boys than they ever did for me. As I watch them relate to one another, I feel a pang of jealousy. The jealousy is a problem of the flesh. I need to understand that there is a spiritual bond between grandparents and grandchildren.

Proverbs teaches us that grandparents are truly delighted by their grandchildren. God provides this extra zest and zeal to help them celebrate. My resentment only attempts to block their blessings. It makes me wonder if I am missing other blessings because of self-centeredness. Ultimately, we must accept the fact that life is not always about us.

Dear God, replace my jealousy with joy and help me see your love in the generations of family members. You have created a world that intertwines the lives of us all for your good. Amen.

JANUARY 7   ENEMIES

"But I say to you, love your enemies, and pray for those who persecute you."   *(Matthew 5:44 NASB)*

Something about this kid at Robby's school sets his teeth on edge. This morning as I dropped him off at school, this kid got out of a car ahead of us, and the mere sight of him sent my son into a rage. He began to mutter angry words and clench his fist. "What could this boy have done to provoke such rage?" I asked. "Nothing, Mom," was his brief answer as he exited the car.

A means of soothing this rage comes from the words of Christ. He had his share of enemies, too. Jesus' response was to pray for them and to love them. Robby's rage and reluctance reminded me of my need to handle my enemies with Christ, too. The negative emotions never solve the problem. We all have enemies, and Jesus is always the best response to them.

Dear God, you are the solution to our enemy problem. Please provide the power to turn to you and not on them in crisis times. Amen.

JANUARY 8   WHAT DID YOU SAY?

He who keeps his mouth and his tongue keeps himself out of trouble.   *(Proverbs 21:23 RSV)*

Middle-school basketball is competitive and aggressive. On the court, a player from the opposing team was guarding Chris and called him a hurtful name. My son had two choices: be the thing he was called and retaliate, or embrace who God made him and keep quiet. Chris kept quiet and kept on playing. If he had retaliated, he would have risked being ejected from the game. This is true in life also. Our opponents realize that sometimes the only way to slow us down is to get us put out of the game. And we can hasten this by losing control over our mouths.

Words have weight because they are sometimes used as weapons. That's why the writer of Proverbs tells us that our tongues need to be monitored. We would experience less turmoil in our world if we truly kept or controlled our mouths.

Dear God, help me control what I say. My tongue needs divine guidance. In your name and in your power I can watch my words. Amen.

JANUARY 9   TALKING BACK

A soft answer turns away wrath, but a harsh word stirs up anger. *(Proverbs 15:1 NRSV)*

After I reminded him twice about his chores, Chris responded with a sassy comment and an aggressive tone of voice. "My favorite television show is on right now," he snarled. That was talking back, which is a no-no in our home. Talking back occurs when a child does not accept what an adult tells him or her to do. Talking back is disrespectful of authority and attempts to put the child and the adult on the same level. After correcting him, I admitted to myself that I am guilty of talking back, too. I often talk back to God when God gives direction to my life that interferes with my plans. There was that hot day when I didn't want to visit the sick with Communion. God was clear, but I responded poorly. Like Chris, something else appealed to me. My talking back was disrespectful of God, and in my own childlike way, I attempted to put myself on the same level with God.

Dear God, when you speak in my life, give me an obedient spirit that responds with readiness and joy. Amen.

JANUARY 10   A FAILING GRADE

I can do all things through Christ who strengthens me.
                                      (Philippians 4:13 NKJV)

Failing at anything is disheartening because it makes us doubt ourselves. Math has always been a failing subject for me, and so it is for
Chris, too. Though he tried mightily, he still failed math this semes-
ter—even with a tutor. What a blow it was to his self-esteem to try
so hard and still not pass the class. As I watched him mope around
the house for days, I thought about an antidote for his predicament.
When we fail in life, we can still find success in Jesus Christ. Paul's
words to us in Philippians speak to anyone who has tasted defeat
and seen no way up. It is not about us, but it is all about Jesus.
When we doubt our own ability, confidence in Christ enables us to
get back up and try again. Jesus is our greatest pick-me-up.

Dear God, when failure invades my world, remind me of your abil-
ity to transcend it. If I keep my eyes on you, I will overcome. Amen.

JANUARY 11   PROPERLY DRESSED

"But when the king came in to see the guests, he noticed a man
there who was not wearing a wedding robe, and he said to him,
'Friend, how did you get in here without a wedding robe?'"
                                      (Matthew 22:11 NRSV)

Who would have believed that the household would be up in
arms over a tuxedo? A tuxedo was the required attire for a fancy
party to which Chris was invited. The problem was that Chris
insisted on wearing sneakers and jeans instead. "Oh, Mom,
nobody really has to dress up for this," he explained. Yet a conversation with the host mom indicated that she envisioned a room
full of dressed-up kids at her daughter's birthday event. We gave
Chris an ultimatum: either wear the tuxedo or forfeit the party. To
him, the matter of what he wore was minor; but the scriptures
offer us a compelling reason to dress appropriately. The tuxedo
battle reminds us of something we learned back in kindergarten:

follow the instructions given, even if they seem minor to us. As moms, we must ensure that we do not override or undervalue another's rules just because they are not our rules.

Dear God, help me see beyond my own priorities and respect those of another. Give me the ability to submit myself to others' rules with a cooperative spirit. Amen.

JANUARY 12   RELUCTANT USHERS

For a day in thy courts is better than a thousand [outside]. I had rather be a doorkeeper in the house of my God, than to dwell in the tents of wickedness. **(Psalm 84:10 KJV)**

The sight of Robby and Chris ushering side by side at church today filled me with joy. It was their first Sunday serving as youth ushers. Their starched, white shirts, navy ties and slacks, and white gloves gave them a crisp, professional appearance. Even though they smiled and eagerly led worshipers to their seats, my sons had dreaded this assignment all week long. They thought it would be an awful experience. Ignorance made them drag their feet. When they took their posts across the sanctuary, however, something took them over. They smiled, threw their shoulders back, and seemed proud to be there. I believe they experienced the joy of God's presence. This is what the psalmist wrote about. God's presence transforms us and gives us an inner peace. As moms, we must be ever mindful of the joy of God's presence and let it saturate us. It is powerful enough to transform us and alleviate our negative situations.

Dear God, thank you for drenching us with your power just when we need it. We confess that we don't always know when we need it, but you are always right on time. Amen.

JANUARY 13   A MESSAGE IN THE MUSIC

And whenever the evil spirit from God came upon Saul, David took the lyre and played it with his hand, and Saul would be relieved and feel better, and the evil spirit would depart from him. *(1 Samuel 16:23 NRSV)*

Music selections can cause conflict. Young people usually prefer something contemporary that speaks to their experiences. Parents often hold on to the music of their generation, making nostalgic selections. My sons and I do not always agree on what they should listen to. The high-tech gadgetry that they own makes it possible to transfer music from the Internet to their listening devices easily and often. They sometimes escape my censoring ears. What I want them to understand most of all is that the music we listen to programs our minds. Negative words create negative thoughts, just as positive words create positive thoughts. This is illustrated in today's passage as David's positive harp playing chased away Saul's evil thoughts. It is vital that we keep positive, uplifting music in our midst to ensure that our thoughts are God's thoughts. God can speak to us through music; we must be open and willing to hear.

Dear God, help me hear you in all situations, especially music. You have the ability to calm my storms and end my trials. Amen.

JANUARY 14   GIVE WHAT YOU CAN

He said, "Truly I tell you, this poor widow has put in more than all of them; for all of them have contributed out of their abundance, but she out of her poverty has put in all she had to live on." *(Luke 21:3-4 NRSV)*

When the collection plate came by our pew, Robby crumpled up his three one-dollar bills and quickly threw them in the plate. "I don't want people to see what I am giving in case they do not think it is enough," he explained. His fear reminded me of the story of the poor widow. She had very little to give, but she gave it with no shame. The rich in her midst put on a show as they gave, but she quietly placed her humble gift in the offering. To the amazement of many, Jesus was most pleased with her small offering because it was a sacrifice.

Sometimes we may feel that we do not give enough, especially if we measure ourselves by others' standards. The good news is that God does not use such a measurement. Our sacrifice is what matters most. Our goal is to sacrifice more and worry less about what others think.

Dear God, please remove the shame I may feel about my giving. Help me focus more on pleasing you, rather than on winning the praise of others. Amen.

JANUARY 15   THE COST OF THE DREAM

They said to one another, "Here comes this dreamer. Come now, let us kill him ... and we shall see what will become of his dreams."   *(Genesis 37:19-20 NRSV)*

On this day, many pause to pay honor to Dr. Martin Luther King, Jr., who dreamed of world peace and freedom for all. The moving tributes on television and radio inspire us all to be of service to the world. I am using this day as a teaching moment on self-sacrifice for my boys. I want them to dare to dream of a better world and what they can do to make this world happen. However, a fact that cannot be overlooked is the price that is exacted from those who dream. This passage on Joseph reminds us that challenging the wrongs of the world is costly. Joseph's brothers envied his dreams and planned his demise. There will always be dream haters. They will hate mine and they will hate yours; but we must never be slowed by their hatred. In spite of the inevitable jealousy, we should all take the risks for the Kingdom.

Dear God, inspire me with your greatness, like those who have gone before. Shelter me from those who would destroy the dreams you have planted in my spirit. Amen.

JANUARY 16   STANDING MY GROUND FOR MY
                                              CHILD'S SAKE

But a woman whose little daughter had an unclean spirit immediately heard about him, and she came and bowed down at his feet.   *(Mark 7:25 NRSV)*

Mothers can summon superhuman strength when their children are in peril. My son was in a difficult situation that required parental leverage. I had to be firm with an administrator at his school. Had I not stepped in, Robby's case would not have been treated fairly. My ability to stand firm reminded me of the mother found in Mark 7. The urgency of this mother's movements always grabs me. She had a sick child and knew that there was only one way to get her healed—through Jesus.

Jesus, in an uncharacteristic stance, initially rebuffed her, and it's painful to read this. Yet the mother somehow summoned the courage to stand her ground and request help again. The second time, she received her request and her daughter was healed. We, too, should recall her tenacity when we need to stand up to daunting situations. When tough times arise, we can be tough because God gives us the strength.

Dear Lord, thank you for your spirit of tenacity. When I need it to stand firm, stand up in me and help me win. Amen.

JANUARY 17   HIDDEN STAINS FOUND

"Nothing is covered up that will not be uncovered, and nothing secret that will not become known."   *(Luke 12:2 NRSV)*

We have rules in the home about no-food and no-beverage zones. Since my sons are prone to spilling their brightly colored beverages and dropping their snack food on the carpet, they are restricted to eating only at the kitchen table. It is not only a cleanliness issue, but also a financial one. Carpet cleaning is costly. One day I discovered several large stains on the den carpet that looked like spills from one of their beverages. These stains were conveniently covered by the easy chair. They thought that by moving the chair over a bit, their spills would be hidden. They were reprimanded and banned again from eating in the den.

In a similar sense, we believe we can hide our missteps from God. Yet God sees all and knows all. Like my boys, we try and rearrange our lives to cover up what we are doing, hoping that we can disguise our actions. We must understand that nothing we do can be hidden from God, and we should strive to live accordingly.

Dear God, keep me mindful that you know all and you see all, and that we should live our lives under your watchful gaze. Amen.

JANUARY 18   BLESSED TO BE A BLESSING

"From everyone who has been given much shall much be required."
                                             (Luke 12:48 NASB)

We require our sons to participate in the church's homeless ministry because they are blessed and otherwise would squander their blessings to ignore the needs of others. They consider it a burden to serve meals to the homeless and sing hymns during the Saturday morning services. "Why do we have to work with the homeless ministry so much?" they often whine. "I don't like how they make me feel. It's sad to go to those events," they say.

My sons are there because they have been given much and the Lord requires that they give much. Their home, clothing, and regular meals make them accountable to those who live without. It is all too easy to sit back and get comfortable with the blessings we have, assuming we have them just to make our lives better. Blessings are our responsibility. God holds us accountable for all that we have. We must be constantly mindful that God does not bless us for nothing.

Dear God, thank you for all the blessings in my life. I realize that they all come from you, and that, in return, I must help others. Do not let me become complacent in my blessings. Amen.

JANUARY 19   DON'T BE ASHAMED

"You are the light of the world. A city built on a hill cannot be hid.... Let your light shine before others, so that they may see your good works and give glory to your Father in heaven."
(Matthew 5:14-16 NRSV)

My boys tend to be shy in public. They clam up in church settings. Our youth pastor noticed this during youth Bible study. He could tell that the boys knew the answers to his questions but would not raise their hands. My sons had to realize that being silent with information about Jesus is like hiding a light under a bushel.

In this text from Matthew, Jesus wants us to know that we are not lights for our own sake, but for the sake of the Kingdom. We are not to hide or deny our light. We deny what God is doing in our lives when we don't give voice to God's action. When we speak up, we give courage to others who may be living in the darkness.

We moms also sometimes forget the importance of being a light, even if we are in the hair salon, the soccer field, or the corporate boardroom. We are to shine.

Dear God, I have a light, and it comes from you. You have given me this light to chase the darkness in my world. Remove my shyness and help me shine for you. Amen.

JANUARY 20   WHAT TIME IS IT?

"And who knows whether you have not attained royalty for such a time as this?"   *(Esther 4:14 NASB)*

Sometimes I struggle with balancing time for motherhood and time for self. Motherhood can feel like never-ending self-sacrifice. I yearn for a modicum of self-indulgence such as a long bubble bath or a solitary walk in the park. Balancing means getting both done, perhaps at different times.

I wonder if that's how Esther felt. She was living the carefree life in the palace, and her uncle Mordecai reminded her of her responsibility to her people. He pointedly says that she had been given much in order to make a difference in the world. Mordecai is also talking to us because we have been given much as mothers.

There will be times in our lives when we must put self to the side and be somebody else's blessing. Living attuned to the voice of God will clue us to such times as those. With God, it is possible to take care of self and take care of others because God provides for all.

Dear God, I thank you for what you have given me and bless your name as I use my blessings for your glory. Amen.

JANUARY 21   ON FIRE FOR GOD

"So because you are lukewarm, and neither hot nor cold, I will spit you out of My mouth."   *(Revelation 3:16 NASB)*

Lukewarm, lackadaisical, and nonchalant best describe Robby's attitude regarding most things. His favorite response is, "Whatever," which unnerves me to no end. I'd like him to be excited and happy about something, because God has been good to him.

I thought I was the only one bothered by the "whatever" attitude until I read this Revelation passage where God gets riled by a lukewarm response. Clearly God is not a "whatever" type of God. Lukewarm Christians make God so angry that he declares they will be spit out of his mouth.

What does God want? God wants excited, on-fire believers who are happy and joyful, not necessarily because life is constantly thrilling, but because God has been constantly good. We must be on guard against coolness toward the goodness of God. Who knows, our joy could change someone else's day. We are too blessed to be blasé.

Dear God, give me a Jesus joy that cannot be quenched by today's challenges. You are good all the time. Amen.

JANUARY 22   THE PAIN OF DEATH

For we know that if the earthly tent which is our house is torn down, we have a building from God, a house not made with hands, eternal in the heavens.   *(2 Corinthians 5:1 NASB)*

Transitioning from life to death is an expected part of the Christian journey. Yet when the mother of one of Robby's classmates suddenly died, it did not matter that death is expected. It still hurt. My son was understandably swept up in the sorrow that engulfed his friend. As a teen with little experience with the death of family members, Robby had few tools to help make sense of this tragedy. I needed to help him help his friend.

The eloquence of Paul makes such a difference. His words tell us that death is not the end, whether it comes without a warning or with a lengthy illness that gives us ample time to prepare. The assurance in this scripture can soften the blow that our departed loved ones have gone not to a nameless place, but to a better place. As moms, we can take comfort in knowing that the scriptures will lead us to answers for life's challenges.

Dear God, death's pain leaves us limp and racked with despair. Thank you for your words of comfort and direction. Amen.

JANUARY 23   DISCIPLINE DILEMMA

Fathers, do not provoke your children to anger; but bring them up in the discipline and instruction of the Lord.   *(Ephesians 6:4 NASB)*

Was Robert too harsh? I wondered one day when he reprimanded the boys. On the one hand, they need firmness and a no-nonsense demeanor. On the other hand, they need hugs and encouragement, too. Mothers and fathers parent differently, usually because of gender differences. The former tend to be nurturing and the latter sometimes can be stern. According to the scriptures, children need discipline and direction.

In this instance, I am prayerful that our sons will accept their father's guidance with willing spirits. In a similar sense, God functions the same way with us. God gives us discipline and instruction. It is our choice to receive it or reject it. As we respect God's right to serve as our heavenly parent, we become better parents.

Dear God, if it were not for your parental oversight in my life, where would I be? You have kept me safe from dangers seen and unseen. Thank you. Amen.

JANUARY 24   INTERRUPTED PLANS

They pressed into service a passerby coming from the country, Simon of Cyrene (the father of Alexander and Rufus), that he might bear His cross. **(Mark 15:21 NASB)**

My family can be rigid about sticking to their established plans. I want them to loosen up a bit and go with the flow because God has an interesting way of interrupting our plans with a greater plan.

That's what happened to Simon of Cyrene. He was on his way to an important destination when he paused to join the throng who watched Jesus struggle under the weight of his burdensome cross. Suddenly a Roman solider grabbed him and forced him to carry the cross for Jesus. It was a gritty and grimy job that offered him the chance to work beside greatness. Simon shows us that the importance of our destinations evaporates when the Lord has need of us. The work of the Kingdom supersedes anything else, whether we like it or not. We should always give God's agenda priority over ours.

Dear God, thank you for including me in your greater plans for the world. Help me be flexible and available when I am needed. Amen.

JANUARY 25   THANK YOU

And Jesus answered and said, "Were there not ten cleansed? But the nine—where are they? Were none found who turned back to give glory to God, except this foreigner?" **(Luke 17:17 NASB)**

Maybe I was too hasty today. While grocery shopping with Chris, we encountered a neighbor who complimented him. In an instant, I barked at him, "Say thank you." Manners mean a great deal to me, and I would have been horrified if he had accepted the compliment without responding with gratitude.

Chris's slowness to respond reminded me of the lepers who Jesus healed. They came to him for healing, and he readily gave it. Most of them went away with their healed lives and did not look back. Only one remembered to say thank you. I wonder, *Am I quick to thank God, or do I allow seconds, minutes, hours, and even days to go by before I say thank you?* I need to be as concerned with thanking God as I was with the neighbor in the store.

Dear God, instill in me an attitude of gratitude that never forgets where my blessings come from. Amen.

JANUARY 26   THE CAR ACCIDENT

"Do not fear, for I am with you; Do not anxiously look about you, for I am your God."   *(Isaiah 41:10 NASB)*

The phone call reporting that our sons were in an auto accident came one quiet evening. Robby had been driving for a year, and we readily trusted him to drive himself and Chris to Wednesday-night youth Bible study; yet two blocks from the church, a left-hand turn at a busy intersection went wrong. An oncoming car slammed into the left side of the car my sons were in, missing Chris on the passenger's side by only inches. As I talked to them on the phone, I felt alone and helpless. Bad news has a way of making us feel separated from others, though the reality is that we are not alone as long as we have Jesus. When I rushed to the accident site, I saw the boys surrounded by the youth directors and youth from the church. I was calmed and reminded that God is with us and we are never alone.

Dear God, when tragedy strikes and caves in our comfort, thank you for consistently showing up and showing out. Amen.

JANUARY 27   THE AUDACIOUS PRAYER

Now Jabez called on the God of Israel, saying, "Oh that Thou wouldst bless me indeed."   *(1 Chronicles 4:10 NASB)*

It takes guts to call on God for a blessing. Some would call it an audacity because you've got to believe deep down inside that you deserve to be blessed. That's how Jabez must have felt. Despite the fact that his name means *born in pain*, he still kept an upbeat attitude. If I am not careful, I will allow the challenges and disappointments of life to beat me down to the point that I can't lift my head and make such requests of God.

There is enthusiasm in Jabez's request, too. That means he was excited about what God would do. His was a leap-of-faith request that closes the chasm between doubt and possibility.

As moms, we constantly need God in our lives to help us meet the myriad of issues that confront us. The Lord welcomes an audacious cry for help; it is a sign that we love ourselves and that we love God.

Dear God, thank you for the ability to come to you with requests. You are the kind of God who loves us more than we could love ourselves. Amen.

JANUARY 28   FAST MONEY

The crown of the wise is their wisdom, but folly is the garland of fools.   *(Proverbs 14:24 NRSV)*

Robby went with the youth group on a weekend tour of colleges and universities. We had planned his budget in advance and had given him enough money for daily meals, along with a little extra for souvenirs. Yet, much to our surprise, we received an urgent phone call from him on the first night of the trip. "All of my money has been spent on a pair of shoes," he said. Obviously we were disappointed in his lack of planning and foresight, and reluctantly we made arrangements for him to receive enough to cover his legitimate expenses for the remainder of the trip.

Similarly, we sometimes squander what God has given us on the wrong things and wind up having to beg for what we need. We are probably a lot more like the fool in this text than we'd like to admit. He could not hold on to his resources either. The lesson that we all must learn is to delay gratification and be mindful of our budgets, knowing that all we have comes from God.

Dear God, keep me mindful that in addition to giving me resources, you give the ability to disperse them carefully. Amen.

JANUARY 29   EMPTY NEST

Trust in the Lord with all your heart, and do not lean on your own understanding.   (Proverbs 3:5 NASB)

I am lodged somewhere between joy and sorrow. Robby is a senior in high school and will be graduating in a few months. This is a bittersweet experience. Sure, graduation is months away, but it is coming, and he will relocate to Virginia to attend college. I should be proud of his educational accomplishments, but sorrow sneaks in. I admit the fact that our mother-son relationship will change forever. He is becoming an independent adult who will leave the nest. I know that I cannot handle this alone, that I need God.

Deep internal emotions like these shake us to the core. That's why the psalmist advised us to "trust in the Lord." Trusting means relying on God's greater power to solve our human situations. If we lean on God, there will be balance to provide equilibrium. The answer to some of our problems comes from letting God take control.

Dear God, I need your soothing power to keep me together. Confusing situations twist my emotions, and only you can straighten out my situation. Hear my pleas. Amen.

JANUARY 30   LET US PRAY

The earnest prayer of a righteous person has great power and wonderful results.   (James 5:16 NLT)

My husband's doctor just informed him that his heart is not functioning properly and he needs major surgery soon. It was hard enough for me to process the news. I was not in a hurry to tell the boys. In fact, I dragged my feet and delayed sharing his medical state for days. I thought they would become distraught, or that their schoolwork would suffer. After summoning all my strength, I gathered them and shared their father's medical condition with them. Much to my surprise, their response was not negative but spiritual. They said, "The best thing we can do for him right now is pray. May we pray, Mom?" Truly this was what James wrote about in this text. My sons showed me that they had options to handling bad news, and prayer is always the best one.

Dear God, in times of confusion, the ability to pray is a blessing. We can come to you with all our hurts, knowing that we are heard and that help is on the way. Amen.

JANUARY 31   STONES IN THE BAG

Then [David] took his staff in his hand, and chose five smooth stones from the wadi, and put them in his shepherd's bag, in the pouch; his sling was in his hand, and he drew near to the Philistine. **(1 Samuel 17:40 NRSV)**

We all have "giants" in our lives. How we handle them makes all the difference. We can run and cower, or we can stand firm and fight. My sons vacillate between male macho and little-boy shyness when it comes to their giants. It is interesting to watch them grow in this area. No matter where they are on the spectrum, I want them to realize that they have a secret weapon: God. Stones were not the only weapons that David had in his battle with the giant Philistine Goliath. He had an unshakable faith that God would deliver him from the giant and any other threats that came his way. For us, as moms, David's kind of faith will serve us well as we choose how to react to our giants.

Dear God, in the face of giants, thank you for your presence and your power. Remind me that in addition to stones in a bag, I have you. Amen.

February

Through a Child's Eyes

LENOIR H. CULBERTSON

FEBRUARY 1   CHILD OF GOD

"Fear not, for I have redeemed you; I have summoned you by name; you are mine." **(Isaiah 43:1 NIV)**

My son had his tonsils taken out today. It's a routine surgery. It would be, except that it is being done to *my* child. That changes everything!

This is part of the mystery of our faith: Somehow this is the way God sees each and every one of us. Regardless of our merit or our loveliness, regardless of our strengths or weaknesses, each and every one of us is God's child. And that changes everything!

As mothers, we tend to focus on our parental role. But we, too, are children. Remembering that we are precious children of God changes our perspective on life. It helps us see everyday experiences through a child's eyes—through eyes of faith. It reminds us that life is so much deeper and richer than our circumstances might lead us to believe. It assures us that we are unconditionally loved and accepted—no matter what.

This month may God help us see through a child's eyes— through eyes of faith.

Most Holy One, help me remember each and every day who I really am—your precious child. And help me see my world through a child's eyes of faith. Amen.

FEBRUARY 2   LIGHT

"I am the light of the world."   *(John 8:12 NIV)*

For most people, the date of February second immediately brings to mind images of groundhogs and shadows; but in one of the ancient liturgies of the church, February second was set aside for a different kind of observance. On this date, priests gathered for the "Candle Mass." This service lifted up words of blessing for all the candles, symbols of Christ as the Light of the world, which would be used in worship for the months ahead. February second—somewhat of a "liturgical black hole," wouldn't you say? By then, Christmas was a fading memory, and the joy and light of Easter were still months away. But when the days were short and the nights were long, when the most violent blasts of winter were howling, the church blessed the gift of light—signs of the promise that the Light of Christ would, indeed, overcome any and every darkness. "The Light has come into the world, and the darkness has *not* overcome it," declares the writer John, a declaration we so often need to hear again when the days are short and the nights are long and the fiercest blasts of winter are howling.

In every moment of darkness, may I be ready to welcome your light, O Christ. Amen.

FEBRUARY 3   ASSURANCE

"Teach these new disciples to obey all the commands I have given you. And be sure of this: I am with you always, even to the end of the age."   *(Matthew 28:20 NLT)*

Living in a parsonage next door to the church, my children grew up thinking the church was an extension of the house. One day my three-year-old marched from room to room in the church. When I asked what was going on, he announced, "This is *not* God's house. I've looked in every room, and I cannot find God's toothbrush anywhere."

I've been with people for whom life or circumstance has pushed them to declare, "God is not here!" I've wondered, *What were you looking for to confirm God's presence? Was it the lack of trouble or sadness, or the need for success or recognition?*

People often declare, "God is not here!" when they are experiencing great pain or disappointment; but if we talk with them in a spirit of compassion, usually the light begins to come on, faintly at first, illuminating the faithful presence of God in *all* times. Sometimes that presence comes in the embrace of a friend. Sometimes it's a surprise gift of calm and hope, but always it is a strengthening assurance: "You are not alone!"

Gracious God, make me a sign of your presence to someone who is hurting and sad. Amen.

FEBRUARY 4   ABUNDANCE

Now to him who by the power at work within us is able to accomplish abundantly far more than all we can ask or imagine, to him be glory in the church and in Christ Jesus to all generations.   (Ephesians 3:20-21 NRSV)

The bread had been freshly baked. The wonderful aroma filled the air as I served Communion that morning. As one little boy popped the bread into his mouth, his eyes widened and he said, "Wow! Can I have some more?" I couldn't help but think that God must be smiling. *Finally, someone understands the gift being offered!* I thought.

Paul talks about knowing the love of God that surpasses knowledge, which allows us to "be filled to the measure of all the fullness of God" (Ephesians 3:19 NIV). That is what God *wants* for us, but God is never pushy. Patiently, God waits for us to recognize our deepest hunger, to open our hands (and hearts), and, with an awareness of the fullness of grace, to say, "Wow! Can I have some more?"

Loving God, may my soul hunger and thirst for the bread of life and the living water you so graciously offer. Amen.

FEBRUARY 5   WAITING

"For this son of mine was dead and is alive again; he was lost and is found." So they began to celebrate. **(Luke 15:24 NIV)**

"Here, wrap this, please," my mother requested.

"What is it?" I asked.

"A shirt for your uncle," she replied.

"Is he going to be here for Christmas?"

"He might. I want something under the tree for him ... just in case he comes home."

I looked into my mother's face. There was no anger or reluctance—just a kind of longing and love.

My uncle struggled with alcoholism most of his adult life, and he would disappear from our family for years at a time; but *every* year there was a new, white shirt wrapped and placed under the tree—just in case.

When I remember my mother's face, I think I see a reflection of God there—that deep longing; that great love; that undying hope that maybe, just maybe, this will be the time the wayward child comes home. The gifts are waiting and ready—just in case. How many times has God been waiting for you and me?

Gracious, awesome God, thank you for eternal patience. Thank you for waiting for us, for welcoming us, and for restoring us to your family. Amen.

FEBRUARY 6   POOR IN SPIRIT

"Blessed are the poor in spirit, for theirs is the kingdom of heaven." **(Matthew 5:3 NIV)**

"Blessed are the poor in spirit." What is blessed about poverty? I grew up in rural East Tennessee, and I had occasion to see poverty firsthand. It was often hollow-cheeked, empty-eyed, and dirty.

But Jesus said "poor *in spirit*." What is poverty of the spirit? Is it not having God, or is it something altogether different? I think Jesus was talking about someone who has a profound trust in the economy of God, which is an economy of abundance. The chief commodity in God's economy is grace. Those who are "poor in spirit" give grace away like there's no tomorrow, for they have great trust in the empowering abundance of that grace. They freely let it go because they know the empty space will be filled by more grace. They are like a burning bush that is never consumed because they never burn themselves out; they are fueled by another resource of grace that allows the fruit of the Spirit to grow and flourish.

I want to have this kind of fruitful life, to be poor in spirit. Then perhaps my children and others will see that the kingdom of heaven is mine, and through me they will get a peek!

God, teach me to be poor in spirit so that my life may be fruitful. Amen.

FEBRUARY 7   COLORS

O LORD, our Lord, how majestic is your name in all the earth! You have set your glory above the heavens.   **(Psalm 8:1 NIV)**

I had an unexpected trip to the beach this week. I always love going. Having grown up in the mountains of East Tennessee, I find the beach such a contrast. And today was so splendid. The sky was clear, and as I sat there looking across the water, I counted thirteen shades of color between the horizon and the sand. It started off with pale lavender, then shades of purple, turquoise, blue, green, and white. When I color a picture, I paint the water blue. Maybe I'll add a few hints of a different shade, but *thirteen* colors? Isn't that just like the extravagance of God! God doesn't only give us blue but lavishes upon us the colors of robins' eggs, delphinium, jasper, sky, cornflower, periwinkle, navy, midnight, denim, steel, aquamarine, teal, and . . .

When the doldrums of daily life threaten to make us ordinary blue, may God's extravagant colors fill us with praise!

Thank you, most glorious God, that your grace is not only amazing but also extravagant! Amen.

FEBRUARY 8   PAY ATTENTION

Be diligent in these matters; give yourself wholly to them, so that everyone may see your progress. Watch your life and doctrine closely. Persevere in them.   *(1 Timothy 4:15-16 NIV)*

I've worn contact lenses for many years, and I have developed a routine for preparing the lenses. I wash them thoroughly with cleanser and rinse them under running water; then I apply conditioning solution and pop them in. But one day I put the first lens in my eye without rinsing it in the cleaning solution. Ouch! I had to quickly remove the lens and flush it with water over and over again.

Maybe I got distracted or was in too much of a hurry. Regardless, this experience reminded me that I am never past making blunders—even in those areas of my life that I consider "set." I must always pay attention, or I might blunder into a painful situation.

Good habits are helpful, but I still must review and evaluate what I'm doing, especially in the area of relationships. Routines and patterns of behavior can help keep a household running, but sometimes they hide the ways a relationship might be changing or evolving. Don't let habits take the place of truly being present in the moment.

Powerful God, help me not to take any moment for granted. Keep my eyes open and my life growing. Amen.

FEBRUARY 9   SAND

"The earth is the LORD's, and the fulness thereof."
   (Psalm 24:1 KJV)

I had been back from the beach for weeks. I'm not sure how those pants missed the laundry basket, but there it was: sand in my pocket. I held the grains in my hand. In an instant, I was transported to the spot on the beach I love so much. I could hear the rhythm of the waves. I could taste the salt. I felt the sun embracing my face. I could see the light dancing off the wings of a gull. I had to take a deep breath and fill myself with this moment of beauty and peace—all because of a few grains of sand in my pocket.

In some way, that's what happens every time I enter a sacred place—whether it's a vesper point at a mountain retreat, a sanctuary, or a quiet spot in my own home. There I find symbols and signs—small things, really, like sand in my pocket—that transport me in a moment into the presence of the living God. They are symbols and signs full of meaning and filled with memory. I must breathe deeply and fill myself with the moment. God is here.

Open my eyes to your presence, O God. Fill me with your glory. Amen.

FEBRUARY 10   BELOVED

"A new command I give you: Love one another. As I have loved you, so you must love one another." *(John 13:34 NIV)*

In the top drawer of my desk at the church, I keep a little metal toy horse. The paint is chipped off in several places, and its back leg is broken off. I keep it in my desk so that I'll see it each day. It is special for two reasons. First, I love horses. I love to watch them run, hear their many voices, and feel their soft noses. I grew up riding and mucking stalls, and those are happy memories. Second, my father gave me that horse as a gift when I was nine. This little horse reminds me that whoever comes through my door today, even if broken or banged up, is special. They all are special because of who they are and because of who has given them to me. God has given them to me and to the world as a gift, and if I love the Giver, I will cherish the gift.

Beyond any merit, I have received your grace-filled love, O Lord. What a wonderful gift! All through the hours of this day, help me love as I have been loved. Amen.

FEBRUARY 11   SALTINESS

"You are the salt of the earth. But if the salt loses its saltiness, how can it be made salty again? It is no longer good for anything, except to be thrown out and trampled."
                                            (Matthew 5:13 NIV)

In a church business meeting, a leader was sharing a devotion based on Matthew 5:13 about being the salt of the earth. I settled back for an "old, familiar journey." She began to share the properties of salt: it preserves things, adds flavor, and has the capacity to melt ice. Wait a minute! That was something new for my imagination—salt melts things!

As those who are called and empowered by Jesus Christ to be the salt of the earth, what should we be melting? Throw me over on the slippery steps of prejudice—let me melt some of that away. Let me thaw out some long, lingering grudge in a cold heart.

What about in our homes? What things should a mother melt? To begin, let us melt away the snows of uncertainty or insecurity in our children's lives to reveal the hidden gifts God desires to utilize for Kingdom causes. There is so much work for salt to do!

Loving God, if you need me to be salt today, please use me for your great purposes. Amen.

FEBRUARY 12   ENCOURAGEMENT

May the words of my mouth and the meditation of my heart be pleasing in your sight. *(Psalm 19:14 NIV)*

After weeks of physical therapy following knee surgery, my therapist announced, "Today is the big day! I want you to get on the stationary bike. You cannot pedal all the way around yet, so I just want you to rock the pedals back and forth."

With a sense of joy at this sign of progress, I climbed on the bike and began to rock the pedals. *I'm getting better,* I thought.

A few moments later, a man walked past and gestured toward my activity. He flatly pronounced, "You won't get far *that* way." Then he walked off.

I was crushed! He didn't have a clue where I had been and what I had gone through to get to this place.

I wonder how often we do this to one another—even our own children. Not taking time to consider or ask where others have been, what trials they have passed through, or what obstacles they might have overcome, we pronounce that they are not where *we* think they need to be.

May we always ask God to grant us a listening ear before we set loose a speaking tongue.

Patient God, when I speak today, may my words be filled with kindness and encouragement. Amen.

FEBRUARY 13   SCARS

"Why are you frightened, and why do doubts arise in your hearts? Look at my hands and my feet; see that it is I myself."
(Luke 24:38 NRSV)

The disciples recognized Jesus when he showed them his hands—the hands with the scars. Whatever the changes were that made him unrecognizable after the resurrection, those scars remained; and those scars told the disciples who Jesus really was.

When our children are little, they can hardly wait to peel off their bandages to show everyone some cut or wound. It means that they have really gone through something. The scars of Jesus announced that he really *had* been through something—death itself—but was back again as a gift of peace and hope for all humanity. As Jesus held out those hands, he was declaring that in God's hands, even scars can become sources of blessings for others. As Ernest Hemingway put it, "The world breaks every one and afterward many are strong at the broken places" (*A Farewell to Arms*).

You know my scars, loving Lord. Take them and make them a sign of hope and blessing to someone who is struggling today—perhaps my own child. Amen.

FEBRUARY 14   LOVE

And over all these virtues put on love, which binds them all together in perfect unity. Let the peace of Christ rule in your hearts, since as members of one body you were called to peace. And be thankful.   *(Colossians 3:14-15 NIV)*

You can read a passage of scripture again and again, and each time God offers up some new insight. This happened the other day as I was reading this text from Colossians. "Put on love," it says. Put on love? Like a comfortable pair of jeans? Suddenly I thought of my favorite article of clothing—a shawl that is deep purple with multicolored butterflies and splashes of gold. It's rather bold, but I love wearing it; and every time I put it on, I just feel happy. I smile more. My heart sings a little more brightly.

Maybe this was the message to the church in Colossae: be intentional about putting on love! When we do, we feel better. We are enfolded in beauty that shines through our words and the work of our hands. Love binds us together in unity. It opens the door so that peace can come in. It reminds us that there is much to be thankful for.

Loving Spirit, today while I'm busy putting on my clothes, remind me to be intentional in my desire to put on love—especially for my children. Amen.

FEBRUARY 15   DUST AND ASHES

Then the LORD God formed man from the dust of the ground, and breathed into his nostrils the breath of life; and the man became a living being.   *(Genesis 2:7 NRSV)*

When you are introducing yourself to someone, what do you say about yourself? What comes to mind first? Do you say that you are a mother, a wife, a businesswoman, a woman of God?

Who am I? It's one of those perpetual human questions. Ash Wednesday, which we celebrate about this time of year, gives us an answer. Like the tolling of a funeral bell, the response pours over us: "Remember, you are dust. From dust you came and to dust you shall return."

But even as we hear those sobering words, we are called to remember just what God did with dust. In the story from Genesis, we find God down in the dust of creation, carefully shaping and forming it into humankind and then bending low to breathe into the dust the very breath of life, the breath of God. And from that point on, God says two things about these frail children of dust: "It is good" and "You are mine."

As we prepare for the season of Lent, we are invited to begin a journey with Jesus—a dusty journey that calls us to remember not only who we are, but also who we are called to become through the profound love and grace of God in Christ.

Lord, help me remember not only who I am, but also whose I am and who I might become if I open myself to your power and grace. Amen.

FEBRUARY 16   TRUTHFUL WORDS

Let your "Yes" be yes, and your "No," no.   (James 5:12b NIV)

Growing up, I had a doctor who had one passion greater than medicine—horses. He would come to the clinic clomping about in his cowboy boots and smelling of farm dirt. At one point, he named one of his horses "Consultation" so that he could leave word with his staff that he was "out on Consultation."

I sometimes think of this doctor when I find myself not saying what I really mean. Why is that so hard? Why can't our no be a no and our yes be a yes? Sometimes we're afraid that we'll hurt someone's feelings, or we're afraid that we'll appear foolish. We're afraid that others will not understand—including our own children. We are afraid, and our fears—instead of our hearts and minds—begin to rule our words. How I need to focus my heart and my mind on Christ so that I may learn again to speak the truth in love.

May the words of my mouth and the meditation of my heart be pleasing in your sight, O LORD, my Rock and my Redeemer (Psalm 19:14 NIV). Amen.

FEBRUARY 17   SOUNDS

For you shall go out in joy, and be led back in peace.
(Isaiah 55:12a NRSV)

What is the most beautiful sound on earth? Is it the sound of the ocean waves, or that of water tumbling down rocks in a mountain stream? Is it the sound of birds singing their way into spring? Is it the sound of children laughing or the sound of a congregation singing? For the longest time, for me, it was the sound of the engine of a little pickup truck, a vehicle driven by my teenage son. When I'd hear that sound in the driveway around midnight, I knew that a promise had been kept and that a child was safe; and nothing could bring me greater joy or deeper peace.

Gracious God, thank you for all the sounds that bring me joy, and for the extra special ones that bring me peace. Amen.

FEBRUARY 18   LOST

If only you had paid attention to my commands, your peace would have been like a river. *(Isaiah 48:18 NIV)*

At one time or another, we've all temporarily lost a child—in a store or in a crowd. It's a terrible, sinking feeling, isn't it? It's also a terrible feeling to feel lost yourself: Has this ever happened to you? You're traveling away from home, and you spend the night in a hotel. Then, sometime in the middle of the night, you wake up and don't have a clue where you are. There comes that momentary flash of panic—I'm lost!

Unfortunately, there are many in our world who wake up in the middle of their lives with the same sensation. Where am I? How did I get here? Somehow life and circumstance has swept them to a place they never imagined. Suddenly, that line from the Beatles song reflects a deep hunger and longing: "Once there was a way to get back home." For that hunger and longing there is a response: "Come to me, all you who are weary and burdened, and I will give you rest" (Matthew 11:28 NIV). "Do not let your hearts be troubled" (John 14:1 NIV). There is a place prepared for you called home.

Thank you, welcoming God, for always offering "home" to your children. Amen.

FEBRUARY 19   WAITING

Those who wait for the LORD ... shall walk and not faint.
(Isaiah 40:31 NRSV)

There have been days I could not soar. All I could do was a little running. And there have been days I couldn't even run. All I could muster was a shuffle. But isn't it wonderful to know that if I wait for God, I'll at least not faint.

Waiting looks so inactive, so passive; and we are not a people who wait well! Hurry up! Get moving! That's the kind of agenda we admire. But waiting? Oh, I don't have time for that!

But waiting for God is far from inactive or passive. Waiting for God means I'm preparing myself for a holy presence. It means I'm listening for the approach and the agenda of that presence. It means I trust that presence so much that I won't leave home (or any other place) without it. And when I'm in that presence, there's no power in heaven or on earth that can shake me.

"Who shall separate us from the love of Christ? Shall trouble or hardship or persecution or famine or nakedness or danger or sword?...No, in all these things we are more than conquerors" (Romans 8:35, 37 NIV).

Lord, I don't want to run off on my own again. Grant me the wisdom to wait for you. Amen.

FEBRUARY 20   PATIENCE

"Choose this day whom you will serve."   *(Joshua 24:15 NRSV)*

Why does it always seem to happen then? Two o'clock in the morning: Crash! Bang! Bang! It was at this hour that my seventeen-year-old son decided to bleach his (black) hair when the cat (the black cat) jumped in the middle of the table. The result was having to live for months with a child crested with orange hair and a polka-dotted cat—outward and visible signs of a very bad choice.

Obviously, there are many people who bear visible signs of their bad choices, but there are so many more whose wounds and hurts are hidden inside, invisible to the outside world. How much more patient we would be if we could just remember that *everyone* is struggling with *something*, and everyone could use an extra word of kindness and encouragement. When we show patience and offer kindness, we choose to serve God rather than ourselves.

Forgive me for my lack of patience with others. I know, loving God, that you've been so patient with me. May I serve you by loving others. Amen.

FEBRUARY 21   PLEASING GOD

"Hallowed be your name. Your kingdom come. Your will be done."   *(Matthew 6:9 NRSV)*

At vacation Bible school one day, a nine-year-old girl offered this prayer: "God, thank you for letting us have such a fun time at Bible school this week. We hope you've had fun, too. Amen."

Can you imagine a more powerful prayer? What if every church, before beginning a worship service or starting a meeting or planning an event, would say, "We hope this will be fun for you, God"? In other words, "We want this to be pleasing, first and foremost, to you, God. It doesn't have to please me, or the power brokers, or the world; but God, this *has* to please you." Can you imagine how that prayer would transform church budgets and staff development and ministry focus?

What if we mothers said a similar prayer every morning before beginning our day? "Lord, I want everything I do today to be pleasing to you. Some things may not be pleasing to me or to my children, but this day *has* to please you, God."

Can you imagine how such a prayer would transform our values and priorities and time management and families?

Lord, you have taught me to pray. Help me today to avail myself to this means of grace. Amen.

FEBRUARY 22   SABBATH

"Get up and eat, otherwise the journey will be too much for you." *(1 Kings 19:7b NRSV)*

I have always loved stories about Elijah, especially the one in which he waits through the wind, the earthquake, and the fire to finally hear the voice of God. But have you ever noticed what Elijah did to get ready for this grand spiritual encounter? The instructions are for him to sleep, eat, and drink. These are some very ordinary, physical activities that open the way for a life-changing, spiritual reality.

As women and as mothers, I think we need to remember Elijah. We get so busy and torn in so many directions. There are so many demands and so many people who count on us. How are we to make prayer or faith fit into such a schedule? Often we rob ourselves of encounters with God simply because we have not taken the time to sleep and to eat. From the beginning, rest was in God's design for us.

Loving God, this day may I experience anew your Sabbath rest so that I may more clearly hear your still, small voice. Amen.

FEBRUARY 23   WANTS

"Ask ... seek ... knock." *(Luke 11:9 NIV)*

What a great promise we have from Jesus, but it looks so self-serving. I ask God for something, and I get it. The emphasis here lies in "what I want" and "what I get." The emphasis of Jesus, however, was God. The point is not what I'm asking for, but that I am asking God. If I am in a conversation with God, then that will totally transform what I will ask for and seek after.

Why don't I get what I ask for sometimes? In the Letter of James we read, "You ask and do not receive, because you ask wrongly" (4:3 NRSV). There are many good things to ask for, but God always demands that we seek after the best. Oswald Chambers once wrote, "The good is always the enemy of the best." Jesus pushes us to "seek first the kingdom of God"—the best—and then "all these things will be added to you" (Matthew 6:33 NKJV). Maybe the question should not be what are you asking for, but to whom are you speaking? If you're speaking to God, know that God desires the best for you!

Purify my desires, O God, with the purity of your love. Amen.

FEBRUARY 24   FAMILY LIKENESS

You are a chosen race, a royal priesthood, a holy nation, God's own people.   *(1 Peter 2:9a NRSV)*

What's the first thing people say when they see a new baby? "Why, he looks just like his father!" Or, "She's got Aunt Amy's eyes!" Or, "Look, he's got the family nose!" But there's no greater compliment than, "Wow, she looks just like you!"

   One of the realities we proclaim as Christians is that we, through grace, are part of God's family. We are God's sons and daughters, God's beloved. How much of a family likeness is there? How often have you heard, "Wow! She looks just like Jesus!"

Gracious Lord, give me eyes like your eyes that can see the potential in each person. Give me a heart like yours that is filled with compassion. Give me feet like yours that are willing to walk a second mile. Give me hands like yours, hands that reach out to serve and lift up the fallen. Amen.

FEBRUARY 25   FEAR

"Do not fear, little flock, for it is your Father's good pleasure to give you the kingdom."   *(Luke 12:32 NKJV)*

"How many times do I have to tell you . . . !" How often have you uttered those words as a parent? How do you most often fill in the blank: ". . . tell you____"?

As a heavenly parent, God must utilize that phrase every minute, and one of the most frequent "fill-in-the-blank" phrases is, "How many times do I have to tell you, 'Do not be afraid!'"?

The angels had to calm the shepherds with those words. Gabriel said it to Mary. Jesus said it to individuals, to the disciples, to the crowds—"Do not be afraid." When we operate out of fear, we tend to resort to self-preservation, self-protection, and downright selfishness. Fear leads to fretting. Even the psalmist said, "Do not fret—it only causes harm" (Psalm 37:8 NKJV). But when we operate out of our hopes or our assurance, what different people we become!

"Those of steadfast mind you keep in peace—in peace because they trust in you" (Isaiah 26:3 NRSV).

May all my fears be lost in my assurance of your power and grace, O God. Amen.

FEBRUARY 26   FORGETFULNESS

"Though she may forget, I will not forget you!"
(Isaiah 49:15b NIV)

My oldest son was just a few months old when, one day, I needed to run to the grocery store. I very carefully buckled him into the car seat, got behind the wheel, and went over my list: bread, milk, and orange juice. I parked the car. Bread, milk, and orange juice. I walked into the store. Bread, milk, and orange juice. I got my cart and was cruising aisle number one. Bread, milk, and orange juice . . . Ben! I had left him in the car! At that point in my life, he was the most important human being on the planet to me, and I had forgotten him because he wasn't on my list.

I wonder how many times we leave Jesus like that? The One we claim is supremely important to us gets left behind while we rush about in our busyness. He's just not on the list.

Thank you, loving Parent, for never forgetting me, even in those times I have forgotten you. Amen.

FEBRUARY 27   MIGRATION

***Hearken unto me, ye that know righteousness, the people in
whose heart is my law.*** ***(Isaiah 51:7 KJV)***

When my younger son was about four, he was discussing bird
migration with my mother. (Yes, leave these topics to the grand-
mothers!) "Well, how do they know to fly south?" he wanted to
know. "We think God put something in their heads to let them
know where to fly so they can stay warm in the winter," she
answered. After a pause he mused, "God didn't put anything in *my*
head to know how to go south. I can't even fly!"

God may not have put anything in our heads, but God certainly
did put something in our hearts: a kind of homing device that
whispers to us through all the ups and downs, twists and turns of
life, calling us to come to a place of safety, to come to a place of
peace, to come home.

***Help me today, Gracious God, to listen to the message you've
written on my heart. Amen.***

FEBRUARY 28   HOPE

"You will weep and mourn ... but your pain will turn into joy."
(John 16:20 NRSV)

"What is it?" I asked, taking the bucket in my hand. It looked like
some wilted brown leaves attached to a clump of dirt. "Just plant
it. You'll like it," my friend answered. Somewhat reluctantly, I
stuck the clump in the garden patch in the front of the house.
Wiping my hands on my jeans, I said, "You're on your own!"

In late February, after a snow, I went out to pick up some twigs
in the yard, and to my great surprise, the dead-looking clump was
exploding with the pale cream blossoms—seventeen of them—of a
Lenten rose.

I guess that was an act of faith to put in the ground something
that looked dead and trust that inherent in those roots and leaves
and earth and sun was the possibility of life, glorious and new.
That's the kind of faith we need to carry us to through the coming
weeks to the great news of Easter.

Lord, I believe! Help my unbelief. Amen.

March

Loving Life Together

REBECCA LAIRD

MARCH 1   REVELING IN THE MOMENT

*"Consider the lilies, how they grow: they neither toil nor spin;
yet I tell you, even Solomon in all his glory was not clothed like
one of these."*   *(Luke 12:27 NRSV)*

When my daughters were very young, I found filling the days
with perpetual activity for their short attention spans a challenge.
I had worked for a number of years in publishing and was used to
ordering my days by hours of reading and interesting conversation
with coworkers. Now there was little time to pause and think!

I remember well the day I realized that I could invite my children to enjoy what I enjoy rather than filling their days with toys
and videos and activities. We went outside to look for "signs of
spring" at the end of winter. "Mommy, look! A thighn of thpring!"
I'll never forget the moment when my oldest excitedly bent over a
tiny daffodil shoot. We reveled in the moment. We weren't just
keeping busy. We were loving life together.

This month we will consider some ways we can teach our children—by our words and by our example—to love life, as well as
ways we can enjoy loving life together.

*God, remind me each day this month that I can pass on what I
love to my children. Amen.*

MARCH 2   REVELING IN GOD'S GLORY

And God said, "Let there be lights in the dome of the sky to sep-arate the day from the night; and let them be for signs and for seasons and for days and years."   **(Genesis 1:14 NRSV)**

Morning and evening make a day. The sun rises and sets, and sometimes I am aware of the passing of time; but often I miss these daily markers as I rush from place to place. A few years ago I read a quote from environmentalist Wendell Berry who said that the earth follows its own "diurnal liturgy." He was saying that the earth pauses twice a day to worship and show forth God's glory in bursts of light and color in displays of silent wonder. If the ground I walk upon and the air I breathe somehow are created to pause twice a day to pray and revel in God's glory, then maybe I'd be wise to join in.

This morning I saw a purple crocus in my neighbor's yard. How magnificent is God's handiwork. This evening, I watched the sky turn from pink to gray.

May we remember to revel in God's glory each day, teaching our children to do the same.

God of all creation, stop me in my tracks this month whenever I am tempted to rush past the beauty that is all around me. Amen.

MARCH 3   LISTENING TO GOD'S VOICE OF LOVE

Hearken unto the voice of my cry, my King, and my God: for unto thee will I pray.   **(Psalm 5:2 KJV)**

Prayer is described as many things, but I favor Henri Nouwen's definition: "Prayer is listening to God's voice of love." Life is so busy and noisy that it's easy to bypass the sterling moments found in God's silence. When I slow down and pray, I start by pouring out all my anxieties and worries and joys and concerns in an unedited rush. I often feel like a young child seeing her mother for the first time at the end of a day spent physically apart. There is so much to tell. Then I breathe deeply and still my mind and wait. I know I'm in the best of company. I know that the one who has heard me out loves me beyond measure. I tell all, and then I can just be for a while—safely heard, held, and loved beyond measure.

Dear God, thank you for loving me. Let your love toward me sink in to the soil of my soul. I pour my heartfelt cries out to you. Amen.

MARCH 4   DIVINE APPOINTMENTS

My voice shalt thou hear in the morning, O LORD; in the morning will I direct my prayer unto thee, and will look up.
(Psalm 5:3 KJV)

What do you do when you first open your eyes? I usually steal a close, furtive look at the clock and try to remember what day it is. Do I have time to roll over and catch a few more moments of sleep? Do I need to jump up and shift myself into overdrive? Do I hear any family-related noises in the house that demand I jump to attention? Once I have my bearings, most days, I take a long moment to pray about the day ahead. Who will I spend it with? What appointments, projects, or errands are on my to-do list? I preview the day in advance, asking God to walk with me and nudge me to do what matters rather than just let the time pass without me fully living into the hours ahead. Then, not only is it time to get up, I'm ready for life.

Dear God, today will be busy. There are a lot of people in my life today. Help me keep my divine appointments—help me look my kids, husband, and friends straight in the eyes and offer myself to them with an open heart. Amen.

MARCH 5   ROLE REVERSAL

Then he poured water into a basin and began to wash the disciples' feet and to wipe them with the towel that was tied around him.   *(John 13:5 NRSV)*

What do you want to be when you grow up? The way children answer this question often shifts over the years, but each wished-for-future holds a special clue to who they are.

When my youngest was seven, she wanted to grow up and have her own foot massage business. She printed business cards and created a price list. For a quarter, I could have my feet rubbed with lotion until all my stress evaporated. Her love showed in her hands. With a serious look on her face, she would usher me into her room, show me where to sit, and ask me to remove my shoes. The first time, the role reversal took me by surprise. After all, I was the one who had powdered and pampered her for many years. Being on the receiving end of my child's care taught me about her capacity to care for others. I saw that she had learned how to show the full extent of her love to me and, in time, would do so for others.

Dear God, help me let others serve me today. Let me feel how much those around me love me, too. Amen.

MARCH 6   GOD'S EVERLASTING ARMS

The eternal God is your refuge, and underneath are the everlasting arms.   *(Deuteronomy 33:27 NIV)*

After a long day of housework, yard work, and cooking, I found my back aching and my spirits lagging. We had hopefully hung the hammock in our backyard even though the weather was not yet predictably warm. That hammock beckoned to me. My first thought was to be practical. It was too cold for a hammock. I had more work to do. But I was tired. I grabbed a throw from the armchair, wrapped it around me, and walked to the hammock. As I settled in, I sunk into the support of the swinging hammock. I felt cradled. The sun was warm on my face, and the sky was blue and crisp. For those few moments, I remembered that my life is more than just completing a long list of things that need to be done. My life is held in God's everlasting arms. There is a refuge, a place of solace and refreshment. I need to go there often. The chores can wait a bit.

Dear God, cradle me in your love today. Slow me down and remind me who is my refuge and my true dwelling place. Amen.

MARCH 7   A LEGACY OF PRAYERS

For I am mindful of the sincere faith within you, which first dwelt in your grandmother Lois, and your mother Eunice, and I am sure that it is in you as well.   (2 Timothy 1:5 NASB)

When mail comes to my mailbox, I don't have to open letters from my mother or grandmother to know who they are from. Their handwriting is as familiar to me as their voices. My mother's tidy handwriting is careful and precise, just as she is. My grand-mother's is more slanted, and her words are always brief but sincere. That's how she is in person, too. Their handwriting differs, but the way they sign cards and letters is the same: "With love and prayers." They both have passed on to me the knowledge that family love and faithful prayers are not to be separated. If you love someone, you pray for them. The legacy of their faithful prayers is something solid to lean into as the years pass. It is also something solid to pass on to the next generation. I want my children to know that my love for them is constant, as are my prayers to the God of my mothers.

Dear God, care for my children today. May the faith that dwelt in earlier generations grow to be sincere and strong in them, too. Amen.

MARCH 8   RUNNING THE RACE

Therefore, since we have so great a cloud of witnesses surrounding us, let us also lay aside every encumbrance, and the sin which so easily entangles us, and let us run with endurance the race that is set before us.   (Hebrews 12:1 NASB)

Recently, I walked around my church and looked at the pictures. I'd noticed the photos of the male senior pastors who had served the church for more than a century. But I hadn't really looked at the handwritten list of charter members and the black and white photos that showed more women's faces than men's.

I looked in the library where a photo hung of the beloved woman who had served for decades as Director of Christian Education. On a nearby shelf, a booklet listed the women associate pastors who had predated me during the past twenty-five years. I realized the committed energy of many who had kept the church's doors open to me and mine. They could have just focused their energies in their own homes, but instead they chose to love widely.

The best way I can say thank you is to run my race with perseverance. I can run with joy and cheer on the other women who run, too. I can take time to extend myself beyond the doors of my own home. What I do matters not just for today, but for tomorrow, too.

Dear God, prompt me to say thank you to the women in my life who have shown me what faithful love and service really are. Amen.

MARCH 9   LEARNING FROM OTHER WOMEN

Older women likewise are to be reverent in their behavior, not malicious gossips, nor enslaved to much wine, teaching what is good, that they may encourage the young women to love their husbands, to love their children, to be sensible, pure, workers at home, kind, being subject to their own husbands, that the word of God may not be dishonored.   (Titus 2:3-5 NASB)

In a group of young mothers who swap stories and suggestions for surviving the toddler years, we sat down with colored paper and markers to make mosaics. We had read Paul's advice to older women and decided to honor what our elders had taught us. We tore small pieces of paper, wrote on each the name of a person and the characteristic he or she embodied for us, and glued them on a sheet of paper. We laughed as we learned of one's Aunt Maude who taught audacity in life and fearlessness with fashion; another's mother cultivated daily humor in a life filled with caring for a disabled child. As we shared, we noticed we had learned from both the quirks and the strengths of those we loved. As the years went by, we had come to appreciate how they had taught us what was good.

Free me today, O God, from trying to be anyone else than the person you made me to be. Amen.

MARCH 10   USING YOUR AUTHORITY

Tell them all this. Build up their courage, and discipline them if they get out of line. You're in charge. Don't let anyone put you down.   *(Titus 2:15 Message)*

The day I walked into my first Daisy troop meeting, I was terrified. I had confidence to speak before large crowds of adults, but a roomful of five-year-olds was a different matter. I reminded myself that I had a lot of craft supplies and stories. I was the grown-up here.

I looked into those young faces, so full of trust, and registered those who had the most mischief in their eyes. A couple challenged me right away, and I smiled as I instructed them to sit outside the circle until they were ready to participate. Within minutes we all were happily getting to know one another.

For seven years, those kids ended up often in my care. Through creative chaos and a lot of fun, I learned that being the grown-up and setting the standard by being clear, kind, and firm was a gift both to me and to them.

God, allow me to use the authority you have given me with kindness and confidence for the good of my family and friends today. Amen.

MARCH 11   COMPETING PRIORITIES

Hear, O Israel: The LORD is our God, the LORD alone. You shall love the LORD your God with all your heart, and with all your soul, and with all your might.   *(Deuteronomy 6:4-5 NRSV)*

When our church was trying to sort out our Sunday morning schedule with multiple worship services and education classes, we asked the young parents for feedback. The survey results showed that all church activities had to be done by noon to accommodate youth sport leagues. I was surprised. I had put aside the team sign-up flyers my daughters had brought home when I saw the games were on Sundays. I didn't want our family to find ourselves rushing from church to games just like we rushed every other day.

A group of parents met to discuss how many extracurricular activities were good for kids and how we could know when we were overdoing it. A few of us banded together and said, "Not on Sundays." One mom said, "I can't let my child get behind. I have to sign him up!" She left that meeting wondering if the bigger worry was telling that child by her actions that loving and serving God with all your might was less important than another sports trophy.

Dear God, competing priorities are everywhere. How do I decide? Help me order my life and my family's life in ways that honor you. Amen.

MARCH 12   MORE "CAUGHT THAN TAUGHT"

Keep these words that I am commanding you today in your heart. Recite them to your children and talk about them when you are at home and when you are away, when you lie down and when you rise. **(Deuteronomy 6:6-7 NRSV)**

I came to a meeting at church to find a huge vase with thousands of colored gumballs in it on the table. Next to the vase was a small glass jar with only a few gumballs in it. A wise Christian education director soon came in the room and explained that the large vase represented the number of hours a parent spends with a child at home, in the car, at breakfast, or before bedtime. The small jar represented the average number of hours a child regularly attends a Sunday school or Christian education class. She said, "We've got to help parents become the primary teachers of faith in their families." She showed us in an unmistakable way that faith is more "caught than taught," and that those priceless moments of talking about faith are primarily found within the walls of home.

God, I'm not sure how to best teach my children about my faith and values. Give me courage and sensitivity to find words and actions to lead them to you. Amen.

MARCH 13   GOD IS WITH US

Bind them as a sign on your hand, fix them as an emblem on your forehead, and write them on the doorposts of your house and on your gates.   *(Deuteronomy 6:8-9 NRSV)*

A family moved into a big, new house and decided to have a house blessing. I was invited, and I loved watching the grand-mother present a tray of bread, oil, and salt—a housewarming cus-tom from her Italian upbringing. One of the children sang a favorite song. A Jewish relative brought a mezuzah, a door plaque, to remind all those coming in and going out of God's presence and blessings. We all gathered at each of the doors and prayed for God's care before affixing the mezuzah to the entrance the family would use most. The family wanted to mark their move, not just with celebration and food, but also with a holy reminder that a home is a place where God is present in each and every room.

God, be with my family today as we come and go. Remind me to pause at the door and remember you are with us, each and every one. Amen.

MARCH 14   BLESSINGS MULTIPLY

Do what is right and good in the sight of the LORD, *so that it may go well with you, and so that you may go in and occupy the good land that the* LORD *swore to your ancestors to give you.*   *(Deuteronomy 6:18 NRSV)*

The envelope held a thank-you card and a check. The family for whom I had offered a house blessing wanted me to pass on the blessing to some children through our church's mission program. I prayed for guidance and decided to give the check to one of our mission team leaders who was taking a group to Bolivia. "Find some children who need their house blessed by love and report back," I told him.

When he returned some months later with a photo of a group from our church standing alongside a daycare in a remote Andean village of Bolivia, tears sprang to my eyes. More than a dozen brown-eyed beauties were smiling shyly for the camera. With those donated funds, not just one family but an entire village raised a roof to shelter all their children during the days, while the parents labored in the fields. Blessings received and blessings shared always multiply.

Dear God, how shall I pass on the blessings I've so graciously been given? I want to be a channel for goodness, too. Amen.

MARCH 15   A HIGH AND HOLY CALLING

God chose you to be his people, so I urge you now to live the life to which God called you.   ***(Ephesians 4:1b NCV)***

When I was young, I thought to be called meant to go somewhere for God. It always seemed that people who talked about calling traveled to exotic lands and did things that made the rest of us seem ordinary. Although the adventurous aspects really appealed to me, I didn't see, after I had my children, how I was still called by God to my tamer, more home-based life. A nun, a woman without children who lived her life nearly silently without clutter or distraction, came to speak to a group of us one day. She said, "Your vocation is to your family. You are called to cultivate that part of the body of Christ with all your heart, mind, and soul. Yours is one of the hardest callings of all." She recognized that family life, with love at the center, is not a distraction to faith; it is the place where, indeed, we are formed by it.

God, help me see today that my life with my family is a spiritual practice and that when I show love to them, I am indeed living out a high and holy calling. Amen.

MARCH 16   "JOINED" TO OTHERS

Always be humble, gentle, and patient, accepting each other in love. You are joined together with peace through the Spirit, so make every effort to continue together in this way.
(Ephesians 4:2-3 NCV)

Humility means getting down on all fours to heed a small child's clamoring for yet another horsey ride. Gentleness means a soft, restrained hand on the shoulder to remind a pokey child to move along when you have the power and the will to push hard to hurry things along. Patiently accepting each other means sitting in the passenger seat, holding your hands calmly in your lap, and keeping the tone even in your voice as your teenage child tries again to back out of the driveway. You know you could act differently and put your own desires or power or knowledge on display, but you also know that peace comes through a spirit-infused life that says I want to live "joined" to others. This asks of me what only God can help me do.

God, grant me self-restraint when I want to move faster and do things my own way. Help me keep my family joined in peace today. I know it will take effort on my part, but I acknowledge my need for your graceful spirit. Shower it on me. Amen.

MARCH 17   SPECIAL GIFTS

However, he has given each one of us a special gift according to the generosity of Christ. *(Ephesians 4:7 NLT)*

When my children turned thirteen, the extended family gathered for a coming-of-age ritual. Each child in the family was asked in turn to describe the person they hoped to become. Then, one by one, aunts, uncles, cousins, Grandma, Grandpa, sister, brother, Mom, and Dad described the gifts of the young person as they neared adulthood. With amazing alacrity, even the youngest cousin could always name the gifts they saw in their older cousins. "You always take time to play with me." "You are creative." "You are willing to listen to me." "When you tell a story, I want to stop what I am doing every time." The list of wonderful gifts and attributes is always long and highly celebrated.

God doesn't forget anyone when doling out the gifts. It's up to us to stop often to name and celebrate them.

God, thank you for giving each child such wonderful gifts. Prompt me to say thank you out loud in my child's presence today. Amen.

MARCH 18   SPIRITUAL MATURITY

We must become like a mature person, growing until we become like Christ and have his perfection. Then we will no longer be babies. . . . No! Speaking the truth with love, we will grow up in every way into Christ, who is the head.
(Ephesians 4:13b-14a, 15 NCV)

In our church, we baptize babies on the same wooden step where our teenagers stand during confirmation. That spot is holy to us. At either of these rituals we are reminded out loud that the promises we claim at baptism are those we claim at confirmation. It's hard to imagine when a burbling baby is walked down the center aisle that this same child will one day struggle to understand and affirm what he or she will believe and build a life upon. It's equally hard to see when a teenager is standing in front of us with shifting feet and a distracted aura that a full measure of Christ is inside that gawky body, but indeed it is. Spiritual maturity follows a process just as physical maturity does. Sometimes slowly and imperceptibly and sometimes with great growth spurts, we are all growing up into Christ.

God, work in my child to bring maturity of body, mind, and spirit. I want to be your partner in speaking the truth with love and offering my time to help my child grow. Amen.

MARCH 19   A MORE PERFECT LOVE

Be kind and merciful, and forgive others, just as God forgave you because of Christ. Do as God does. After all, you are his dear children. Let love be your guide.   (Ephesians 4:32–5:2a CEV)

My daughter stayed out too late, and I worried. She didn't return my phone call, and I felt my fear mutate to anger. Was she okay? Why didn't she call? What should I say when she finally came through the door? I began to rehearse my speech. Then I stopped myself and prayed for wisdom. I breathed deeply a few times. I remembered the innocence that still played often across my beloved child's face. Yes, I would need to clearly restate her curfew, my expectations of a courtesy call if running late, and the importance of a fully charged cell phone. But no, I did not need to blow up. I could stand at the door ready to welcome her home. My embrace was real and my frustration and relief must have played across my face. She said she was sorry. She was happy to be received with the calm truth rather than fury. Love is hard to live out, but I do love this kid, no matter what.

God, help me find a more perfect love that sees through your eyes when my own eyes are full of fear. Amen.

MARCH 20   CHILDREN OF THE LIGHT

For once you were darkness, but now in the Lord you are light. Live as children of light—for the fruit of the light is found in all that is good and right and true. Try to find out what is pleasing to the Lord.   (Ephesians 5:8-10 NRSV)

My kids are, thankfully, terrible liars. Their smiles flatten and an emotional veil comes down over their eyes when they lie. Their voices go distant. When I ask, "Did you have a good day?" I can tell with a quick look or a tuned ear if that "yeah" is for real or not. When they come into view with a broad smile and something they can't wait to tell or do, I know I'm getting the full sunlight of their lives. I suspect they see and hear the same in me when I'm hiding my truer feelings, deeper beliefs, or real desires. I want my children to be children of the light. As their teacher in how to live, I have to tend my own light of honesty and truthfulness in matters big and small. My light will help them fan their own lights of truth.

God, help me be honest and true with what I feel and what I believe so that my light may shine in my home. Amen.

MARCH 21   DON'T BE FOOLISH

Do not be foolish but learn what the Lord wants you to do.
(Ephesians 5:17 NCV)

One of the youngest in the group came up to me and voluntarily confessed, "I was just doing what the older boys told me to do!" I knew something was up. It took very little prompting to find out that a whole group had climbed the three-story ladder to the nearby rickety rooftop of the church bell tower. While playing hide-and-seek, they had ditched the game and explored the forbidden territory. Oh, it had been so tempting and so much fun. When they were all found and gathered together, they tried to make up excuses: "We didn't know we couldn't go up there." Of course they did. We'd talked about it and even put it in the ground rules for playing together. When I asked, "What would you like me to tell your parents if you do that again and fall three stories to the ground?" They had no answers. I made sure that ladder was removed and the area secured. I was not going to let a group of kids in their foolishness take that chance again. Then I'd be the fool.

God, help me take a good look around my house and my life to make sure that I am using good sense and not being foolish about my family's or neighbor's well-being. Amen.

MARCH 22   PUT OTHERS FIRST

Honor Christ by submitting to each other.   (Ephesians 5:21 TLB)

It seems somebody or something else gets to go first all the time: first in the shower, first to get the hot coffee, first to go to work, first to get the potatoes passed, first to get homework help, first to put another event on the calendar, first to get a load of clean clothes folded into a drawer. The list of all the ways a mother puts others first seems awfully long sometimes. It's hard to see how all the giving and deferring has to do with faith, but learning to look out for others has worked off some of my selfish edges. Being first in line or pushing my own kids to the front of the line of life no longer drives me. Somehow, in all the serving that we all do, life gets a little more focused. There is enough time and love and opportunity to go around, at least most of the time.

OK God, I surrender any impulse I have to be first or best or fastest today. Can you help me relax and trust that today will take care of itself if my priorities are fixed on you? Amen.

MARCH 23   YIELDING AS TO THE LORD

Wives, yield to your husbands, as you do to the Lord.
                                        (Ephesians 5:22 NCV)

The Bible sure is countercultural sometimes. Every advice column I read says I'm to put myself first and find ways to fulfill my own needs. Being married often reminds me that my needs and the needs of my husband can't really be separated into two distinct lists on a page. He needs to be respected and appreciated. I need to be listened to and valued. When I take time to ask questions about his day at work and thank him for picking up the kids and inviting friends over for my birthday, he naturally listens and values me in return. Maybe putting my husband first is good for me, too. In the warp and woof of relationship, giving and receiving, when done frequently, are hard to tell apart.

Thank you, God, for the daily relationships in my life. What can I do today to show my love to those closest to me? Amen.

MARCH 24   LOVING BY SERVING

And you husbands must love your wives with the same love
Christ showed the church. He gave up his life for her.
                                                    (Ephesians 5:25 NLT)

It was such a simple act of kindness. While traveling, my family
took an early morning swim at a hotel. A dad, mom, and small
daughter shared the pool with us. Most of us were still just wak-
ing up, but the little girl was lively and full of energy. While her
mom watched, the dad bobbed up and down playing games and
racing around the pool. When the little girl slowed down briefly,
he went to get his wife a drink of water and then grabbed the keys
when she asked if he'd get the swimming ring from the room. He
did all of this with such a smile on his face. He clearly loved his
family. He sent his wife looks of kindness from the pool. He served
her with ease. I noticed. My kids noticed. We all took note of what
serving one another in love looks like in family life. Laying down
one's life doesn't usually happen in dramatic ways, but in daily
ways.

Dear God, give me eyes to see how I can serve others today, and
help me say thanks for the ways others love me in my daily life.
Amen.

MARCH 25   GIFTED FOR GOOD WORKS

For we are His workmanship, created in Christ Jesus for good
works, which God prepared beforehand, that we should walk in
them.   *(Ephesians 2:10 NASB)*

When my first child was born, I thought she was a blank slate
that the world and we would mold. I thought all babies were social
magnets that drew strangers in (and many are), and that "having
a way with people" was common. As my daughter grew and another
child joined our family, I began to see how much of a child's personality and gifts are really hardwired or, to use a more religious
term, foreordained. My oldest, as she grew, continued to just

understand people and be a kid who included others when it wasn't the group thing to do. She simply revels in being around people; and without fanfare or drawing attention to herself, she finds ways to offer welcome to others. She's been doing this since she was cooing at people from the backpack she was carried in from infancy. She didn't like the backpack facing in; she wanted to see all the people. She came from God with a relational gift. She's doing well by it.

God, show me the special gifts that my children and I have so that we may do the good work in the world that we are naturally made to do. Amen.

MARCH 26   KEEPING SHORT ACCOUNTS

For He Himself is our peace, who made both groups into one, and broke down the barrier of the dividing wall.
(Ephesians 2:14 NASB)

"She took my flip-flops without asking!" "She won't get off the computer, and it's my turn!" "I was watching the other channel before anyone else was in the room!" "How could you tell somebody that? I told you that was a secret!" There are so many opportunities in family life for slights and betrayals to build up. I remember a wise person advising me to keep short accounts in relationships. "What does that mean?" I asked. It means owning up to taking flip-flops without asking on the day it happens. It means clarifying how much time each family member has on the computer or watching television the day the squabble erupts. It means asking for forgiveness and praying for healing whenever we betray one another's trust. If we keep small accounts on small things, God can help us keep the walls between us from getting so high that only miracles of grace and perseverance can knock them down.

God, be the peace in our family. What small burdens can I clear away from our relationships today? Amen.

MARCH 27   FELLOW CITIZENS

So then you are no longer strangers and aliens, but you are fellow-citizens with the saints, and are of God's household.
                                              (Ephesians 2:19 NASB)

Church is such a good leveling place. When my kids were small, the church we attended was in the center of town. Homeless men from the local mission often walked over on Sunday mornings. A homeless woman who refused help came into the church lugging her bags and used the church bathroom to wash up. The presence of those in need who had different levels of social skills and economic means led to some debates: Were our kids safe? Who was going to clean up after that woman? What about our coffee and bagel time after church?

Some were eating more than their share and not contributing. Should we encourage them to keep coming? What if we were over-run with people in need? What about our own needs for safety and calm worship on Sunday mornings?

When we were driving around town, I remember the pleasure I felt when one of my kids pointed to the homeless woman and remarked, "Hey, that woman goes to our church." Yes, indeed, she and we are members of the household of God.

God, make room in my heart today for someone who might make me uncomfortable. I know your household has more room for strangers than mine often does. Give me boundaries and love in equal measure. Amen.

MARCH 28   GOD'S DWELLING PLACE

[Through Christ] you also are built together spiritually into a dwelling place for God.   *(Ephesians 2:22 NRSV)*

One year at church we had a family Seder service prior to Easter. We set up many tables, boiled a lot of eggs, washed bunches of parsley, and set out matzos. We gathered family style, and there was much talking and laughing and singing. We divided out speaking parts for the service and decided to ask two brothers to split the part of the youngest son. The elder would ask the question, "Why is this night different from all other nights?" and the younger would go at the end of the service and open the door for Elijah. The younger boy was fixated on the empty chair we left for Elijah. The idea that the prophet was to be welcomed at our table just opened up his imagination. We made room at the table for God's prophet and later, after the service was over, it was clear the young boy understood that not only God's prophet but also God's presence were present with us—and in us, too. Our families, our church family, and we were a habitation, a place where God dwells.

Lord, be present at our table. Be our guest. Amen.

MARCH 29   ROOTS

[May] Christ ... dwell in your hearts through faith, as you are being rooted and grounded in love. **(Ephesians 3:17 NRSV)**

Why do roots matter? Knowing who you are, what you believe, and where your strength comes from becomes essential when the winds of trouble blow. When life is smooth, shallow roots don't show; but when trials come, they do.

When my youngest daughter was diagnosed with cancer, the roots of my faith were sorely tugged at and shaken. But thanks be to God, my faith was intertwined with the faithful roots of an extended family, many friends, and a caring church. The strength of that holy tangle of prayers grounded me and kept my family and me standing firm until health and hope returned.

There is no better day than today to push down roots of faith and foster shoots of hope in our children.

God, be my ground of being today. Water me with your spirit and push my spiritual roots deeper into the soil of your love. Amen.

MARCH 30   POWER WITHIN

Now unto him that is able to do exceeding abundantly above all that we ask or think, according to the power that worketh in us.
(Ephesians 3:20 KJV)

How does she do it? There is a mother of two special needs children in our town who provokes awe. The special need of one of her children is a matter of amazing giftedness: he can sing like Luciano Pavarotti. The other child has physical challenges that baffle doctors. Rather than looking at her life with dismay, this mother tackles each day with prayer; and most days her positive spirit radiates as she grapples with the day's pile of obstacles. Somehow she finds time to organize a Bible study group at church. When she shares stories about her life, it is so obvious to the rest of us that God is at work through her. She sometimes can't see it; she is too close to her own life. We all are like that sometimes and need others to remind us. Those of us who are blessed to count ourselves as her friends know where her power comes from; and even when she can't see it, we can.

Lord, pour your power through me today. I need it. Amen.

MARCH 31   EXCHANGING ANXIETY FOR MEDITATION

For surely, O LORD, you bless the righteous; you surround them with your favor as with a shield.   *(Psalm 5:12 NIV)*

I once heard that meditation is a lot like worrying. Both require a tumbling and polishing of thoughts. I can worry over my child who is staying overnight with a new friend, turning it over and over in my mind and heightening my anxiety and solving nothing. Meditation differs from worry in that what I focus on is not my problems but God's promises. When I exchange my anxiety for meditation on God's promises of faithfulness, such as "For surely, O LORD, you bless the righteous; you surround them with your favor as with a sheild" (Psalm 5:12 NIV). I can focus my thoughts on God's promises toward me and my family and let my thoughts be tumbled in the polishing waters of prayerfulness. That does accomplish something: It strengthens my faith in the One who does provide, protect, and prompt to action.

Dear God, take my thoughts and polish them as prayers today. Amen.

April

Splashes of Grace

LAURA LEIGH PARKER

APRIL 1 THE PROVERBS 31 WOMAN

Charm and grace are deceptive, and beauty is vain [because it is not lasting], but a woman who reverently and worshipfully fears the Lord, she shall be praised! **(Proverbs 31:30 AMP)**

I have a confession to make: I don't like the Proverbs 31 woman. In my world of rearing four boys, I struggle to complete the most basic chores. Her list of accomplishments makes me feel inadequate—and irritable!

But what if she's not someone we must try to emulate but a promise of who the Lord is making us into? The precious Holy Spirit is at work in us, conforming us to the image of Jesus. Our task is to listen for God's voice and respond in obedience. As we do, the Lord is creating us into the women he has planned us to be.

This month I offer "splashes of grace"—reflections on times when the Lord has convicted me of something, comforted me, or taught me through scripture. You have these splashes of grace, too. And when we respond to these little revelations of God's work, we are changed. You may not see it, dear sister, but like a patchwork quilt, each little piece is part of a beautiful creation—you!

Lord, help us walk in the beauty of your promises of what you are creating us to be. Amen.

73

APRIL 2   GOOD GUILT

"Those whom I [dearly and tenderly] love, I tell their faults and convict and convince and reprove and chasten—[that is], I discipline and instruct them."   *(Revelation 3:19 AMP)*

In the verses preceding Revelation 3:19, the Lord lists several grievances he has with a particular church, including being "lukewarm," rich, self-sufficient, and unable to see their own faults. Then he balances those grievances with the words from today's verse. Have you ever said something similar to your children? Listen to the rest of the verse: "So be enthusiastic and in earnest and burning with zeal, and repent—changing your mind and attitude" (Revelation 3:19 AMP).

Why should we be enthusiastic and burning with zeal about hearing our faults and being convicted? Doesn't sound like much fun to me! Why does God convict and reprove? Because he loves us and wants our best. God always convicts or reproves with a specific purpose in mind—our good.

Dear Father, we thank you for your discipline because we know it means that you love us dearly. Help us see it as a doorway to deeper intimacy with you. Amen.

APRIL 3   JUMPING JEHOSHAPHAT

Then Jehoshaphat feared, and set himself [determinedly, as his vital need] to seek the Lord; he proclaimed a fast in all Judah.
                                              (2 Chronicles 20:3 AMP)

When I was facing a situation that overwhelmed me, the Lord led me to this story.

Jehoshaphat was king, and he tried to walk according to the ways of God. But he had a problem. The Ammonites, Moabites, and Meunites had banded together and were marching against him. Jehoshaphat was afraid, but he set himself to seek the Lord. All the people fasted and began to gather together to seek the Lord and pray. King Jehoshaphat prayed: "God, . . . we have no might to stand against this great company that is coming against us. We do not know what to do, but our eyes are upon You" (2 Chronicles 20:12 AMP).

When the Lord brought me to this story, I realized I had been trying to solve my problem alone. How sweet it was to give the problem to my loving, capable Lord. Dear sister, are you facing something that's too big for you? Jehoshaphat's God is your God, and he loves you.

Dear Father, thank you that you know what to do and have the power to do it. Amen.

APRIL 4   JUMPING JEHOSHAPHAT, CONTINUED

He said, Hearken, all Judah, you inhabitants of Jerusalem and you King Jehoshaphat, the Lord says this to you: Be not afraid or dismayed at this great multitude; for the battle is not yours but God's.   (2 Chronicles 20:15 AMP)

As the people assembled to seek God, the Spirit came upon a man named Jahaziel, and he comforted them with these words. The Lord also told the people to go out and meet the enemy—but not to fight.

Wouldn't you love to know what King Jehoshaphat must have thought? Nevertheless, the king obeyed. In fact, he appointed a group to go before the warriors and sing praises to God for his mercy and loving kindness.

On their way to meet Jehoshaphat, the Ammonites, Moabites, and Meunites began to quarrel and suspect one another of betrayal. This led to a battle between the attackers. By the time Jehoshaphat's group got to the meeting place, all the enemies were dead. It was finished before Jehoshaphat's group even got there.

Are you trying to take control of a battle that should be the Lord's? Give it to him, praise him, and look for his hand.

Mighty God, we thank you that you are willing and able to fight our battles. Help us release these hard places to you and wait for your direction. Amen.

APRIL 5   WHAT THE BEST-DRESSED WOMAN IS
                                    WEARING THIS SEASON

For you have stripped off the old (unregenerate) self with its evil practices, and have clothed yourselves with the new [spiritual self].   *(Colossians 3:9-10 AMP)*

We women spend a lot of time on our appearance; and I think looking attractive in a modest and tasteful way is a good thing— for ourselves and for our loved ones. Do we, though, put too much emphasis on dressing up the body in comparison with the time we spend on clothing ourselves spiritually? And how do we go about putting on the spiritual self, anyway? The stores I shop in don't sell that outfit!

First, we need to strip off the evil things that belong to our old selves. If God isn't happy with it, dump it! Then we must clothe ourselves with behaviors such as tenderhearted pity and mercy, kindness, humility, gentleness, patience, and endurance (see Colossians 3:12).

Gentle lady, you are God's chosen one, and through his grace you are purified, holy, and well beloved! So, clothe yourself accordingly. Clothing yourself with behaviors that are pleasing to God will make whatever you are wearing look fabulous!

Our Father, help us desire to be women who are clothed with behaviors that display we are yours. Amen.

APRIL 6   BEAUTIFUL PEOPLE

But as it is, God has placed and arranged the limbs and organs in the body, each (particular one) of them, just as He wished and saw fit and with the best adaption.
                                          (1 Corinthians 12:18 AMP)

I know some people I would describe as "beautiful people"— people who are recognized for accomplishing great things. I'm not one of those. Even in my role as a mother, I feel like my efforts at doing the laundry, feeding everyone, and keeping the bathrooms halfway clean are pretty unimportant compared with the lists of accomplishments of the "beautiful people."

If you, like me, feel a little "ordinary" sometimes, take heart. We are all parts of a body. Whether it's our church body or our family body, our role in that body is crucial. What's more, verse 24 says that we "ordinary" parts are to receive greater honor.

So, don't fret if you are not appreciated in your role in your home, or if you are not in an up-front position in your church. Your role has value and honor. Our job is to be obedient in being the part God has chosen us to be. If we do that, we will be "beautiful people."

Lord, help us be obedient in playing the part you give us and seeing the beauty and significance of it. Amen.

APRIL 7   WHERE'S YOUR FOCUS?

And He arose and rebuked the wind, and said to the sea, Hush now! Be still (muzzled)! And the wind ceased [that is, sank to rest as if exhausted by its beating] and there was (immediately) a great calm—a perfect peacefulness.   ***(Mark 4:39 AMP)***

Three of my boys participate in Bible quizzing in our church. They study a book of the Bible to be able to answer multiple-choice questions about it. One day I was studying with one of my boys when I came across this question:

When Jesus quieted the storm on the lake, did the disciples say

A. "Why did you let a storm come?"
B. "Who then is this, that even wind and sea obey Him?"

I knew the answer was B, but the Holy Spirit drew my attention to the first answer. I realized that when even small emergencies or irritations occur in my life, I often begin to question and say, "Lord, why did you let that happen?" My focus is on the storm—the thing that frightens, exhausts, or worries me—rather than on the Lord.

Just as God revealed a new facet of himself to the disciples that day, so God is revealing himself to us all the time, particularly in our times of greatest need. Look back at your own storms. What was he revealing to you about himself in those places?

Dearest Lord, help us see what you are revealing to us about you in our storms. Amen.

APRIL 8   OUTSTANDING

But Daniel determined in his heart that he would not defile himself by eating his portion of the king's rich and dainty food or with the wine which he drank.   *(Daniel 1:8 AMP)*

Daniel and his friends were young men when their country was invaded, and they were taken as captives to a land with a radically different set of moral and religious standards. With only the convictions of his path firmly planted in his heart, Daniel decided to live counterculturally.

Daniel had been granted a good deal for a prisoner of war. Any rejection of their hospitality could have been seen as ungratefulness. But to Daniel, it was a matter of not compromising his beliefs. When Daniel and his friends were introduced at the Babylonian court, they stood out from everyone else. Because of their "outstandingness," God began to reveal himself to a pagan people.

Like Daniel, we are to be different from those around us—so different that people notice. What is God calling you to "stand out" for? How can God use you to reveal himself to a pagan world around you?

Master, we live in a world that shrinks from convictions. Call us back to those convictions that are dear to your heart—even if it makes us stand out. Amen.

APRIL 9   UNDER AUTHORITY

As soon as [Jesus] got out of the boat, there met Him a man out of the tombs [under the power of] an unclean spirit. This man

continually lived among the tombs, and no one could subdue him any more, even with a chain. **(Mark 5:2-3 AMP)**

This man was someone's son—perhaps someone's husband. How did this happen to him? The scripture says he was "under the power." We're all under someone's authority. The question is, *Whose?*

Little by little, this man must have given authority to evil thoughts, which led to evil decisions and actions. Finally, he wandered around friendless in the midst of tombs.

We must walk carefully in this matter of authority. It begins with being willing to set all our thoughts and purposes under the lordship of Christ. That, in turn, affects our daily decisions. We are creatures made to worship. And we won't be satisfied until we put the right One on the throne!

At the end of the story, we see the man clothed and in his right mind (see Mark 5:6). He has put the right One on the throne. It was, and is, a question of authority.

Most High God, our hearts are satisfied only when you are on the throne. Help us guard against anything that would attempt to usurp your authority in our lives. Amen.

APRIL 10   GO HOME TO YOUR OWN

[Jesus] said to him, Go home to your own [family and relatives and friends], and bring back word to them of how much the Lord has done for you, and [how He has] had sympathy for you and mercy on you. **(Mark 5:19 AMP)**

The man who had been under the power of unclean spirits was now under the authority of the One who loved him. As Jesus stepped into the boat, the man begged to go with him. But Jesus asked him to go home.

We often think about sharing the gospel with someone who doesn't know the Lord. But the people we rub shoulders with every day need to hear what the Lord is doing in our lives. Are our children hearing how God has been good to us? Are we sharing answered prayers with our friends? What happens when we do?

Let's look at what happened to our friend. Mark 5:20 tells us that as he publicly proclaimed what Jesus had done, people were astonished and marveled. That sounds like God, doesn't it? The Lord may ask us to speak of him in many places, but we must not overlook the desperate need people we live with have to hear our story of faith.

Dear Lord, help us be faithful to go home to our own, proclaiming your sympathy, mercy, and love. Amen.

APRIL 11   SEIZED WITH ALARM

And they came to Jesus, and looked intently and searchingly at the man who had been a demoniac, sitting there clothed and in his right mind, [the same man] who had had the legion [of demons]; and they were seized with alarm and struck with fear.
(Mark 5:15 AMP)

The word must have gotten out quickly that something big had "gone down" out at the tombs! When the townspeople got there, they looked "intently" and "searchingly" at the man to see if this was "for real."

The scripture says they were afraid. Apparently, they knew that a work of great power had been done; but instead of rejoicing, they asked Jesus to leave! It makes me want to shake those silly, scared people. My heart aches for them, too, when I think of what Jesus might have done among them. Yet they asked him to leave because they were afraid of something they couldn't understand.

Are you ever afraid of the movement of God? I must admit that I fear change. So did the townspeople. But look at what they missed! Oh, sister, let's not let fear rob us of an encounter with the Living God!

Where is God inviting *you* to experience his power?

Most High God, help us follow you in trust, knowing you to be good and trustworthy. Amen.

APRIL 12 — GUARDING THE CITY

He who has no rule over his own spirit is like a city that is bro-ken down and without walls. **(Proverbs 25:28 AMP)**

Even in a family of males, I manage to carve out "girl time" to drink a cup of tea, garden, or anything that meets the need of my female chromosomes. Being female, however, brings its own set of challenges. Like most women, I tend to be a little undulating in my emotions.

Do moods ever color the way you speak to your children or affect how easily you get your feelings hurt? Our scripture says that a woman who has no control over her emotions is like a broken-down city without walls. Uncontrolled emotions leave us open to attack, making us vulnerable to the environment around us. A stressful situation, a cranky child, a late appointment, and we become "putty in the hands" of our circumstances.

We need to slow down and respond, not react. God understands what makes us tick, and we can take our emotions to him. Tell God about your anger, jealousy, or irritability. Confess and ask him to be Lord of your feelings. Proverbs 16:32 says that when we exert rule or restraint on our emotions through the strength of the Holy Spirit, we become better than the mighty!

Dear Father, help us not be ruled by our emotions but give our emotions into your safe authority. Amen.

APRIL 13 — DO VERSUS DO NOT

Rejoice and exult in hope; be steadfast and patient in suffering and tribulation; be constant in prayer. Contribute to the needs of God's people—sharing in the necessities of the saints—pur-suing the practice of hospitality. **(Romans 12:12-13 AMP)**

There are a lot of "do nots" in the Bible. Just check out the Ten Commandments. To be sure, there are many things God doesn't want his children to do. But have you ever thought that we Christians tend to recognize ourselves not by what we do but by what we don't do?

If people think we're Christians simply because we don't _____ (fill in the blank), then they have missed a huge part of what it means to be living the Christ life. Romans 12 lists a few of the things we are to take part in: rejoicing, exulting, being steadfast in suffering, being constant in prayer, contributing to God's people, pursuing hospitality.

In the Old Testament, the people of Israel were known as a peculiar people not only because they didn't follow the ways of the civilizations around them, but also because their practices, habits, and attitudes were different.

Let's not reduce our faith to a list of don'ts. Instead, let us be about the business of acting out what we believe.

Dear Lord, help us engage in the activities and actions that would mark us as your own. Amen.

APRIL 14   FAMILY MOTTO

May the God Who gives the power of patient endurance (steadfastness) and Who supplies encouragement, grant you to live in such mutual harmony and such full sympathy with one another, in accord with Christ Jesus, that together you may (unanimously) with united hearts ... praise and glorify the God and Father of our Lord Jesus Christ, the Messiah.
                                                            (Romans 15:5-6 AMP)

Have you noticed that the families of today's sitcoms are sarcastic and abusive? Perhaps people feel better when they can say, "Well, at least I am doing better than that!" Yet we Christians should get our standards from God, not culture.

The standards of today's verse are high, but you don't orchestrate this harmony by yourself. God is granting patient endurance and supplying encouragement to your family as you seek to live in harmony and sympathy with one another.

Your family is a little Body of Christ. Many days, between the brotherly bickering and the cranky-mom responses, I don't think our family resembles this picture. But now and then, God gives me a glimpse of this sweet harmony taking place in our little Body of Christ. That encourages me.

Let's be burdened for harmony and sympathy in our homes. Discarding the standards set by what is "normal" around us, let's look at the picture the Lord gives of a body of united hearts.

Dear Lord, help us look at your standards and not be discouraged but inspired. Amen.

APRIL 15   A PICTURE OF GOD

Beloved, if God loved us so [very much], we also ought to love one another.   *(1 John 4:11 AMP)*

As children, we know we're "supposed" to love others. Yet as we get older, this gets harder. Not everyone is nice. Not everyone is particularly likeable, and some are downright irritating! Even those we are closest to can be hard to love sometimes.

Today's verse tells us that we are "beloved," and that because we are so loved through no merit of our own, we should love one another. The next verse gives us another insight about why we should love others: "No man has at any time [yet] seen God. But if we love one another, God abides (lives and remains) in us and His love [that love which is essentially His] is brought to completion" (v. 12).

Though no one has seen God, others can see what God is like when Christians love one another. As we love the cranky and the bossy, God is displayed and lifted high for all to see.

Who around you is hard to love? Pray to love people with the love of the Lord Jesus. Our little trickle of love can be flooded with the mighty river and unending supply of God's love.

Dear Father, fill us so full of your love that we overflow onto other people's lives. Amen.

APRIL 16   BRIMFUL

I have great boldness and free and fearless confidence and cheerful courage toward you; my pride in you is great.   *(2 Corinthians 7:4 AMP)*

I am proud of my four boys, but sometimes I struggle with a critical spirit. Sometimes we women do so much teaching and training and guiding that we forget to say "well done" every once in a while. The end result becomes the goal instead of the countless lessons learned in attempting to get there.

This passage, written by Paul, tugs at my heart. He is talking about his church and how he feels about them. Did they have their problems? You bet. Did they always get things right? Definitely not! But, the affection and love Paul had for them bounces right off the page. Paul goes on to say that, despite all their trials, he is overflowing with joy. We need to speak such life-giving words to those we love.

Oh, the sweet comfort of being full of cheerful courage about the people we invest our lives in. Let's ask the Lord to make us so brimful of boldness, courage, and pride for those we love that we spill over and splash all over them!

Father, help me love with abandon. Fill me up, Lord, so that I can offer cool water to the thirsty. Amen.

APRIL 17   WAYS TO GIVE

Let each one [give] ... not reluctantly or sorrowfully or under compulsion, for God loves (that is, He takes pleasure in, prizes above other things, and is unwilling to abandon or to do without) a cheerful (joyous, prompt-to-do-it) giver—whose heart is in his giving.   **(2 Corinthians 9:7 AMP)**

The way we give matters to God. We are to give without reluctance, sorrow, or being under compulsion. That last one makes me cringe a little bit. Do you ever give because you feel "guilted" into it? Me, too. So, what's wrong with that? Simply put, it's not what God likes.

God loves a cheerful giver. The Amplified Bible indicates that God loves this type of giver so much that he is unwilling to do without her. God also likes a giver who purposes to give and then does it. Here is where I struggle. I can think of wonderful things to do for my friends and family, but if I don't purpose a certain plan of action, they just stay ideas.

Ask the Lord how to best use your time and who needs your particular ministry most. God is very practical, and he will guide you.

Dear God, soften our harried hearts with your touch so that we can be women after yours. Amen.

APRIL 18   ABUNDANCE

God is able to make all grace (every favor and earthly blessing) come to you in abundance, so that you may always and under all circumstances and whatever the need, be self-sufficient— possessing enough to require no aid or support and furnished in abundance for every good work and charitable donation.
(2 Corinthians 9:8 AMP)

D o you believe God has the power to help you with a cranky two-year-old or a grouchy boss? Is God able to meet the needs of the parents of a wayward teen? And what, I ask you, about someone struggling with hormones? (That one makes me laugh!)

Often I find myself murmuring things such as, "I can't help it," or "What can I do about it?" But this verse blows those excuses out of the water. Basically it says that God can supply us with everything we need for every circumstance we find ourselves in. What's more, he can supply us with *abundance*.

A little later in the same passage, we find a sound promise: God will multiply our resources and increase our fruit (v. 10). I like that. Let's let the Lord furnish us with his grace. How much do we need? An abundance!

Gracious Lord, remind us to slow down and call upon you, trusting that you will multiply our resources and increase our fruit. Amen.

APRIL 19   UNBELIEF

And He was not able to do even one work of power there, except that He laid His hands on a few sickly people [and] cured them.
(Mark 6:5 AMP)

Jesus had gone back to his hometown, and the people had not been receptive. They acknowledged his wisdom and his mighty works of power, but they just couldn't get past the fact that they had known him as a boy. So, their reaction was one of disapproval and offense.

In this verse, the lack of belief was credited as the cause for the lack of miracles. Hmm. Could our belief—or lack of it—affect how the Lord works in our lives? Scripture clearly makes the connection. Go back and read the miracles in the Gospels. When Jesus drew out individuals for a work of power, he frequently questioned their state of heart and mind on the issue of belief.

What about you? Do you believe that the Lord who worked miracles with a touch or a word is the same Lord who works in your life? He is drawn to believing hearts—even honest hearts that acknowledge their unbelief and cry out for help (see Mark 9:24).

O Lord, help our weak hearts to be stirred up to mighty belief! Amen.

APRIL 20   THE CHURCH OF ACTS

And they worshipping Him went back to Jerusalem with great joy, and they were continually in the temple celebrating with praises and blessing and extolling God.   (Luke 24:52-53 AMP)

Jesus had just been taken up to heaven after his resurrection. The disciples were instructed to wait for the promised Holy Spirit. Did they act like defeated people? Scripture says they went with joy and were always in the temple celebrating!

In the book of Acts, we see that after Pentecost the disciples devoted "themselves constantly to the instruction and fellowship of the apostles, to the breaking of bread [including the Lord's

Supper] and prayers" (2:42 AMP). Another passage tells us that they "regularly assembled in the temple with united purpose, and in their homes they broke bread [including the Lord's Supper]. They partook of their food with gladness and simplicity and generous hearts" (2:46 AMP).

These men studied together, ate together, and prayed together. Jesus' resurrection and the coming of the Holy Spirit changed everything. It was obvious that they were full of the Lord. And since they were in the temple all the time, everyone saw them! I'm sure there were some who thought they were just plain weird. That's OK. We could use a little more of that in our churches today. Amen?

Dear Lord, embolden us to live obviously different lives. Amen.

APRIL 21   BLESSINGS

Now we have not received the spirit (that belongs to) the world, but the (Holy) Spirit Who is from God, [given to us] that we might realize and comprehend and appreciate the gifts (of divine favor and blessing so freely and lavishly) bestowed on us by God. **(1 Corinthians 2:12 AMP)**

In the past when people would tell me of a material or financial blessing, I would think, *So where is my blessing?* Then God began to deal with my jealousy. Look at the verse above. Since we do not have this world's spirit, we should be able to perceive things differently. So, I began to ask God to help me "see" his blessings. If we feel lavishly blessed and adored, it's hard to feel envious!

Having good health is a blessing. Having children is a blessing. A blessing could be something as simple as a delicious meal eaten with people we love. One of the reasons we have received the Holy Spirit is so that we might know we are a blessed people. So, ask God to make you aware of his many gifts. Open your spiritual eyes and thank him. And the next time a friend tells you of a blessing, you'll have one to share as well!

O Father, it's hard not to compare. Change our focus. Help us feel your lavish love. Amen.

APRIL 22   HOME BUILDING 101

You are built upon the foundation of the apostles and prophets with Christ Jesus Himself the chief Cornerstone. In Him the whole structure is joined (bound, welded) together harmoniously; and it continues to rise (grow, increase) into a holy temple in the Lord—a sanctuary dedicated, consecrated and sacred to the presence of the Lord. **(Ephesians 2:20-21 AMP)**

The cultural trend is for us to be mere *decorators* of our homes rather than *builders*. Just look at the number of home decorating magazines, television shows, and stores.

It's a good thing to want our homes to be places of beauty; but if we are giving more time to redecorating than to laying a sound foundation through family prayer, personal devotions, and Bible study, it may be time for a reevaluation. The very things we want for our homes—peace, warmth, happiness, and love—are gifts of God that can only be gained from obedience.

So, as we contemplate a new couch, let's remember that one of our primary callings is to partner with the Lord in home building. Let us nurture our homes so that they are places that are dedicated to the presence of the Lord.

Lord, don't let us get so caught up in the trappings of our homes that we lose sight of what is important to you. Amen.

APRIL 23   PURSUING GOALS

Knowledge causes people to be puffed up—to bear themselves loftily and be proud; but love, [that is] affection and goodwill and benevolence, edifies and builds up and encourages one to grow [to his full stature]. **(1 Corinthians 8:1 AMP)**

The articles in women's magazines tend to focus on organization, beauty, health and fitness, one's sex life, and home decor. A tremendous amount of our energy goes into running after these things—and they're not necessarily bad in themselves. However, they can get in the way of pursuing the qualities God admires.

When you're talking with friends, how often do you hear, "She's so loving, I wish I were more like her"? Well, love certainly is a quality God esteems. Our verse says we could have knowledge (be in great shape, have a neat house, be organized), but if love (affection, goodwill, and benevolence) doesn't define our lives, we might be "barking up the wrong tree."

Are you more loving than five years ago? What would your children answer? Are you spending more time and energy pursuing your next work-out goal than seeking hard after love? Let's ask God for an edifying, encouraging, building love that spills over on those we live among. That's a goal worth pursuing!

Dear Lord, shift our focus onto the things you deem of vital importance. Amen.

APRIL 24   RULES OF THE TRAIL

And cut through and make firm and plain and smooth, straight paths for your feet—[yes, make them] safe and upright and happy paths that go in the right direction—so that the lame and halting [limbs] may not be put out of joint, but rather may be cured.   (Hebrews 12:13 AMP)

Our family likes to hike. We've tried to ingrain in our boys the importance of being aware of the hiker behind you. Frequently, one of our boys would push aside a branch only to let it snap back on the person behind him. Trailside talks would follow! Gradually, we began to see our young naturalists consider those around them.

As women, we have an influential touch on the lives of so many. Do you know any people who are lame? What about people who are weak or fragile? What about the young? Possibly, you know people who are strong and capable but who are going through a difficulty and need your guidance.

We are called to be path makers. What kinds of paths are you cutting for younger women to follow? What about your family? Remember the rules of the trail: Always consider the hiker behind you. And remember, all the while we are following a Leader who always makes a path for us.

Lord, help us bravely follow you, and help us be trustworthy women and tender lovers of the ones who follow us. Amen.

APRIL 25   ADOPTION OR SLAVERY?

God sent His Son, ... to purchase the freedom of (to ransom, to redeem, to atone for) those who were subject to the Law, that we might be adopted and have sonship conferred upon us—be recognized as [God's] sons.   *(Galatians 4:4-5 AMP)*

Jesus came to redeem we who were under the Law so that we might be adopted as his children. A later verse tells us, "Therefore, you are no longer a slave (bond servant) but a son; and if a son, then [it follows that you are] an heir by the aid of God, through Christ" (v. 7).

Before Christ, we were living as slaves; now we are children of God. What a rags-to-riches story! All of our Father's resources are available to us. We have a Father who loves us; and because of his love and grace, we are his rightful heirs.

How often do we find ourselves living in slavery? Do we say things such as, "I just can't help it"? Do we go out to meet our days in a spirit of defeat? Do we allow people or things to take places of authority over us when they have no right to? Take your rightful place as a child and heir. You are chosen and wanted, and your Father's resources are available to you.

Lord, help us walk out in full confidence of your love and provision because we belong to you. Amen.

APRIL 26   DANIEL'S GOD

Then King Nebuchadnezzar fell on his face, and paid homage to Daniel [as a great prophet of the highest God].... The king answered Daniel, Of a truth your God is God of gods and Lord of kings, and a revealer of secret mysteries, seeing that you could reveal this secret mystery!   *(Daniel 2:46-47 AMP)*

Nebuchadnezzar had a strange dream, and he was troubled. The king demanded that his royal advisors interpret his dream—without him telling them what the dream was! And he told them that if they could not do this, he would have them killed. Talk about pressure!

Daniel was included in this group of unfortunate advisors, so he immediately brought the matter to his friends and asked them to pray with him. God revealed the dream and its meaning to Daniel. It was obvious to everyone—even a pagan king—that this was a miracle. Nebuchadnezzar fell on his knees, declaring that Daniel's God was the God of all gods, because Nebuchadnezzar encountered something only God could do.

When we pray, do we expect miracles? Well, sweet sister, Daniel certainly did! And look what happened! You have a big God! So, lady, pray like it!

Most High God, forgive us for our small prayers of weak faith. Let us pray boldly, expecting you to do what only you can do. Amen.

APRIL 27   SPIRITUAL ATTENTION DEFICIT
                                                    DISORDER

And He said to them, Be careful what you are hearing. The measure [of thought and study] you give [to the truth you hear] will be the measure [of virtue and knowledge] that comes back to you.   *(Mark 4:24 AMP)*

Sometimes I find myself spiritually distracted. I'm moved with a profound insight only to forget it days later. It's like I have spiritual Attention Deficit Disorder!

This verse indicates that the measure of effort, thought, and focus we put toward God's revelations of truth has a direct bearing on how much fruit we receive from it. What the Lord says to us is worthy of being recorded, displayed on index cards, pondered on, and prayed over. And the Lord is so bounteous with us. He promises: "More [besides] will be given to you who hear. For to him who has will more be given, and from him who has nothing, even what he has will be taken away (by force)" (vv. 24-25 AMP). God not only gives us fruit according to the measure we use; he gives more!

So, let's get serious about hearing from God and then allowing the truth to have its full work in our lives.

Gracious Lord, help us treat your revelations with reverence.
Give us a crystal-clear focus that cuts through the things that
would distract us from the insights you give us. Amen.

APRIL 28   TEMPLES

Do you not know that your body is the temple—the very sanc-
tuary—of the Holy Spirit Who lives within you? . . . You are not
your own, you were bought for a price—purchased with pre-
ciousness and paid for, made His own. So then, honor God and
bring glory to Him in your body.   (1 Corinthians 6:19-20 AMP)

I struggle with this verse, because I find myself drawn to foods
that are not healthful for me. I stay up late at night to read and
then drink too much caffeine to compensate for my tiredness. I
overplan and get irritable because of the frenetic pace I'm leading.

   This verse calls me to something higher. My daily habits of eating, sleeping, exercising (or not) are not just about me. I am
instructed to honor God and bring glory to him *in my body*. This
means we're under authority even on personal things such as what
we eat and wear, how much sleep we get, and how we use our
time.

   God has a right to "get in our business." Are there things you
need to do more of or less of to glorify God in your body?
Remember, we are God's own—purchased with preciousness.

O Lord, help us listen and obey even in small, daily choices.
Amen.

APRIL 29   BEARING UP AND WALKING OUT

Bear (endure, carry) one another's burdens and troublesome
moral faults, and in this way fulfill and observe perfectly the
law of Christ, the Messiah.   (Galatians 6:2 AMP)

When you hear the word *burden*, do you think of a heavy weight
or an oppressive load? Scripture says we're to cast those burdens

on the Lord. This verse, however, instructs us to bear one another's burdens. I thought that meant to help one another with our problems, but the Amplified Bible describes it as "troublesome moral faults." It appears that bearing one another's burdens includes a certain amount of "putting up with" a person's less attractive qualities.

In Galatians 6:5 we read: "For every person will have to bear [be equal to understanding and calmly receive] his own (little) load [of oppressive faults]" (AMP). As we're bearing up with others' burdens and faults, they're bearing up with ours.

What person are you having to "bear with"? Perhaps you are called to bear with them through grief or sadness. But it also could mean loving in spite of a personality you find difficult. Trust, though, that as you do this, you are observing Christ's law, and that someone is loving you in the same way.

Dear God, expand our minds to what it means to bear with one another. Then give us the strength to walk it out. Amen.

APRIL 30   ALL ABOUT GRACE

[All] are justified and made upright and in right standing with God, freely and gratuitously by His grace (His unmerited favor and mercy), through the redemption which is [provided] in Christ Jesus.   (Romans 3:24 AMP)

As mothers, we often hear, "It's not fair!" Our wants and needs may be bigger, but our attitude is often the same.

One of the things I struggled with was the desire for a bigger house. As a family of six, we were walking all over one another in our little house. The problem wasn't my desire; it was that many of my friends had a bigger house and fewer children, and I found myself in an attitude of "it's not fair."

One day my boys and I went to a strawberry patch to gather berries. Soon I began to notice thick, black clouds gathering over us. "No, Lord, not yet; they're having such a rich time. Please, just let us finish."

The rain held off until we got into our van. I marveled that God would hold back the rain just for us. He spoke to my heart, saying, "You didn't earn this rain-free time; I just graced you with it."

I'd been so busy proving why I "deserved" a bigger house that I'd forgotten it's all about grace. None of us deserves anything; we're just receivers of God's goodness.

Trust God with your desires. Beware the comparison game. And the next time you feel you've not been treated fairly, remind yourself that, indeed, you have not. Praise God!

Dear Father, sometimes we must sound like whiny two-year-olds. Help us put our desires into your safekeeping. Amen.

May

Gifted to Be a Mother

GINNY UNDERWOOD

MAY 1   LOVE

Beloved, let us love one another, for love is of God; and every-one who loves is born of God and knows God. He who does not love does not know God, for God is love.   (1 John 4:7-8 NKJV)

Carrying the title Mother is both wonderful and challenging. This month we will be exploring the extraordinary gifts and skills that God has given us women to become great mothers. We will consider these gifts in relationship to our own families as well as to our global family.

First, we mothers are to love. I heard the best definition of a mother's love during a brief airplane conversation several years ago. I had been married only a couple of years and wasn't considering starting a family. The woman sitting next to me told me about her children and asked if I planned to have any. At the time, I said no. She gasped and started to tell me about her experience as a mother. She said, "It's like a whole other part of your heart opens up that you didn't even know you had."

I often reflect on that conversation and thank God for the experience. She was right. A mother's love is a never-empty treasure box. You find strength, love, hope, and patience when you need it the most.

Today, enjoy knowing that God has equipped you with exactly what you need to face the day.

Dear heavenly Father, thank you for the abilities you give us to be loving mothers. Amen.

MAY 2   GIVE

Give thanks to the LORD, for he is good; his love endures forever. *(1 Chronicles 16:34 NIV)*

During a business trip to Mutare, Zimbabwe, I witnessed some extraordinary things mothers were doing to support their children. In a small rural area facing extreme economic hardships, mothers were finding ways to make a difference. They were not able to contribute financially to the education of their children, so their payment and support came in the form of sweat equity. Many mothers were helping to build a new room for the high school. In the United States, such an endeavor would involve contractors and heavy equipment. In Zimbabwe, it meant that everyone in the community had to pitch in. Many mothers helped make bricks from natural resources and then transport them by wheelbarrows to the new site. I even witnessed some women carrying stacks of bricks on their heads. From watching the work of their mothers, the children who will be enjoying the new classrooms have already learned priceless lessons about love and sacrifice.

Thank you, Lord, for giving us the desire and strength to meet needs and to make meaningful contributions in the lives of our children. Amen.

MAY 3   INSPIRE

"Let your light shine before [others], that they may see your good deeds and praise your Father in heaven." *(Matthew 5:16 NIV)*

For me, inspiration from my mother has not been confined to a single moment. It has been a chain of events. My inspiration was in seeing my mother work diligently to provide for the family financially and emotionally. It was in her quiet presence as we learned how to do things for the first time. It was in her calming voice that wiped away tears and set us back on our feet. My inspiration has come from watching a woman live her life in a Godlike fashion.

Now that I'm a mother, I ponder at how she was able to keep such a graceful exterior while dealing with the heaviness of responsibility and duty. For my entire life I have watched this vision of inspiration; but I was unable to see its full beauty until it was my turn to inspire my own children.

God has such a plan for us. He has so many gifts to give us in his own time.

Father, thank you for the inspiration you give mothers. Help us feel inspired and renewed by the gifts of the Holy Spirit. Amen.

MAY 4   CARE

"A new command I give you: Love one another. As I have loved you, so you must love one another."   *(John 13:34 NIV)*

Mary is a missionary and a social worker in Senegal. She spends her time working with young women who either left school early or never attended at all. This situation is common in a country where 65 percent of women are illiterate. Breaking economic and cultural barriers is difficult. Figures show that in most countries, women actually do twice as much unpaid work as men and work longer hours, according to "Paddling in Circles While the Waters Rise" by Angela M. Kuga Thas (APC Women's Networking Support Programme, 2005).

As the scripture says, we are called to be in relationship with all our brothers and sisters around the world. As mothers, we have the opportunity to stand in solidarity with others who are struggling for ways to better their situation and provide for their families. Please be in prayer for women like Mary, who work on the frontlines against poverty and hardship, trying to make a difference.

Father, you know our hearts and our desires. Please give us the will to care for all of your children and to glorify you in our daily efforts. Amen.

MAY 5   SUPPORT

When I said, "My foot is slipping," your love, O LORD, supported me. When anxiety was great within me, your consolation brought joy to my soul.   *(Psalm 94:18-19 NIV)*

After a recent softball game, my daughter pulled me aside and said, "Momma, you are embarrassing me." My enthusiasm and vocal support seems to be wasted on my six-year-old slugger. She says she can hear me all the way in the outfield. I gingerly say, "That's my job." I'm her number one fan. I will always be her number one fan.

We all know that in life it's nice to have someone rooting for you. As we get older, pats on the back or vocal acclamations are harder to come by and probably more needed than ever. Support for our children is one of the greatest gifts we can give. A little support early on gives them a strong foundation to be able to step out on their own later in life.

Remember, our number one fan is God. He, too, is standing on the sidelines ready to offer support whenever we ask.

God, thank you for the foothold you give us every day. Thank you for anchoring us with your love and giving us the strength to lead our families. Amen.

MAY 6   PROTECT

Love does not delight in evil but rejoices with the truth. It always protects, always trusts, always hopes, always perseveres.
                                        (1 Corinthians 13:6-7 NIV)

I overheard an interesting conversation between two colleagues about one daughter's diary. The teenage daughter left the diary open in her bedroom. The mother read everything, claiming it was her duty to do so. It's a very compelling topic. Is the right to privacy more important than the parent's right to know what is going on? The mother has an understanding with the children that her job is to protect them. If that means prying into their private lives, so be it. A family therapist I know says that a parent's job is to be involved. She says, "Children need to have a parent who is willing to say, 'No'; hear their child say, 'I hate you'; and then turn around to their child and say, 'OK, but I love you.'"

God has given us a responsibility to protect our children. Today that means tough talks about diaries, online chats, and text messaging.

Dear Lord, please give us the strength and courage to talk with our children about difficult issues. Please bless us with guidance and wisdom. Amen.

MAY 7   MOTIVATE

Let us not become weary in doing good, for at the proper time we will reap a harvest if we do not give up. (Galatians 6:9 NIV)

Motivating a three-year-old and six-year-old to listen to Mommy is simple right now. All I have to do is start counting to three. It's understood that the worst possible consequence will occur if Mommy ever gets to three. Fortunately for all of us, that has never been tested. However, direct threats are not the way I want to motivate my children. My husband and I spend long conversations helping the girls see the big picture to their actions. Most of the time, we are helping them think about other people. We want their motivation to be about kindness, love, and support. It may seem like mature subject matter at this age, but they understand the basics of being happy and helping others.

These are important talks to have with our children, for we are raising children in an age that is heavily influenced by consumerism and commercialism. Consider "unplugging" for a day to discuss with your children how Christian values motivate us in different ways, remembering that we "do all things through Christ who strengthens [us]" (Philippians 4:13 NKJV).

Thank you, Father, for making a promise to us for everlasting life. There is no stronger motive to do your will.

MAY 8   GUARD

And the peace of God, which transcends all understanding, will guard your hearts and your minds in Christ Jesus.
                                                 (Philippians 4:7 NIV)

Satellite technology has been launched around the world to track endangered species, criminals, and your car. It won't be long until we'll be able to track our children online from anywhere in the world. Wouldn't it be nice to also have a magic button to buzz our children when we think they are making bad decisions? Although that might be a reality someday, we can't make decisions for our children all the time. Empowering them with knowledge is the best guard against bad decisions. Teaching them how to include prayer in their decision-making processes and to consult with appropriate people is vital.

   Work to create an environment that allows your children to talk about difficult scenarios, and help them think about how to negotiate the issues before they happen.

Lord, help us equip our children with knowledge to make good decisions. Protect and keep them while we are apart. Amen.

MAY 9   TEACH

But the fruit of the Spirit is love, joy, peace, patience, kindness, goodness, faithfulness, gentleness and self-control.
                                               (Galatians 5:22-23 NIV)

Downtown in the city where I live, it's not uncommon to see people standing at intersections asking for money. I see this so often that I have trained myself to not even look at the people who are standing outside my car window. One afternoon, my daughters were with me on an errand. We came to a light, moving very slowly. My daughter

Avery did not look away from the man on the corner. In fact, she wanted to know what his sign was about. I explained to her that it said he was homeless and needed money. We pulled through the light and went to our destination. As I opened the door, I realized that she was weeping. I asked her what was wrong. She said, "Momma, he needed help and no one was helping him." What a teaching moment for me. Her innocent expression melted my heart and helped me remember the mandate to love one another.

We went back to the corner and made our donation to the homeless man. Avery also promised to pray for him.

Father, thank you for the teaching moments you give us each day. Help us open our hearts and minds to understand the lessons you put before us. Amen.

MAY 10   FORGIVE

"For if you forgive [others] when they sin against you, your heavenly Father will also forgive you." (Matthew 6:14 NIV)

When I was preparing to be a mother, I did the usual things such as take vitamins and eat healthier. I also was concerned about my spiritual wellness. I was aware of ill feelings that I had had toward one person for several years. The rift came from my parents' divorce. I blamed my father's second wife for the struggle we all went through. I held these feelings for at least a decade. As I thought about becoming a mom, I knew I had to let those feelings go. I didn't want my child to know that kind of hate or dislike from me—feelings we all learn too quickly in this world. So, I finally did what God had been calling me to do for many years: I forgave her and all involved. What a great feeling to let all of those burdens go forever. I can't believe I spent so many years allowing myself to feel so bad about a situation when God gives us the power to forgive.

God, thanks for your forgiveness and for loving us with all our imperfections. Help us remember to be like Christ on our journey and to love all of our brothers and sisters. Amen.

MAY 11   MINISTER

"I needed clothes and you clothed me, I was sick and you looked after me, I was in prison and you came to visit me."
                                            (Matthew 25:36 NIV)

I met Lynette, a social worker, in Zimbabwe. She detailed the hardships children in her community are dealing with. The effects of a harsh economic situation, health challenges, and an unstable government are at the fiber of families there. In many cases, she is dealing with HIV/AIDS orphans. By the year 2010, the World Health Organization is projecting that eighteen million children in Africa will be orphans because of the disease. Lynette's work is cut out for her. She serves as a mother to hundreds of children. She says that it's critical to reach out, even if the most she can offer them is a meal and a prayer.

Please remember in prayer women around the world who are ministers of love and compassion. Let us celebrate their work and contributions to the greater good of society.

Today, Lord, we ask for strength for the women working around the world to better the lives of children. Give them wisdom and courage to carry on. Amen.

MAY 12   NURSE

Therefore confess your sins to each other and pray for each other so that you may be healed. The prayer of a righteous man is powerful and effective.   *(James 5:16 NIV)*

Both of my daughters were prone to ear infections as babies. For me, as their nurse and caregiver, this meant many nights with no sleep and tired arms from holding them upright. I remember the turmoil I would go through trying to troubleshoot in my head what could be wrong. Though both of them have outgrown the ear infections, I still vividly remember holding them close and stroking their hair. I even remember the gurgles of relief they would make when the medicine kicked in and they were able to sleep.

As mothers, we truly carry our children's burdens with them. Whether they are eight months or eighteen years old, we pray and hope that they are healed and safe. This is the same prayer our heavenly Father makes for us. He is always there with a prescription of comfort and love whenever we need it, no matter what ails us.

Thank you, Lord, for modeling love and compassion. Give us the patience and ability to nurse and comfort our children when they need it the most. Amen.

MAY 13   PASS ON TRUTH

Only be careful, and watch yourselves closely so that you do not forget the things your eyes have seen or let them slip from your heart as long as you live. Teach them to your children and to their children after them.   *(Deuteronomy 4:9 NIV)*

We live in a challenging time to raise children. My three-year-old daughter wants to wear crop-top shirts "like Barbie." My seven-year-old is already concerned about her weight. They are heavily influenced by the bombardment of media images they see every day. Balance is critical in helping to shape how they perceive themselves and how much they "buy" into secular culture.

I wasn't quite ready to have conversations about appropriate clothing and the principles of beauty this soon. Nonetheless, I find myself prayerfully explaining Christian principles in an effort to fight back against television networks and advertising companies. We must teach our children not only right from wrong but also how to discern truth in modern messaging—a difficult task when truth seems to be airbrushed to an unobtainable perfection.

There is only one perfect thing, and that is the love of God.

Father, we give thanks for the transforming power to take all of our imperfections and make them great for your glory. Amen.

MAY 14   SPOIL

But the needy will not always be forgotten, nor the hope of the afflicted ever perish.   *(Psalm 9:18 NIV)*

As my daughter and I walked through the back-to-school section one year, we loaded up on brand-new pencils, crayons, glue, and scissors. We also went through a series of shopping trips to find back-to-school clothes and accessories.

Recently I had the opportunity to travel to Zimbabwe and spend time at a primary school there. At this school of five hundred students, one-third of the students are AIDS orphans. What we would call basic school supplies are not options there. Some of the children are barefoot and wear shorts in the middle of winter. Because of the difficult economic situation, children can expect no coat drives, no allotment of shoes, and sometimes only one meal a day.

I write about these things to create an awareness of need and to put our own situations in context. Living in America, our children are very blessed. In this culture that teaches us to consume, may we give our children balance by teaching them to have a global perspective of human need around the world.

Father, thank you for the many blessings you have bestowed upon us. Help us share the wealth you have given us with those who are in desperate need. Amen.

MAY 15   SERVE

And it shall come to pass in the day that the LORD shall give thee rest from thy sorrow, and from thy fear, and from the hard bondage wherein thou wast made to serve.   *(Isaiah 14:3 KJV)*

When my oldest daughter, Avery, was born, I thought the instincts of motherhood would automatically kick in. I had always envisioned the idealized version of motherhood with smiles, a lot of cuddling, and each moment filled with pure happiness. It wasn't exactly like that for me. I had to work pretty hard to make things such as feeding and sleeping happen. It took some time for Avery and me to teach each other how to be mommy and daughter. I quickly figured out that if she lay close to me, we could both sleep a little longer. I also realized that time as I knew it no longer existed. We were now on "baby time," and that has no regard for daylight or convenience. I learned that motherhood parallels the concept of the convenience store: you are open twenty-four hours.

As we serve our children, we must also take time to draw from the well of strength God provides us. Thankfully, it, too, features around-the-clock service.

Give us strength today, Lord, to serve you with all of our abilities. Help us find humility as we do your work. Amen.

MAY 16   INDULGE

"Remember the Sabbath day by keeping it holy."
(Exodus 20:8 NIV)

For most of us, the daily routine is fast paced and arduous. It's a race to make lunches, get out of the house and off to school and work, pick up the kids, run taxi service to team sports, eat dinner, help with homework, and go to bed. There's little, if any, quiet time. Our children see us as a driver, cook, tutor, and coach. It's important, however, for them to see another side of us as well. How about Mom the person? She likes long walks, fresh flowers, prayer time, and an occasional massage.

Indulge yourself without guilt. Think about the lessons you teach your children about taking personal time and being balanced in all aspects of their lives. You will feel better, and they will appreciate your renewed strength and spirit.

Father, as you know, we mothers have a difficult time taking breaks. Please remind us of the Sabbath. Help us remember to renew ourselves physically and spiritually each day. Amen.

MAY 17   PLAY

Find rest, O my soul, in God alone; my hope comes from him.
He alone is my rock and my salvation; he is my fortress, I will
not be shaken.   *(Psalm 62:5-6 NIV)*

One of the greatest lessons my children have taught me is how
to play. Somewhere along the way, I lost the ability to simply
play. I tend to focus on getting things done, which means laundry, cleaning, meals, and errands. I wake up with a plan for the
day. Thankfully, that may not jibe with Barbie's makeover needs
or a stuffed animal's spontaneous birthday party. It's hard for
me to put down a laundry basket to play patty-cake, but as I find
out after a few moments of laughter, I need it as much as my
daughter needs my attention and time. I like to think of these
playful breaks as "Sabbath moments." We mothers are called to
lay down our burdens and rest our souls, because finding down-
time is difficult. We must seek "Sabbath moments" whenever
we can.

Today, look for opportunities to play and take a break.
Remember your own personal need for spiritual renewal.

Thank you, Lord, for opening our hearts to the lessons you
teach us through our children. Help us remember the Sabbath
and renew our strength so we may glorify you. Amen.

MAY 18   FOLLOW *AND* LEAD

Guide me in your truth and teach me, for you are God my
Savior, and my hope is in you all day long.   *(Psalm 25:5 NIV)*

In my work for a church-related communications organization,
I'm frequently asked to travel a couple of times a month. I often
spend hours thinking about the time away from home, because it
involves the hassle of lining up babysitters, meals, and activities
for the week. More important, it means I'm sacrificing precious
time away from my two girls and my husband. Yet God has called
me to this work, and I must follow where he leads. I always come

down to the same conclusion: God has a purpose through my work not only for my life, but also for my family.

I take comfort in the belief that because I am following God's call, my family is learning important lessons about visiting new places and people through my work experience. Through my example, I hope my children are learning that the only limitations they have are in their minds. Through my example, I hope the girls will see and explore all the beauty God has created in this world.

Are you leading your children by following God's call on your life?

Father, give us courage to follow your call. May we lead our children by example. Amen.

MAY 19   NOURISH

"And the King will answer them, 'Truly, I say to you, as you did it to one of the least of these my brothers, you did it to me.'"
(Matthew 25:40 ESV)

During a work trip to Zimbabwe, we took students out to practice photography at some rural schools. A woman and her sons were sitting on the porch of their home watching us. We were given sack lunches for the day. The economic conditions in the area were such that it was not uncommon for people to have only one meal a day. Knowing this, I offered my lunch to the mother. She graciously took it and went inside. The boys casually filed into the home. I realized I had more to give and went back. I saw the mother frantically looking for plates as the boys jumped up and down in delight. I was deeply touched. It was a small gesture in a place where need was so great. The nourishment was physical to them but spiritual to me.

Today, remember mothers who must rely on spiritual nourishment more than physical. Let us be in prayerful solidarity with them.

Father, thank you for providing us with physical and spiritual nourishment every day. Help us remember the least and forgotten today. Amen.

MAY 20   COMFORT

"Peace I leave with you; my peace I give you. I do not give to you as the world gives. Do not let your hearts be troubled and do not be afraid."   *(John 14:27 NIV)*

When I was a young girl, we would often stay with my grandmother and grandfather. Everyone was expected to get up early. I remember my grandfather walking the halls trying to rally everyone out of bed. As the youngest in the family, I would wait until he passed me, and then I would dash down the hall and crawl into bed with my grandmother. The flannel sheets were warm, the room smelled like fresh flowers, and she always hid me until we were ready to get up. She made me feel special and loved.

It's truly a gift to know that kind of comfort. I believe it's a kind of comfort that parallels the presence of God. What a blessing to know that feeling and be able to share with my own children and others.

Today, take time to remember a moment in which you found great comfort. Seek an opportunity to pass along a sentiment of peace and comfort to someone in need.

Thank you, Father, for being a comforting force in our lives. May your love wrap around us today and remind us to whom we belong. Amen.

MAY 21   HAVE A SENSE OF HUMOR

Our mouths were filled with laughter, our tongues with songs of joy. Then it was said among the nations, "The LORD has done great things for them."   *(Psalm 126:2 NIV)*

We are avid moviegoers in the Underwood family. We like to see all of the "kid movies," usually on the day they come out. One afternoon, a movie trailer had my girls and me in a roaring laughter. When the sound went off, we realized that we were the only people in the entire theater laughing. I wonder if humor is hereditary. If that's the case, my children will have a lifetime of giggles and awkward humorous moments.

One of the most important attributes and gifts God has given to mothers is the ability to laugh and find humor in many things. Sometimes we find ourselves in situations where all we can do is laugh. Laughter relieves tension and helps us keep things in perspective.

As author G. K. Chesterton wrote in his book *Orthodoxy,* "Angels can fly because they can take themselves lightly." Try to find humor in the things that burden you, and see if you can find a lighter outlook.

God, help us be able to lay down our burdens and find humor to lift our spirits. Amen.

MAY 22   PROVIDE

If anyone does not provide for his relatives, and especially for his immediate family, he has denied the faith and is worse than an unbeliever.   *(1 Timothy 5:8 NIV)*

Grandparents, according to U.S. Census data, are raising more than six million children—approximately one in twelve. My mother-in-law falls into this category. She is raising my twelve-year-old nephew. It's a challenge for her on a limited income. However, this being her "second time around," she is able to provide a bit more in terms of shelter, food, and clothing than she was able to provide for her own children. My nephew also has the luxury of computers, video games, and cable television. Most important, she gives him love and discipline. She provides him with a constant presence, which he is unable to get from either of his parents. However, like many grandparents who are raising children, she faces challenges such as finances, health, and isolation.

Today, please pray for women who find themselves in this growing trend of second-time-around mothers.

Today, Lord, please renew the strength of women who are raising children for a second time. Fill them with wisdom and courage to guide a new generation on a path to righteousness. Amen.

MAY 23   BE PATIENT

***There is a time for everything, and a season for every activity
under heaven.***   ***(Ecclesiastes 3:1-3 NIV)***

At the end of kindergarten, my daughter Avery's teacher recommended that she go to "transition one" instead of first grade. This was a bit of a shock to my husband and me—the very idea of red-shirting our daughter so early in her educational career. She proceeded to tell us that Avery needed time to mature. Being the competitive parents we are, we retorted that she was perfectly capable of moving on. After a lot of reflection, we began to ask ourselves, *What is the big rush?* I know in my own life I have pushed myself hard to reach whatever goal is before me. In that process, I have missed out on important experiences along the way. So what if Avery has an extra year to be a kid and enjoy the simpler things in life? We had to put aside our own aspirations for our child and find the patience to support her need to develop and grow at her own pace.

***Help us remember that life is not a race, Lord. Be patient with
us, and give us the patience to support our children and meet
their needs in their own time. Amen.***

MAY 24   BE HUMBLE

***He has showed you, O man, what is good. And what does the
Lord require of you? To act justly and to love mercy and to
walk humbly with your God.***   ***(Micah 6:8 NIV)***

I would like for you to meet Gena. She lives a humble existence with her six children in a rural town in Oklahoma. Imogene is a faithful member of her church. If the church doors are open, you will find her there.

One evening, Gena was perplexed about the fact that she had nothing to bring to the church dinner. She was debating whether she would attend at all. It was getting close to service time, so she went outside to consider her options. At that very moment a truck went by and something fell off the back. Gena sent one of her children to see what was lying on the road. Directly in front of this humble woman's home was a large sack of potatoes. She considered it a delivery from God as she prepared potato soup for the congregation. That night she stood up and gave thanks to God for providing for her.

Gena is an example of humility. With meager things, she still gives all the glory to God.

Heavenly Father, you know our hearts and our needs. Thank you for people like Gena who live by your commands and inspire all of us. Amen.

MAY 25   HOPE

But those who hope in the LORD will renew their strength. They will soar on wings like eagles; they will run and not grow weary, they will walk and not be faint.   (Isaiah 40:31 NIV)

My daughter Avery came home from school perplexed one day. Her teacher had asked the students what they want to be when they grow up. Many said they want to be veterinarians and doctors. Avery told the truth. She wants to be a rock star. She said, "Mom, why did everyone laugh?"

Tough question, I thought. Here's my chance to either give her a somewhat brutal reality check or support her in her efforts to dream big. I told her sometimes people are going to laugh at your hopes and dreams. They may not understand where you are coming from. But that's OK. If you believe in your dreams, that's all it takes to keep hope alive.

Keep hope alive today. Think of ways to help your children think big.

God, help us remember that all things are possible by believing in you. Help us remember the power of your love and wisdom. Amen.

MAY 26   HAVE RESOLVE

There are different kinds of gifts, but the same Spirit.
(1 Corinthians 12:4 NIV)

Limping along and rubbing her knees as we exited a roller-skating rink, Avery had an epiphany. She said, "Mom, roller skating is not one of the gifts God has given me." She was not sad or disheartened. She seemed at peace with this realization.

We often discuss the fact that God has given all of us many gifts. Throughout our lives we will unwrap those gifts and discover ways to put them to use. With great gifts comes great responsibility. God gives us skills and opportunities to further his Kingdom. The gifts may be as small as conquering roller skates or as great as finding a cure for cancer. The challenge is keeping our minds and hearts open to the gifts that God wants to give us.

With this knowledge, Avery has not hung up her roller skates entirely. Wearing kneepads, she continues to roll along looking for her next gift to unwrap.

Father, please help us be open to receive the gifts you wish us to have. May we glorify you and live in a manner that furthers your Kingdom. Amen.

MAY 27   PREPARE

For we are God's workmanship, created in Christ Jesus to do good works, which God prepared in advance for us to do.
(Ephesians 2:10 NIV)

At the end of a tear-jerking kindergarten graduation, my daughter's teacher handed us an excerpt from the essay "All I Really Need to Know I Learned in Kindergarten," by Robert Fulghum. This essay alludes to the fact that the most important things in life we learn at age five—things such as "share everything" and "say you're sorry when you hurt somebody." It's amazing to me that we forget basic concepts such as cleaning up our own messes and the value of cookies and naps.

I believe God also has equipped us early in our lives with critical knowledge of right and wrong. Romans 2:14-16 tells us that basic Christian values are written into our hearts. In addition to giving us the Word of God, God has implanted in us an innate understanding of his teachings. He has prepared us for doing his work; it's up to us to use this knowledge and make right choices throughout our lives.

God, thank you for preparing us to be soldiers for Christ. Help us listen to the teachings you offer us and benefit from the gifts you want to give us. Amen.

MAY 28   ENDURE

May you be made strong with all the strength that comes from his glorious power, and may you be prepared to endure everything with patience, while joyfully giving thanks to the Father, who has enabled you to share in the inheritance of the saints in the light. **(Colossians 1:11-12 NRSV)**

My mother-in-law is a fine example of what it means to endure. She has lived through a difficult, abusive marriage. She raised her children and is now raising her grandchildren. She has also been known to take in brothers, sisters, nieces, and nephews as they need help—all on a salary that is barely above the poverty level. She's had a harsh existence, to say the least. Still, she endures. She makes every effort to help people find their footing and to get them going while juggling to keep her own head above water. Still, she endures. She's a bold example of many single women who are forced to take challenges with no one but God at their side. Their burdens are heavy, but their gifts and abilities are great.

Today, thank God for women who have such strength and heart to inspire us all.

Dear heavenly Father, sometimes our burdens seem so heavy, and we are so weary. Renew our strength today so that we may endure and give assistance to those depending on us. Amen.

MAY 29   TOLERATE

"The second is this: 'Love your neighbor as yourself.' There is no commandment greater than these."   *(Mark 12:31 NIV)*

One of the most important gifts we can give our children is an understanding of tolerance.

Tolerance is defined by the *American Heritage Dictionary* as "the capacity for or the practice of recognizing and respecting the beliefs or practices of others." Tolerance is a skill we use every day—from negotiating traffic to handling work relationships to participating in Parent Teacher Association meetings. Tolerance is also synonymous with compassion, broad-mindedness, and kindness.

Today, model the behavior of tolerance, and speak to your children about being kind and compassionate to their friends and neighbors, especially those who are different from them.

Father, thank you for the diversity you have created in this world. Help us embrace differences and learn from one another today. Amen.

MAY 30   UNITE

Make every effort to keep the unity of the Spirit through the bond of peace.   *(Ephesians 4:3 NIV)*

What would you do if your child came home and told you that he was now in a gang? This very incident happened to Queen Mother Falaka Fattah in Philadelphia. Her story ran on *True North*, a news magazine show. Queen Mother Fattah struggled with how to deal with her son. Instead of casting him out, she invited fifteen gang members to move into her home. She told reporters that it wasn't easy; she had to give away all of her furniture on the first floor and have the boys camp in. This was the start of the House of Umoja.

Thirty-plus years later, Queen Mother Fattah is still operating the boys' safe haven and is known as a mother to more than three thousand sons. She has earned the respect of the community and the children she serves by showing love, patience, and endurance. Queen Mother Fattah told *True North* that her experience proves that although no one person can do everything, any one person can start something.

Lord, help us see the vision you have for our lives. Give us courage to answer your calling and to use our gifts and talents to benefit your Kingdom. Amen.

MAY 31   CHERISH

He tends his flock like a shepherd: He gathers the lambs in his arms and carries them close to his heart; he gently leads those that have young.   *(Isaiah 40:11 NIV)*

My grandmother stood up during every Christmas Eve service to pledge money to the church. And every year she would openly weep as she spoke the names of her children and grandchildren whom she was honoring. At that stage in her life, she knew that all material things would pass away and the thing that mattered most was her family—the family she created, loved, and supported. She taught all of us how to love, live, and cherish one another. She showed us how to stay in touch and how to come together in good times and bad. She showed us how to talk and laugh together. I am very grateful to have experienced her love and to be able to share it with my own children.

And thank you for allowing me to share it with you this month. May God bless and keep your family safe.

Thank you, God, for mothers. Thank you for the skills and attributes you have blessed us with. Guide our hearts and minds to glorify you in all that we do. Amen.

June

It's All About Love

LILLIAN C. SMITH

JUNE 1   "WHAT'S LOVE GOT TO DO
WITH IT?"

*"This is my commandment, that you love one another as I have
loved you."*   *(John 15:12 NRSV)*

A popular song asks, "What's love got to do with it?" Everything, if you are a Christian! The Scriptures call us to love God and neighbor—even our enemy. Easier said than done, right? But that's the point. God wants and needs us to do what seems impossible.

What would happen in the world if love became the predominant mode of action and being? Love melts hearts and transforms lives. Love provides hope, affirms our humanity, and gives us confidence to keep on keeping on. Love moves us to provide for those we don't know because they need us in order to survive another day.

This month's meditations deal with love. I don't know about you, but as a mother I often feel stretched to love even more. We all can and need to grow in our ability to love.

Loving God, help me love others. I need your Spirit to work within my heart and life so that I can be an instrument of your love. Amen.

JUNE 2   LOVE IS PATIENT

Love is patient.   *(1 Corinthians 13:4a NRSV)*

Patience may be a virtue, but it hasn't been one of mine. After reading the words "love is patient," my response is, "Ouch, God." You mean to tell me that to be patient is to be loving?

Patience. Life for me moves at breakneck speed. I'm a woman on a mission. I've got people to see and things to do. The truth of the matter is that I was moving too fast. In my haste to get things done, I had become impatient with others, especially my children. I would get frustrated when they weren't moving or answering fast enough. I came to understand that it was my impatience that was the problem.

If this description sounds like it could be you, here are some words of advice. Slow down, sister friend. Life moves too fast already. You will blink, and these children will be grown. Enjoy your children and encourage them to love life. Let your love be expressed through your patience this day.

God, help me love others through my patience. Amen.

JUNE 3   LOVE IS KIND

Love is kind.   *(1 Corinthians 13:4b NRSV)*

My boys, ages three and five, had just spent time with me playing, reading, and laughing. As they turned to walk to the other room, I was impressed by their kindness. My heart broke as I realized that my sons would encounter many unkind expressions in life.

Life will not always be kind to our children. My two African American sons are being raised to love and respect everyone. In their short lives they have been taught that God's family is multicultural. It hurts me to know that someday they will encounter pain from people who will judge them not by their character, but by the color of their skin.

All of our children, regardless of ethnicity, may encounter unloving responses from persons who will dislike them because of their country of origin or their religion or some other "difference." Let us teach our children to be strong and kind. We mothers need to model kindness in our day-to-day interactions with others and with our children. God calls us to love one another. One way to love is through kindness.

Dear God, thank you for your kindness to us. Help me to be kind to others and to teach my children to be kind in an often unkind world. Amen.

JUNE 4   LOVE IS NOT . . .

Love is not envious or boastful or arrogant or rude. It does not insist on its own way.   (1 Corinthians 13:4c-5 NRSV)

If love is not envious, boastful, arrogant, or rude, then love must be excited when others do well, and be respectful of others, and never condescending. The task is so challenging that it almost seems crazy and impossible.

Yes, this kind of love is crazy, but in the Gospels we see Jesus—the personification of God's love—loving friend and foe in ways that respect the humanity of all. In our own power, love as God demands is impossible. But through the power of the Holy Spirit working in us, we *can* love.

Dear woman, pray now and ask God to work within your heart to give you the ability to love. If we allow and invite God to work within us, God will mold us more into the image of Christ and gift us with the ability to love.

Our children will be influenced by our ability to love as God desires. What a spiritual inheritance we will give them. What a witness they will give to an often unloving world.

Dear God, help me love as I should, and work within my children so that they may also share Christian love. Amen.

JUNE 5   LOVING GOD

"Love the Lord your God with all your heart, and with all your soul, and with all your mind, and with all your strength."
(Mark 12:30 NRSV)

Honestly speaking, there are times when I feel that I don't have anything else to give. As a woman who works in and outside of the home, sometimes I think, *What else can I do?* With responsibilities as an employee, a wife, a mother, and a daughter, I often feel I can't possibly do another thing.

In reality, God wants the totality of our love. God desires us to love God with our whole being, withholding nothing. God wants us to spend time with God. God desires that we live our lives and vocations in ways that give honor to God. God wants us to love God with our thoughts, intellect, and even our questioning.

Of all my responsibilities, the call to love God is the most refreshing and replenishing. Its reward is a strengthened relationship with my heavenly parent. If I make time to love God, God's love makes me better able to handle everything else in life.

God, in your love I find peace. In loving you I find freedom. Please prompt me when I get too busy to remember to love you. Amen.

JUNE 6   GREAT IS THY FAITHFULNESS

The steadfast love of the LORD never ceases, his mercies never come to an end; they are new every morning; great is your faithfulness.   *(Lamentations 3:22-23 NRSV)*

God has been working through families from the beginning of time. Luke 3:23-37 and Matthew 1:1-17 detail the genealogy of Jesus. The lineage of Jesus gives us insight into the working of God through generations. From Adam and Eve to Abraham and Sarah, down through the generations to David, and on to Mary and Joseph, God was working through families to redeem humanity.

God through Jesus Christ turned the world upside down! God wants your children and grandchildren to be agents of transforming love and change in the world. We mothers have the responsibility of making sure that our children learn about God through church school, Bible study, and family devotions. We need to tell our children what God has done for us and for our families through the years.

God wants to show faithfulness to our families. Let us not be guilty of not passing the faith on to our children and grandchildren.

Dear God, you've been faithful and loving to my family through the generations. Help me pass that story on to the next generation. Amen.

JUNE 7   PASS IT ON!

When your son asks you, "What is the meaning of the stipulations, decrees and laws the LORD our God has commanded you?" tell him: "We were slaves of Pharaoh in Egypt, but the LORD brought us out of Egypt with a mighty hand."
(Deuteronomy 6:20-21 NIV)

Telling our "God story" to our children is so important. Children watch everything we do, taking it all in like sponges. So that it never appears that we are going through the motions in our faith, let's tell them *why* we do what we do.

God has been good to me. Yes, life is sometimes hard and I have cried many tears. My father died when I was a very young child, and my mother raised me alone. Life was sometimes painful, but just as God promised, God never left me. In fact, as I look back, I can clearly see how God was making a way for me.

I will tell my children why we go to church and why we pray. I will tell them how God delivered our ancestors from the Middle Passage, slavery, and Jim Crow. I will tell them how God has blessed them.

What is *your* story? Pass it on to your children and grandchildren, your nieces and nephews.

Dear God, help me pass on my story. Amen.

JUNE 8   WE'VE COME THIS FAR BY FAITH

And without faith it is impossible to please God, for whoever would approach him must believe that he exists and that he rewards those who seek him.   (Hebrews 11:6 NRSV)

Memories of homecoming at my mother's childhood church flood my mind as I remember hearing the opening song of the worship service: "We've come this far by faith, leaning on the Lord."

While participating in a retreat/work team experience in New Orleans, I heard people talk about their experiences after Hurricanes Katrina and Rita. A pastor talked about how people from all walks of life lost everything. Rich, poor, and middle class stood in line for food stamps. She recounted her experience when she returned to her home. Even as a woman of faith, she felt hopeless as she saw the devastation of her home. Sitting on her front steps, crying and hopeless, she heard the Holy Spirit say, "O you of little faith." Shortly after that, a car of people drove down her street, stopped in front of her home, and asked her if she knew anyone they could help. Those people helped her begin her life of recovery after the hurricanes.

Through it all, we go forth in faith, leaning on the Lord.

Dear God, help me remember your faithfulness and teach my children to trust you even when life is hard and seems unfair. Amen.

JUNE 9   TRUST IN THE LORD!

When you are disturbed, do not sin; ponder it on your beds, and be silent. Offer right sacrifices, and put your trust in the LORD.
(Psalm 4:4-5 NRSV)

In Daniel 3, three faithful men—Shadrach, Meshach, and Abednego—were told to worship a golden statue or be thrown into a fiery furnace. The three men chose to face the fiery furnace rather than worship a false god. They were thrown into the furnace, but they were not harmed. God sent an angel to withstand the heat for them. They trusted God.

The thought of trusting God while facing danger makes no logical sense; but that is what we believers are called to do. When the pressures in life are beyond "boiling point" and it appears all hope is gone, we are to trust God anyway. God never promised us lives without problems. God did promise to be with us.

Is life getting rough? Trust God! Is stress pushing you beyond the breaking point? Trust God! Are you ready to give up? Trust God! Just like God delivered the three Hebrews from the fiery furnace, God will deliver you. Let's teach our children to trust God. God will always be with them, even when we are not.

God, thank you for your presence and deliverance. Amen.

JUNE 10   YOU'VE GOT TO GO THROUGH IT
TO GET TO IT

For surely I know the plans I have for you, says the LORD, plans for your welfare and not for harm, to give you a future with hope.   *(Jeremiah 29:11 NRSV)*

God has a destiny for you! Your calling will place you in places of leadership and ministry. This calling utilizes your giftedness. But guess what? Getting to your destiny is not easy. In fact, if you knew what you had to go through, you probably wouldn't do it.

You are going to go through some stuff to get to your destiny. Some of the stuff will include heartache and disrespect. You may find yourself in some seemingly hopeless situation. Take heart; God still has a plan for your life and will see it through to fruition.

To get to the Promised Land, the people had to go through the Red Sea. To assume his rightful place as king, David had to go through persecution and attempts on his life by King Saul.

God has something in store for you! God has plans for you— plans to give you a future with hope. As my husband preached in a sermon, remember that when things look bad, you've got to go through it to get to it! Pass that on to your children!

God, keep me mindful that I'm passing through the storms of life to get to your destiny. Amen.

JUNE 11   FEAR NOT, PART 1

Fear thou not; for I am with thee: be not dismayed; for I am thy God: I will strengthen thee; yea, I will help thee; yea, I will uphold thee with the right hand of my righteousness.
                                          (Isaiah 41:10 KJV)

Fear is a serious thing. It can paralyze us so that we declare defeat. Throughout the Scriptures, God instructs, "Fear not" and "Do not be afraid." Repeatedly we encounter scriptures that instruct us not to fear.

Fear has been defined as *False Evidence Appearing Real*. Fear is a tool of the enemy designed to defeat us. Fear is an evil spiritual force designed to destroy us.

Don't fear! Tell your children, friends, and colleagues not to fear, either. When we feel afraid, we are to run to God in prayer, seeking direction and strength and trusting that God will help us handle the situation.

Overdue bills to pay? Don't be afraid! Marriage on the rocks? Don't be afraid! Under fire at work? Don't be afraid! Remember that God is greater than anything we will ever encounter.

Dear God, in my fears I'll run to you in prayer, seeking your comfort, wisdom, and power. Amen.

JUNE 12   FEAR NOT, PART II

For God has not given us a spirit of fear, but of power and of love and of a sound mind.   *(2 Timothy 1:7 NKJV)*

In my household, little people sometimes sleep with their parents. On one particular night, my oldest, who will not remember this, was used by God to calm my fear. The situation at work was hard. It felt as if spiritual attacks were coming from every side, and I did not know how to protect myself. A coworker was undermining my leadership and inviting others into the situation.

My stress was high, and so was my fear. Even though I remembered the many scriptures that told me not to be afraid, I was afraid.

That particular night, as I lay in bed thinking and praying, my sleeping child put his hand on my head and said, "God said, 'Don't be afraid.'" Wow! God worked through a sleeping child to minister to me in a serious time of need.

Even now, God says to you, "Don't be afraid."

Lord, I am afraid of _____. Yet, as my loving Parent, you have told me there is no need to be afraid. Help me let go of my fear so I may be filled with your peace. Amen.

JUNE 13   STOP WHINING AND START WINNING!

If you have raced with foot-runners and they have wearied you, how will you compete with horses? And if in a safe land you fall down, how will you fare in the thickets of the Jordan?
(Jeremiah 12:5 NRSV)

Life's not fair. People are often unkind. Situations often are unjust. That's the reality in our fallen world. For Christians, the frustration can be unbearable. We try to live faithful lives and still have to deal with heartache and trouble.

The prophet Jeremiah faithfully shared what God wanted him to tell the people, yet they ignored and mistreated him. Jeremiah repeatedly called the people to turn from their sins to God, but many would not listen.

Sin influences all of humanity. Although life is messed up, strive to remain faithful like Jeremiah—no matter how hard life becomes. Don't whine. Instead, win. God wants to bless you in spite of the mess. The challenge you now face is preparing you for an even greater challenge in ministry. Remember, you are more than a conqueror through Christ who gives you strength. You are an overcomer who, through the power of the Holy Spirit, can do the impossible.

Is your situation rough? Ask God to help you. Then trust God. Don't whine; win!

God, you have said that I'm more than a conqueror, so I'm claiming that reality right now. Amen.

JUNE 14   JESUS LOVES THE LITTLE CHILDREN

Jesus said, "Let the little children come to me, and do not stop them; for it is to such as these that the kingdom of heaven belongs."   *(Matthew 19:14 NRSV)*

Children are really amazing. They love to play with other children. Differences of ethnicity or physical abilities don't instinctively stop children from playing with one another. No, adults bear responsibility for teaching children not to love other children. Adults tell children not to play with other children because of prejudices and hatred. Our mistreatment of one another must hurt the heart of God.

No matter what we feel about people of different ethnicities, you are called to love them. If Jesus loves children of all shades, why don't we? We must teach our children to love people of various backgrounds and ethnicities. The world would be a whole lot better off if we could truly love one another. Every mother would have more peace knowing that other children are learning to love her children.

Dear God, I confess my prejudices to you today. Please work in my heart. Help me love as you do. Help me teach my children to love others also. Amen.

JUNE 15   RAISING OUR CHILDREN TO PLEASE GOD

Train children in the right way, and when old, they will not stray.   *(Proverbs 22:6 NRSV)*

From the first time you set eyes upon your child, whether it was when you first held the child after delivery or when you first touched your adopted child, you wanted the best in life for that child. Your love for your child was overwhelming. How would you raise the child? Would life be kind to the child? How would you protect the child? As life would have it, we parents are not able to hold our children all of their lives. They grow up. As they grow, our parental care also grows.

We have the honor and responsibility to raise our children in ways that please God. It is our parental responsibility to pray for our children and teach them to pray for themselves. We have the responsibility to teach them to love God and others. We have the responsibility to teach them discipline. Parenting is an awesome responsibility that requires a whole lot of "sweat equity."

Let us raise our children to live as loving, bold disciples of Jesus Christ. Let us pray continually for them and their well-being.

Dear Lord, help me raise my child(ren) in a way that pleases you. Amen.

JUNE 16   KEEP ON STEPPIN'

Whenever you face trials of any kind, consider it nothing but joy, because you know that the testing of your faith produces endurance; and let endurance have its full effect, so that you may be mature and complete, lacking in nothing.
(James 1:2-4 NRSV)

At a funeral, I was impressed by the words of a pastor who is now deceased. He said that when his younger brother would come to him complaining about life, he would say, "That's no pace for a stepper!" In other words, don't give up and keep on going! That encouragement has taken on special meaning for me.

The phrase alludes to show horses, who keep their pace and exhibit strength and dignity at all times. Oh, that we can teach our children to keep stepping during life's heartaches and setbacks. We need to help our children learn to persevere and thrive.

Many young people are ready to give up too fast. Many are ready to complain that life is not fair, but they are unwilling to work for the change they want. Life will be hard and cruel at times, but our babies will, with God's help, need to keep on steppin'!

Dear God, help me teach my children to persevere when life becomes hard, so that they may grow into individuals of deep faith, character, and integrity. Amen.

JUNE 17   TAKE THE LIMITS OFF!

"Oh, that you would bless me and enlarge my territory! Let your hand be with me, and keep me from harm so that I will be free from pain." And God granted his request.
                                         (1 Chronicles 4:10 NIV)

Could it be that we ask God for too little? Do we, in our human imagination and understanding, limit God?

Anytime we think God can't help us, we limit God. Whenever we want to give up or just don't ask God to enlarge our territory, we limit God.

Stop saying or thinking about what God can't or won't do. God created the world and raised Jesus from the dead. God has an excellent track record! Each day for the next month, pray the prayer of Jabez in 1 Chronicles 4:10.

In the song "Take the Limits Off," the group Israel and New Breed shares a prophetic message from God to each of us: "Take the limits off of me."

Don't limit God! Expect great things from God!

Dear God, forgive me for the times when I have limited you. Please forgive me when I have forgotten your awesome power. Amen.

JUNE 18   DARE TO TRUST

Now the Lord said to Abram, "Go from your country and your kindred and your father's house to the land that I will show you."   *(Genesis 12:1 NRSV)*

"You're leaving Ur, huh?"

Those were the words a clergy sister and T-ball mom said to me after learning that my family was moving to another state.

God told Abram to leave his home in Ur and all that was familiar, including family, and go to a new place. Following God's direction required a lot of trust, to say the least. In life, we all must go where God leads.

As we prepared to leave the familiar to go to the unknown, things got a little hard. In less than a month, I had to find a place to live and a school for the kids, pack, and arrange to move. At every turn, God said to me, "Dare to trust." I could hear the words clearly. When I felt like giving up and my stress level would rise, I'd say, "God, I'm trusting you." As I trusted God, God showed up again and again.

God wants to be strong on your behalf, too. Dare to trust God today.

Dear God, I will trust you through whatever happens and wherever you send me. Amen.

JUNE 19   TRUSTING THE LORD

You who live in the shelter of the Most High, who abide in the shadow of the Almighty, will say to the LORD, "My refuge and my fortress; my God, in whom I trust."   *(Psalm 91:1-2 NRSV)*

In this world of drive-by shootings and terrorist plots, we need to trust in the Lord. Danger abounds, and we can't always protect ourselves.

As I write this meditation, I've just learned of a terrorist plot to blow up an airplane in midair. Tomorrow I'm scheduled to fly home. In my anxiety and fear, I choose to trust God. I've told God, "I've got to get on a plane in the aftermath of this discovery. Truthfully, I have no choice but to trust in you. I can't protect myself from dangers seen or unseen. I choose to trust you when I can't see my way through. In good times and bad times, when my stress is high, when my back is up against the wall, my only way out of the situation is with your help."

Let us choose to trust the Lord.

Dear God, I'm trusting you to take care of my family and me. Please keep us safe, and help me teach my children the importance of trusting you. Amen.

JUNE 20   GOD'S DIRECTION

Trust in the LORD with all your heart and lean not on your own understanding; in all your ways acknowledge him, and he will make your paths straight.   *(Proverbs 3:5-6 NIV)*

"This doesn't feel like the right direction," I said to myself. It was late and I was traveling from a meeting to my new home. The GPS device's return directions were different from the directions to the meeting site. "Does this machine really know how to get me home?" I wondered aloud.

The GPS device was all I had at the moment to get home. So, I trusted it and followed every directed turn. As I drove, I remembered various times before I had a GPS device when I would somehow happen upon the needed street even if it wasn't on the driving directions I had printed off the computer.

Going with God is a lot like driving with a GPS device. On our journey with God, we don't always know where we're going or how we'll arrive. We have to trust God. Trusting God is both unsettling and comforting. Yet we have the gift of knowing that God is always with us, directing us at all times.

Take comfort in knowing that God directs your path.

Today I acknowledge you, God. Please make my path straight. Amen.

JUNE 21   LOVE YOUR NEIGHBOR AS YOURSELF,
                                                         PART 1

" 'You shall love the Lord your God with all your heart, and with all your soul, and with all your mind.' This is the greatest and first commandment. And a second is like it: 'You shall love your neighbor as yourself.' "   *(Matthew 22:37-39 NRSV)*

This portion of the great commandment is a difficult one for many women. We usually don't have problems loving others. Many of us do have problems, however, loving ourselves. This is especially true for mothers.

Motherhood requires self-sacrifice. As soon as we hear our children's first cries or hold them for the first time, our thoughts immediately focus on them. Double lattes and "that pair of shoes" take a backseat to the immediate needs of our children. We are wired to love. The challenge is that often we love others at our own—and others'—expense.

I'm as guilty as the next person. There have been many times when my attempts at self-care have been cancelled because of others—family, children, husband, mother, and so on.

Our care for our children will never end—nor should it. Yet we mothers also need to love ourselves. In some ways, loving ourselves will increase our ability to love others.

Loving God, let me receive your love as I give it. Help me love myself. Amen.

JUNE 22   LOVE YOUR NEIGHBOR AS YOURSELF,
                                                    PART 2

"'You shall love the Lord your God with all your heart, and with all your soul, and with all your mind.' This is the greatest and first commandment. And a second is like it: 'You shall love your neighbor as yourself.'"   *(Matthew 22:37-39 NRSV)*

"Love your neighbor." OK, I've got that. "As yourself . . ."

Wait a minute, God. Does that mean I'm supposed to love myself?

Sister in motherhood, yes, it does! In reality, your ability to love others is impaired by your inability to love yourself. Only when you learn to love yourself—unconditionally, imperfections and all—will you be able to love others—imperfections and all.

Love yourself today. You're not perfect. No one is. Yet God is working through you in your imperfections. Can't attend to everything on your to-do list? Love yourself by not overscheduling. The kitchen floor still needs cleaning at 11:00 p.m. Take time to pray, have some quiet time, laugh a little, go to bed, and tackle the floor tomorrow.

God, please help me truly love myself. Amen.

JUNE 23   'TIS SO SWEET TO TRUST IN JESUS

For he will command his angels concerning you to guard you in all your ways. *(Psalm 91:11 NRSV)*

OK, it is truth-telling time. Do you *really* trust God to take care of you and your family? My lack of complete trust in God was one of the hardest things for me to acknowledge as a new mother.

I wanted to protect my children and provide for them. I had to remember that God loves my children more than I do, and that God would care for my children in and out of my presence. God would even care for my children if I transitioned to everlasting life.

Trust God with your children. Pray and ask God to bless your children all the days of their lives. Pray for their well-being in all areas of their lives.

God, I love _____ (insert your child's name, each in turn if you have more than one). You love this child more than I do. I trust you to care for _____. Please provide, protect, teach, and guide my child through all of life. Amen.

JUNE 24   SOMEBODY PRAYED FOR ME

Therefore confess your sins to each other and pray for each other so that you may be healed. The prayer of a righteous man is powerful and effective. *(James 5:16 NIV)*

"Somebody prayed for me, had me on their mind . . ."

The words of this song speak loudly to my experience. Too much has happened in my life for me not to know that people have prayed for me. Heartache and disappointment were not allowed to destroy me. Bad relationship choices didn't derail me. Too many unexpected blessings and opportunities have come my way for someone not to have prayed for me. Someone must have prayed for me!

Has life been perfect? No. But I believe that God continues to honor the prayers of ancestors who prayed for me to make it. Those individuals prayed for me to survive and thrive.

Are you praying for your children? Are you making time to pray for your children's future? Are you praying for future generations? They need your prayers, too. Today, intercede for your children and your children's children. Ask God to take care of them all the days of their lives.

God, I've heard your call to pray. Today I pray for my children and the children of the community and the world. Please bless them with a peaceful and prosperous future. Amen.

JUNE 25   LOVE AIN'T EASY

I am not writing you a new command but one we have had from the beginning. I ask that we love one another. And this is love: that we walk in obedience to his commands. As you have heard from the beginning, his command is that you walk in love.   **(2 John 5-6 NIV)**

There are times when loving someone else is not so easy. Differences in opinions can distance us from others. Some people are downright hard to love because of difficult personalities. It is extremely hard to love a person who has intentionally hurt you.

God calls us to love everyone—enemies and neighbors. We all know that it's hard. We all know that there are many times we feel anything but love toward some people. That's reality. When we are having a difficult time loving others, we need to pray, asking for forgiveness and for God to help us love.

God wants us to love when it is easy and when it is hard. God, who is love, wants us to reflect that love in this world. God wants us to be transformed because of that love.

God, your love for me is unconditional. Help me love others unconditionally. Amen.

JUNE 26   REST IN GOD

"Come to me, all you that are weary and are carrying heavy burdens, and I will give you rest."   **(Matthew 11:28 NRSV)**

"I'm tired" is the mantra I hear from many women. Personally, the term *sleep deprived* is the constant, definitive descriptive for me right now. Let's not even talk about the responsibilities I carry. It's like I'm juggling life's responsibilities and can't afford for any of the balls to fall. I'm tired all the time.

If you're like me, you probably don't go to God with the issues of life as quickly as you should. We women in the "Superwomen Anonymous Association" think we have to do so much by ourselves—that we have to be strong.

God doesn't want or need us to be Superwoman. Instead, God wants us to rest in God's love. God wants us to come with all our stuff—our heartaches and burdens. God calls us to come, and God promises to give us rest.

We can trust God with our concerns. We can trust God with all that life has dealt us. God wants to give you rest.

Right now, tell God everything from which you need a break. Tell God about everything that burdens you. Give everything to God right now. Receive God's rest.

Dear God . . .

JUNE 27   SHOW YOUR LOVE!

Praise the LORD!
O give thanks to the LORD, for he is good;
for his steadfast love endures forever.   (Psalm 106:1 NRSV)

My oldest son has learned a lot about professional sports. He knows that a lot of people like one football team and others like another. Watching games and listening to people talk, he has learned that people praise or celebrate the things or people they like.

Isn't it interesting that many people will offer praise to football teams or jobs or money before offering praise to God? That is so odd. God has answered so many prayers and delivered us from so many situations. Yet we often seem reluctant to praise God.

God deserves our praise. Take a praise break today! Ask your children to share reasons to praise God. Tell your children why you praise God. Together, praise the Lord.

God, you have always been faithful and kind. Today, our family praises you for your loving ways. Receive our praise and thanksgiving. Amen.

JUNE 28   TEACH YOUR CHILDREN TO PRAY

"Pray then in this way ..."   *(Matthew 6:9a NRSV)*

Prayer is talking to God. If we don't do anything else, we need to teach our children to pray. Prayer will keep them connected with their heavenly Parent. Prayer will calm their fears and get them out of countless situations. Prayer will strengthen them. Prayer will remind them of their dependence on God.

It is never too soon for children to learn to pray. Teach your children to pray. In your family devotions, ask your children to pray. Allow younger children to freely lift up petitions for Mommy, Daddy, the pets, and more. Ask older children to lift up joys and concerns to God.

Don't hinder their prayer lives. I have met many an adult who was too intimidated to pray. How sad. God has given us the gift of prayer for our good.

As a family, pray the prayer that Jesus taught his disciples:

Our Father in heaven, hallowed be your name. Your kingdom come. Your will be done, on earth as it is in heaven. Give us this day our daily bread. And forgive us our debts, as we also have forgiven our debtors. And do not bring us to the time of trial, but rescue us from the evil one. Amen. (Matthew 6:9-13 NRSV)

JUNE 29   GOD HAS A PURPOSE FOR
                           YOUR CHILDREN!

But the LORD said to me, "Do not say, 'I am only a boy'; for you shall go to all to whom I send you, and you shall speak whatever I command you, Do not be afraid of them, for I am with you to deliver you."   *(Jeremiah 1:7-8 NRSV)*

The Bible has numerous instances when God used a young person to accomplish something big. The who's who list of young people God used includes Jeremiah, Samuel, Esther, Timothy, and Mary the mother of Jesus. From generation to generation, God has used people of all ages. Jesus himself began his ministry as a young person.

Let's prepare our children to be used by God in ministry. Read them the stories of the faith. Invite them to pray for people. Encourage them to share in ministry by making cards for shut-ins and those who are sick. Tell them that God has a purpose for their lives.

Like Paul said to Timothy, tell your children not to let anyone look down on them because of their age. Rather, they should set the believers an example by their speech and conduct.

Loving God, you have called my children to a purpose. Bless them so that they can be strong disciples. Amen.

JUNE 30   KEEP YOUR JOY!

"The joy of the LORD is your strength."   *(Nehemiah 8:10 NIV)*

Life's ups and downs can make us feel like we are on a roller coaster. Emotionally, we can find ourselves up one minute and down the next. It can be so easy to feel unhappy.

Sisters in motherhood, work to keep your joy. External forces influence happiness. Joy is something that resides on the inside of you. Joy comes from God.

Choose today to have God's joy residing in you. Like the psalmist, tell the world in every situation, "This is the day that the LORD has made; [I will] rejoice and be glad in it" (Psalm 118:24 NRSV). Choose to embrace the goodness of God despite the situation.

The tears will come, yet God's faithfulness will remain. Frustrations will come at you from every side. God is still good and worthy of your praise. Illness may come knocking at your door. Let the joy of the Lord be your strength. Natural disasters and other threats remain, but God's joy is here for you.

God's joy is like salve to the hurting heart and strength to the tired. Let the joy of the Lord keep you!

Loving God, I need your joy to be my strength. Help me keep your joy whether times are good or bad. Amen.

July

An Open Letter

HILDA DAVIS-CARROLL

JULY 1   A DAY OF NEW BEGINNINGS

I am about to do something new; even now it shall come to pass, suddenly you shall perceive it: I will make a road through the wilderness And rivers in the desert. (Isaiah 43:19 TANAKH)

My daughter graduates from college today! I wonder, When did this happen? Not graduation, but when did she become this beautiful, smart, and confident young woman? I look at her and see the baby taking her first steps, the toddler demanding that I let her do it, and the teen who moved multiple times between elementary and high school.

These meditations are an open letter to the young woman who gave me a new identity: mother. They are reflections on my life—spent in large part as a single mother—with my daughter, who has taught me and changed me so much that my family breaks my life into "before Erin" and "after Erin." They also are an open letter to all mothers who, like me, want to pass on valuable life lessons to their children.

One of my favorite hymns, written by Brian Wren, says, "Christ is alive and goes before us to show and share what love can do. This is a day of new beginnings; our God is making all things new" ("This Is a Day of New Beginnings," copyright © 1983, 1987, Hope Publishing Co.). This open letter presents my thoughts on the "new beginnings" my daughter and I are now facing, yet it also speaks to the new beginnings that every mother and child face at every age and stage—beginnings that also are opportunities for learning the life lessons God has for each of us.

Loving God, thank you for new beginnings. Help us prepare for the new experiences and lessons you have for our children and us. Amen.

JULY 2   WORDS TO LIVE BY

Take to heart these instructions with which I charge you this day. Impress them upon your children.
(Deuteronomy 6:6-7a TANAKH)

Dear Erin:

You are starting a new phase of life, and though you often say to me, "Mommy, I am grown," I know even "grown" people can be instructed. So, I ask you to indulge me as I try to put into words some of my own learnings over the past half-century. Maybe something will be of value to you.

I'd like to tell you about some values that have meaning for my life. Consider thinking about their meaning for *your* life. Some of my reflections will be lessons I have learned; others will be lessons I am still learning. My hope is that you will find your own way—a better path—to learn these lessons.

First, love God. I know you have heard this all of your life; however, you have to grow into what it means to love God in your own life. I try to show it by loving people. Scripture asks how we can love God, whom we haven't seen, if we can't love other people, whom we can see (John 4:20). Learn how to love God.

Love,
Mommy

Dear Lord, may we show our children how to love you with body, mind, and spirit. Amen.

JULY 3   YOU ARE SPECIAL

Keep me as the apple of your eye; hide me in the shadow of your
wings.   *(Psalm 17:8 NIV)*

Dear Erin:
  God loves you.
  You're special to God, and God will keep you through all that
happens in life. This doesn't mean you won't experience disappointment, grief, and heartache—though I pray those times are
few. Rather, God is with you to shelter you and give you a safe
place to rest.
  What does it mean to rest in God? When I was faced with the
decision of divorce, I looked at you and thought, *What should I do?*
I had been laid off, needed a place to stay, and was heartbroken
that my marriage had not worked. So, I took you back to my home
church where we were welcomed, helped, and loved. They let me
rest in their "wings" until I was strong enough to make the move
I needed to make.
  God will always place people in your life who love you and see
you as special. Trust those relationships provided for you by a loving God.

Love,
Mommy

Loving God, bring people into our lives who will remind us that
we are special when we forget. Amen.

JULY 4   FREE TO BE A BLESSING

You, my brothers, were called to be free. But do not use your
freedom to indulge the sinful nature; rather, serve one another
in love.   *(Galatians 5:13 NIV)*

Dear Erin:
  Serve others.
  When I was growing up, I watched my mother collect dimes for

the March of Dimes. She also taught Sunday school and worked in a women's mission league. Your father's mother taught piano and was a faithful musical presence in her church while rearing a family and working full time. You have role models for service. I, as clergy, pass on to you the legacy of service your grandmother passed to me.

You have already begun serving in our church, the community, and your university. As an honor student, it would have been easy for you to spend so much time on your studies that you had no time for anyone else. You could have fallen into self-pity and expected others to help you get what you needed just because you grew up in a single parent home. Instead, you served others out of gratitude for your blessings.

On this Fourth of July, we celebrate our freedom as a country. Today I want to celebrate you, because you show that freedom is a privilege that comes with an obligation to serve.

Love,
Mommy

Our Lord, thank you for your blessings. May we use our blessings to bless and serve others. Amen.

JULY 5   GIVE THANKS

Do not be anxious about anything, but in everything, by prayer and petition, with thanksgiving, present your requests to God.
(Philippians 4:6 NIV)

Dear Erin:
   Have a grateful heart.
   At Christmas I would say, "Sorry, daughter, but I can't get you anything for Christmas this year." As a child of six and seven, you would look so wise and say, "That's OK, Mommy." Then I would manage to surprise you with gifts that would delight your heart. You were always grateful for anything I gave you.

As you grew, I stopped thinking about gifts of toys and focused more on the gift of family. What I hope I gave you was a spiritual foundation that will help you through the anxious times. I hope you received from our family ritual of attending Christmas Eve service an assurance that God is present in the smallest packages—that you matter to God.

Because you matter to God, God will always hear your prayers. God encourages you to ask without worrying about the outcome. Give thanks and relax, knowing that God will supply all you need (Philippians 4:19). You have seen that over and over—in spite of uncertainty about what was coming next.

Love,
Mommy

O gracious God, you always provide what we need. For this we are grateful. Amen.

JULY 6   LIVE JOYFULLY

Rejoice in the Lord always. I will say it again: Rejoice!
                                                    (Philippians 4:4 NIV)

Dear Erin:
  Take time to celebrate and enjoy life.
  You understand how to work. You have worked hard in school and in jobs you've had. You pay attention to excellence whether you are volunteering or getting paid. I'm proud of your strong work ethic.

But you're coming to adulthood in a society that does not value play or joy. People are just as likely to be released from their jobs and made to carry their boxes of belongings like a thief in the night as they are to be praised for their decades of dedicated service.

Too often we don't take time to enjoy our friendships and the love they bring to our lives. I'm guilty of becoming so busy that I have to schedule "free time" with a friend weeks in advance. Both of our schedules are full of things we *must* do, which makes it difficult to make time for things we would *like* to do.

Please start a new tradition: Celebrate yourself and your

friends. Give thanks through music. Make a joyful noise unto the Lord! Sing! Praise! Rejoice! God intends us to have joy.

Love,
Mommy

Joyous God, help us spend less time in joyless routine and more time in praise and celebration. Amen.

JULY 7   LIVE YOUR PURPOSE

He Who began a good work in you will continue until the day of Jesus Christ—right up to the time of His return—developing [that good work] and perfecting and bringing it to full completion in you.   *(Philippians 1:6 AMP)*

Dear Erin:
    God created you for a purpose that only you can fulfill.
    You have talents and wonderful gifts (writing, singing, teaching, serving, compassion, wit, friendship, courage, perseverance). God will continue to shape, mold, and guide you on the path you were born to take.
    Bible personalities show us that God calls each of us, gives us a particular purpose, and helps us fulfill our purpose. Queen Esther's uncle, Mordecai, said that perhaps she was born for "such a time as this"—to deliver the Jewish people from death. All of us were born "for such a time."
    I know you were born to write. You have been writing stories since you were old enough to hold a pen. You can transform lives with your words by changing public policy; inspiring through healing words; or creating a haunting, human drama. Though you don't know where your path will take you, know that God will direct you to complete all you are intended to be. Listen for God's guidance.

Love,
Mommy

Lord of purpose, draw us closer to your purpose for our lives. Amen.

JULY 8   BE PART OF A COMMUNITY

Her neighbors and relatives heard that the Lord had shown her
great mercy, and they shared her joy.   *(Luke 1:58 NIV)*

Dear Erin:

Build a community.

We moved to Detroit, where my family lives, when you were five
years old. Though it was a difficult time, our family welcomed us.
I joined another church, reconnected with my college sorority sisters, and made new friends. Having a new community made the
change of divorce and moving across country easier. Certainly, living in the same city as my family was a constant source of joy and
comfort for both of us.

In our next two moves, first to Dallas and then to Nashville, we
made new friends. We found communities that helped us celebrate graduations and the buying of our first home. They also
were there when your uncle died and I lost my job; and through
their generosity we were able to manage on a reduced income
when I returned to graduate school.

Wherever you are in life, God is with you—you are never alone.
God shows up in a loving community. We have experienced God's
love and mercy over and over in the sharing of our lives with people who loved us. Take time to build a community where you can
love and be loved. In such a community you will know God.

Love,
Mommy

Loving Lord, help us build loving relationships so we can know
your love. Amen.

JULY 9   GUARD YOUR HEALTH

Do you not know that your body is a temple of the Holy Spirit,
who is in you, whom you have received from God? You are not
your own.   *(1 Corinthians 6:19 NIV)*

Dear Erin:

Treat your body as a sacred object.

In a world of fast food and even faster living, it's easy to over-look taking care of your body—the temple of God.

When you were a child, we often ate our meals together. We talked about your day, and I learned how you were doing emotion-ally and spiritually. I learned who your friends were and how you were being treated in school. I also knew what you were eating because I prepared your food in a healthy way.

Now you make your own choices. Your life moves fast, and the fast-food industry insists they are "helping" you keep up with your fast-paced life by giving you meals on the run.

Slow down and eat meals that are healthy. Slow down and lis-ten to your body tell you when you need to rest. Slow down and hear the Spirit of God guiding you. It's difficult to avoid stress when you're eating on the go and eating foods that are full of fat, salt, and sugar. Slowing down won't make you miss anything. It may help you find yourself.

Love,
Mommy

Dear Lord, help us slow down and eat well so we may live as you intend. Amen.

JULY 10 TAKE CARE OF YOUR MONEY

Of what use is money in the hand of a fool, since he has no desire to get wisdom? (Proverbs 17:16 NIV)

Dear Erin:

Prepare for your financial future.

I can't say this enough: spend wisely. I did not learn as a child how to save money, invest money, and prepare for the future. Somehow as a young adult I realized I had to set some money aside. So I had money taken out of my paycheck every payday and began to accumulate a nice savings account.

However, as the saying goes, "A fool and her money are soon parted." I left the company where I was working to take a lower-paying job, because it was something I loved—which was not a bad thing. But that job abruptly ended, and rather than getting another job, I took some time off. So, my savings were eaten up in day-to-day living.

Take some classes on financial management. Many churches offer seminars that teach you to manage your money. Serving God wisely means that you can care for yourself as well as save enough to share with others.

Love,
Mommy

Giving God, teach us how to be wise stewards of all you give us. Amen.

JULY 11   CONTINUE LEARNING

My teaching, let it fall like a gentle rain, my words arrive like morning dew, like a sprinkling rain on new grass, like spring showers on the garden.   (Deuteronomy 32:1 The Message)

Dear Erin:
Stay curious.

When you were four, we were walking one day on the campus where I was attending seminary and we saw a huge seed the size of a grapefruit. You asked me what it was. I didn't know, but we immediately went to the library and discovered the "seed" was called a "horse apple." It fell from the Osage orange tree. We were excited because we had learned something new.

Stay excited about learning. Whether you continue formal education and get your doctorate or continue learning on your own, just keep learning. If you see something new, find out as much as you can about it. Go to another country and use the Spanish you have learned. Learn about the people and their culture; learn something about yourself on your own in a foreign place. Learning will refresh your spirit like a spring rain and allow you to grow as God intends.

Love,
Mommy

Lord, you have blessed us with curious minds and the ability to learn new things. May we use what we learn to glorify you. Amen.

JULY 12   AVOID NEGATIVE PEOPLE

Troublemakers start fights; gossips break up friendships.
                              (Proverbs 16:28 Message)

Dear Erin:
   Negative people bring negative energy.
   I never heard my mother gossip or say mean things to or about other people. She would say to us, "If you can't say anything good, then don't say anything at all."
   I wish I could hold my peace more. However, I will make a point of not saying anything *about* the person that I could not say *to* the person. I believe in building people up. What we say is very important.
   I teach a workshop to women using the example of the woman in the Bible with a flow of blood (Matthew 9:20). Blood is life, and something was draining the life out of her for twelve years. When you are around negative people who say uncaring words to you, they are draining the life out of you.
   Surround yourself with positive people. Fill yourself with the positive words of God. Just as the woman touched Jesus' hem and was healed, you can touch God any time you need to be reminded of how beloved you are: "I have loved you with an everlasting love; I have drawn you with loving-kindness" (Jeremiah 31:3 NIV). Seek positive energy.

Love,
Mommy

Loving God, help us remember that reading your Word helps us stay positive. Amen.

JULY 13   FIND A CHURCH HOME

Let us not give up meeting together, as some are in the habit of doing, but let us encourage one another.   (Hebrews 10:25 NIV)

Dear Erin:
   Settle into a church family.
   Though I am clergy, I sometimes find myself someplace other than church on Sunday morning. So, I know that we can worship in our gardens, on the seashore, or in our "home chapel." But the way I found my path to God was through a great church home where I could be taught, listened to, and loved.
   As a young adult, I came to my own understanding of God at a church where the pastor and his wife took the young singles into their home and became our surrogate parents. Many of us came from someplace else. They provided that Thanksgiving dinner, Saturday "go-to" place, and Sunday worship home. They modeled a Christian marriage and lifestyle that has stayed with me thirty years later.
   Wherever you go to church, just be sure of three things: (1) that the Word of God is taught by example in how the church treats you and others, (2) that you are given respect for having your own faith journey, and (3) that you are allowed to grow at your own pace—not according to an imposed standard. Find a church home that allows you to hear God.

Love,
Mommy

Blessed Savior, guide our young people to you through compassionate leaders. Amen.

JULY 14   APPRECIATE BEING ALONE

And after he had dismissed the crowds, he went up the mountain by himself to pray. When evening came, he was there alone.
                                        (Matthew 14:23 NRSV)

Dear Erin:

Find time for solitude and prayer.

Jesus was busy. He taught, healed, and preached to thousands of people. After teaching the crowds, he taught his disciples. How did he get so much done in his three years of ministry? He took time to be alone and pray.

Jesus was renewed after he spent time talking to God. He drew courage for the journey ahead. Though he would have preferred not to have to commit his final act of obedience, praying alone to God strengthened him (Luke 22:39-41).

We live in a world where we are expected to do more and find ways to do it faster. Jesus gives us another, healthier model for success: take time to be alone to pray. As you move from campus to workplace and learn how to negotiate the path to success, include fulfillment and peace in your definition of success. When you take time to be alone, to hear the small voice of God, you will have life—abundantly.

Love,
Mommy

God of peace, you always took time for solitude and prayer. Thank you for showing us that if our path does not include taking time for you, we are too busy. Amen.

JULY 15 SEEK AND GIVE FORGIVENESS

And be kind to one another, tenderhearted, forgiving one another, as God in Christ has forgiven you.
(Ephesians 4:32 NRSV)

Dear Erin:

Forgive as you are forgiven.

I continue to work on forgiving others—and myself. When I tell you things I wish I had done for you when you were a baby, you quickly say, "Mommy, get over it. That was more than twenty years ago." Though I can do nothing about the past, I still try to understand why things happened as they did.

The grace of forgiveness, however, says we don't need to know "why" someone behaved a certain way. We need only to ask God to give us the grace to forgive as we are forgiven. God is "faithful and just" (1 John 1:9 NIV) and will forgive our sins. So, we can forgive others when they hurt us. What seems even harder is to forgive ourselves when we have hurt someone—or hurt ourselves.

Jesus said pray for those who persecute you (Matthew 5:44). I tried it, and it works! I pray for their well-being and for God to bless them. My prayers have helped me let go of anger.

The best thing about forgiving others and praying for them is that forgiveness brings peace to your spirit. Forgive yourself, and you will find it easier to forgive others.

Love,
Mommy

Merciful God, thank you for forgiving us before we are able to forgive ourselves. Fill our hearts with your peace as we grow in our ability to forgive. Amen.

JULY 16   USE YOUR TALENTS FOR OTHERS

"To one he gave five talents of money, to another two talents, and to another one talent, each according to his ability."
(Matthew 25:15 NIV)

Dear Erin:
You have skills to offer.
You have always given your talents to build up the community to the glory of God. At age three you were singing in the children's choir. You volunteered two years at a summer camp for young children. You have always had time for the children at church. You willingly helped me work with older adults and people who were homeless. You also made a mission trip to help restore homes devastated by Hurricane Andrew.

God gives us skills to help others. In the parable of the talents, Jesus told of three men who were given gifts to manage while the master was away. Two used their gifts wisely, and their original gift was doubled. The third buried his gift and never realized the rewards that could have come had he used his gift wisely.

Be wise and use your gifts in ways that will allow you to grow and others to be blessed. When you do, your blessings will increase. You also will recognize Jesus in the faces of those you serve.

Love,
Mommy

Dear God, help us celebrate the gifts that our children have to offer others. Give them the boldness and compassion to use their gifts. Amen.

JULY 17   VALUE YOUR SEXUAL HEALTH

Do not be conformed to this world, but be transformed by the renewing of your minds, so that you may discern what is the will of God—what is good and acceptable and perfect.
                                            (Romans 12:2 NRSV)

Dear Erin:
   Make healthy choices.
   I was in college during the sixties when "free love" was the slogan. It seemed that "everybody was doing it," and that I would be left out if I did not join in. I had to pray very hard to make healthy choices.

One year my college roommate wanted me to double-date with her and her boyfriend. She set me up with one of his fraternity brothers. What I thought was a date turned out to be a visit to adjoining suites at a motel. I was furious and made them take me back to the dorm. You can't be afraid to "spoil the party." You have to care more about saving yourself.

You are a beautiful young woman who is coming to adulthood at a time when sexuality as seen in the media is not sacred or private. This is a world that devalues the sexuality of the young. This is a society where sexual behavior can lead to unwanted pregnancies—or to death from AIDS.

You have to resist being conformed to this world. Know that

God's will for you is wholeness and health in mind, body, and spirit. Pray and ask God for courage to value your sexual health.

Love,
Mommy

God, help our children to not be conformed to the world but to live according to your will. Amen.

JULY 18   DONATE TO WORTHY CAUSES

But a poor widow came and put in two very small copper coins, worth only a fraction of a penny.   ***(Mark 12:42 NIV)***

Dear Erin:
Give what you can.
Most of your life I was in graduate school. Part of the time we lived in a graduate students' dorm on campus. Those were some of our happiest times.

During that time we belonged to a small church where the pastor would preach, run over to the piano and play, and sing and lead the hymns at the same time. Some of those who attended were homeless; others (like us) did not have much beyond what it took to care for themselves. However, I made sure we put money in the collection plate. We shared even the little we had, and we always had what we needed.

You may not have fifty dollars, so give five. If you have more, then give more. Whatever you give to a worthy cause, you will find that you have enough of what you need and some of what you want. But, more important, you will help someone else live a better life. You may not be able to give a lot, but even small dollars matter.

Love,
Mommy

Generous God, help us give what we can to others. We know that you will increase even our small gifts. Amen.

JULY 19   LAUGH OFTEN

A cheerful look brings joy to the heart, and good news gives health to the bones.   *(Proverbs 15:30 NIV)*

Dear Erin:
  Enjoy your life.
  When I was a child, we would sit around the dinner table and laugh at my mother's jokes. Even if you aren't able to master the art of telling jokes, enjoy the company of people who make you laugh.
  When we lived in Houston, several of my girlfriends had children your age, and we would have parties together—nothing special, just enjoying one another's company. I miss the unplanned fun we had with them.
  When we moved to Nashville, there were certain rituals we had that did not cost very much and brought us joy. One was having an indoor picnic on the living room floor on a Friday night. We would rent comedies to watch and have a "girls' night."
  What I learned is that you don't have to go anyplace special or have a lot of "things" to entertain you. What matters is having the right people in your life who enjoy you and enjoy having fun. Enjoy the small things: a joke well told, friends laughing together, a picnic on a quilt. Enjoy life.

Love,
Mommy

God, give us the eyes and heart to see the joy and goodness in our lives. Amen.

JULY 20   *MOTHER* IS AN ACTION WORD

She brought him to Pharaoh's daughter, and she took him as her son.   *(Exodus 2:10 NRSV)*

Dear Erin:
  Be grateful for your "other-mother."

154

When your dad remarried, I was given a special blessing when I met his new wife, your "other-mother." When Ms. J. and I met, the first thing she said was, "I love Erin, too." She has shown that in many, many ways since that time almost twenty years ago.

She helped you with your school projects. Every year she made you an Easter basket, decorated with lace and filled with delicious goodies. Whenever you returned home from visiting, you always had a suitcase filled with beautiful new school clothes. I knew it was because of Ms. J.

She gave you a sense of style with her love of decorating and fashion. But also, as the daughter of a pastor, I trusted that her teachings and values supported my own. And as always, Ms. J. was present for special occasions, such as your graduation—taking more pictures than me! Be grateful for her love expressed not only in words but also in deeds. I am grateful she is in both our lives.

Love,
Mommy

Dear God, our parent, thank you for the women and men who are willing to show their love and care for other people's children through their loving actions. Amen.

JULY 21   ACT ON BEHALF OF OTHERS

My soul will rejoice when your lips speak what is right.
(Proverbs 23:16 NRSV)

Dear Erin:
Use your voice for justice.
Today it may be hard to know what is right because of many competing claims for truth, but this verse from Proverbs reminds us that you will do well to speak God's truth. You can't always trust popular opinion to determine what is righteous and just.

Jesus did not let standard religious practices keep him from bringing in a new order of love—not law. He spoke out for the oppressed.

Do you remember when we went to hear activist Angela Davis

speak at Fisk University? She didn't let her status as a college pro-
fessor keep her from taking action against the injustices she saw
in the legal system during the trial of the Soledad Brothers. That
act changed her life and eventually led to her imprisonment. She
was acquitted, but as you remember, she continues to speak out
against injustices and inequality.

You may not have to defend your cause to the point of prison or
the cross. However, believe in something enough that you would be
willing to speak against what is popular. It is the right thing to do.

Love,
Mommy

*God of the oppressed, give us the courage to speak what is right.
We trust that you will direct our words. Amen.*

JULY 22   LEAD A BALANCED LIFE

*Seek first [God's] kingdom and his righteousness, and all these
things will be given to you as well.*   *(Matthew 6:33 NIV)*

Dear Erin:
Put first things first.
Before you experienced the aftermath of Hurricane Katrina,
you were moving toward graduate school and a teaching career at
a major university. Now, after having to evacuate from one of the
worst disasters to hit the Gulf Coast, you are less sure of what you
want to do. Your confidence that events will happen the way you
plan has been shaken.

But one thing has not changed and never will: God loves you
and wants your life to prosper. Seek God, listen for God's voice,
make knowing God's purpose for you a priority, and you will find
all the career direction you need.

How do you know God's purpose? Put first things first. Begin
your day with prayer. Pay attention to what God placed in you
from the time you were born. Hear what is in your heart. Think
about what you would do if you were not paid. God's kingdom is
present when you live fully using your talents.

Hurricanes may force you to move. Disappointments may cause you to question your path. However, when knowing God is first in your life, you can always count on receiving blessings abundantly.

Love,
Mommy

Dear God, help us put you first; then we can know that every-thing that happens works out for our good. Amen.

JULY 23   BAD THINGS HAPPEN

Jesus wept.   **(John 11:35 NIV)**

Dear Erin:
Don't be afraid to grieve.
Jesus was summoned to Mary and Martha's house because their brother, Lazarus, was ill. By the time Jesus arrived at their home, Lazarus had already died.

In John 11:5 we learn that Jesus loved Mary, Martha, and Lazarus. So naturally, when he heard that Lazarus had died, he cried. Jesus had all the power in heaven and earth, yet in his humanity, he cried when he learned his beloved friend had died.

There is a lot of grief in our community. Children and youth die far too young. Older parents who expect their children to bury them often stand at the gravesides of their adult children. As a young person, you don't like to think about death, but too often young people attend the funerals of their friends.

Jesus understands the pain of loss and offers his presence for comfort and assurance that you are not alone. Allow others to share your grief. Talk to friends or family; find a support group or a professional counselor who can listen and offer support. You are never alone in your grief. Jesus cried, too.

Love,
Mommy

O Lord, you know the sadness we feel when we lose a loved one. Help us know you are with us and fill us with your peace. Amen.

JULY 24   BE WILLING TO RISK

For God has not given us a spirit of fear, but of power and of love and of a sound mind.   ***(2 Timothy 1:7 NKJV)***

Dear Erin:

God's love overcomes fear.

Many times over the past two decades I have recalled this scripture when faced with challenges. When I have felt like turning around rather than asking for a promotion, I used this verse to give me courage. When I have been hesitant to speak up and give my ideas, I have used this verse to remind me that I have a spirit of power.

I give this verse to you as one of my favorites. You are going into a world that may want you to be quiet and accept things the way they are. You may find yourself in a job where your creativity may be ignored. That may cause you to doubt your own vision.

Be reminded of this verse during those times when doubt and fear creep in. Also, remember the stories of others who have had to overcome harsh critics to make a difference in the world.

Remember, God gives you your spirit of courage, power, self-control, and love. Because God has deposited this in you, no one can take it away. Draw upon it when you need strength.

Love,
Mommy

God of love, thank you for blessing us with the courage to speak boldly, knowing you will give us the words to say. Amen.

JULY 25   YOU ARE BODY, MIND, AND SPIRIT

I will praise thee; for I am fearfully and wonderfully made: marvellous are thy works.   ***(Psalm 139:14 KJV)***

Dear Erin:

Your body is a miracle.

I have learned that what happens in our bodies affects our emotional and spiritual health. When I was in my twenties, I had a glamorous job, yet it was very stressful. I did not manage my stress well, and eventually my health was affected. I had an appendectomy.

In my thirties, the divorce was emotionally distressing and led to another health problem—and another major surgery.

In my forties, I decided to take better care of my physical, mental, and spiritual health. I began to exercise, make wiser food choices, and get back to my daily Bible reading. I had never stopped going to church, but I had neglected my personal relationship with God. I needed to improve my spiritual health.

Once I got my health back in balance, I had more peace and actually felt better. God made us for wholeness. We cannot overlook any part of ourselves if we want to have well-being. We are a marvelous work of God because we are spirit, mind, and body. Take good care of your whole self. You are a miracle made by God.

Love,
Mommy

Creator God, remind us that our bodies, minds, and spirits all need care for good health. Amen.

JULY 26   HAVE A PLAN

Entrust your affairs to the LORD, And your plans will succeed.
(Proverbs 16:3 TANAKH)

Dear Erin:
  Plan, but be open to change.
  I read an article that said we're expected to get on a career path, stay there, and eventually arrive at a desired goal. The writer warned, however, that this rigid career path does not leave room for chance—or what I would call Divine intervention.

  In grade school I wanted to be a nurse. I left high school wanting to be a psychologist. I entered college with a speech and drama major. I completed my first graduate degree in theology. Eventually, I achieved a doctorate in religion and personality. I'm still trying to figure out how I got from there to here!

I can't give you an outline for career success. But I know this: when you trust God for the direction of your life, you'll never take the wrong path. I believe you can and should have a plan. Prepare for a career that you will love and that will allow you to contribute to society; but stay open to direction from God. Pay attention to those side roads that may not be as popular. Above all, trust God and you will never fail.

Love,
Mommy

Lord, give us the wisdom to plan our future while recognizing that you direct our paths. Amen.

JULY 27   GIVE EXCELLENCE

Finally, [beloved], whatever is true, whatever is noble, whatever is right, whatever is pure, whatever is lovely, whatever is admirable—if anything is excellent or praiseworthy—think about such things.   *(Philippians 4:8 NIV)*

Dear Erin:
Do your best.
   You are an excellent student. As you have moved from elementary school to college, I have watched you do your best even when you wanted to give up. I know how hard you worked to do well in those classes where "the teacher wasn't fair" or the "work was boring."
   We moved across the country several times when you were in junior high school, which made your coursework more difficult. But you didn't give up. You continued to do your best, and I'm proud of you. Your hard work has paid off; you have been an honors student throughout college.
   Continue to focus on excellence; look to what is right and ethical. Live with kindness and see beauty in the unlovely. Respect opinions that are different from your own. Excellence is not just about academics; it's a way of experiencing life. When you seek excellence and do your best, you will not regret the outcome.

Love,
Mommy

Precious Lord, thank you for the courage to work hard even when we feel like giving up. Give us strength to walk in excellence and leave the outcome to you. Amen.

JULY 28   GOD CALLS YOU BY NAME

But now thus says the LORD—Who created you ... Fear not, for I will redeem you; I have singled you out by name, You are Mine.   (Isaiah 43:1 TANAKH)

Dear Erin:
You belong to God.
When you were little, I would ask you, "Who loves you?" and you would begin to name family and friends. We would always remember to say that God loves you, too. In fact, God loved you first and called you by your name—a child of God.

Research has shown that a fetus can tell the difference between her mother's voice and a stranger's voice. The fetus will move toward her mother's voice.

When you spend time with God and grow closer to God, you will turn toward God's voice. As you turn to hear God's voice, you'll find more peace in your life. You'll know that God's will for you is good. You won't be afraid.

You'll hear God's voice through reading Scripture. You'll recognize the voice of God in people who love you. You don't have to go to a special place or do a particular thing to hear God. God says simply, "Be still, and know that I am God" (Psalm 46:10 KJV). God knows you. Listen for the voice of God.

Love,
Mommy

Redeemer God, you have claimed us for yourself because we are your creation. Allow us to be silent and hear your voice. Amen.

JULY 29   CLAIM YOUR INHERITANCE

"What Zelophehad's daughters are saying is right. You must certainly give them property as an inheritance among their father's relatives and turn their father's inheritance over to them."
                                                    (Numbers 27:7 NIV)

Dear Erin:
    You have an inheritance.
    Your inheritance is my inheritance; it comes from the values I gained from my mother. Today the legal world calls that "intellectual property," and lawyers get paid a lot of money to protect it.
    As my sisters and I would leave to visit a friend, our mother would say, "Remember who you are." What she meant was, "I expect you to use the manners I have taught you and to not embarrass me." We were always pleased to give her a good report on our manners.
    Today, good manners are missing from our culture. It seems to be OK to call one another cruel names or to "diss" (disrespect) people. Now manners are taught in corporate boardrooms by highly paid consultants, rather than at home by parents.
    You are a beneficiary of your grandmother's "intellectual property." You have something of value, an inheritance that thieves can't steal. Not only do you know "who you are," but you also know "whose you are." You have an inheritance from God, your grandmother, and me. Pass it on.

Love,
Mommy

Lord, thank you for giving us your love, an inheritance that is priceless. May we pass it on to others as a precious gift. Amen.

JULY 30   LIVE THE FRUIT OF THE SPIRIT

But what happens when we live God's way? He brings gifts into our lives, much the same way that fruit appears in an orchard—things like affection for others, exuberance about life,

serenity ... a willingness to stick with things, a sense of compassion in the heart, and a conviction that a basic holiness permeates things and people. We find ourselves ... able to marshal and direct our energies wisely.
(Galatians 5:22-23 The Message)

Dear Erin:
Bear much fruit.
Do you remember when the pastor would ask the children to come to the front of the church and recite the fruit of the Spirit? I like this expanded version. The writer gives us a picture of abundance—not just fruit appearing on one tree, but fruit filling an entire orchard.

Take the fruit described here—loyalty, recognizing the holiness in all things and people, compassion, willingness to stick to your goals, excitement about life, living peacefully, having affection for others, having wisdom in how you pursue goals—and fill your life with these in abundance. Don't just pick one or two kinds of fruit. Give them all; lavish them on people.

I know it's easier to recite the verses than live them. People can be rude and disappoint us. We can't control how people treat us.

But we *can* control how we respond. If people are mean, treat them with compassion. If your job is boring, volunteer after hours to bring excitement to someone else. When you are fruitful, seeds are planted that will grow into an orchard. Allow them to grow in yourself, and you will have an abundant life.

Love,
Mommy

Gracious God, work on us so we may bear the fruit of the Spirit—in abundance. Amen.

JULY 31   GO WITH GOD

"I charge you: Be strong and resolute; do not be terrified or dismayed, for the LORD your God is with you wherever you go."
(Joshua 1:9 TANAKH)

Dear Erin:

God is with you.

On graduation day I felt such excitement and pride mingled with anxiety and sadness. As you walked across the stage, I saw myself holding you in the rocking chair where I read you to sleep every night. As you reached for your diploma, I saw us stretched across my bed, watching television together until we both fell asleep. As you walked back to your seat, I'm sure I walked beside you as I did when you started kindergarten, junior high, high school, and even college.

Actually, it was God walking with *us*. Surely it was God who got us to the hospital in time before your earache turned into a ruptured eardrum. I know it wasn't just me who guided you through those uncertain days of junior high.

I'm grateful I wasn't the only one walking with you. Our loving families, faithful friends, and merciful God have all been present as you have grown up.

As you marched down the Avenue of Oaks, you began your walk into your future. Take my words with you. Take my love. Most of all, my darling, go with God.

Love,
Mommy

Dear God, give us courage as we move into our future. May we walk with joy and boldness, knowing you are walking with us. Amen.

August

Celebrate Every Day

MARY RITZMAN EBINGER

AUGUST 1   FILLED WITH LAUGHTER

Then our mouth was filled with laughter, and our tongue with shouts of joy. **(Psalm 126:2 NRSV)**

Laughter is a delight. As mothers, we often see something that is funny, which helps us to be happier that day. Life is busy, and everything does not always go right. But even allowing ourselves to laugh when a little event seems humorous can help ease the tension, enabling us to live one day at a time. Always it is a matter of laughing with one another, not at one another.

So, look for the caterpillar that is squiggling down the sidewalk. Laugh together as a child tries to blow out candles on a birthday cake. Look for the humor in life each day. And at night, remember that laughter, hugs, and prayers are a great ending to the day—and that God is smiling, too.

Join me this month as we "browse" through some of my own memories of joy and laughter, and consider how we may celebrate the gift of life each and every day.

Thank you, Lord, for children. And thank you for the laughter and joy of each day. Amen.

AUGUST 2   THE GIFT OF ADVENTURE

So teach us to count our days that we may gain a wise heart.
(Psalm 90:12 NRSV)

Life is an adventure. There are ups and downs. The "ups" are the joys of life: a wedding or the birth of a healthy baby. The "downs" are sad times: sickness; the death of a loved one—even the loss of a child, which is the saddest loss; or an unexpected accident or terminal illness that changes life. But in all this, in the good and the bad, we know that God goes with us on every adventure, whether happy or difficult.

My mother had many adventures. She traveled alone to China when she was seventeen to be a missionary. She tells of traveling in a ship and sailing through a typhoon, which was very scary. Then, when she arrived in China, she found that someone had broken into her trunk and stolen many items. Yet she saw all of this as an adventure—as she did with all of her life. She taught me a Chinese Christian song, "I Will Not Be Afraid," which I think of often.

My mother met my father in China. He was also a missionary there, and later they were married in Shanghai. My parents gave me the gift of adventure—the spirit to face anything that happens in life. May we give this gift to our children.

Thank you, Lord, for the adventure of life and for being with us each day. Amen.

AUGUST 3   A LITTLE MONEY, A LOT OF LOVE

"Therefore I tell you, do not worry about your life, what you will eat or ... what you will wear.... And why do you worry about clothing? Consider the lilies of the field, how they grow."
(Matthew 6:25-28 NRSV)

We had little money when I was a child, but we never worried. My mother amazed us with what she was able to do with it. I remember the smell of delicious cherry pie baking in the oven, fried chicken cooking on the stove, and the delightful aroma of fastnachts—doughnuts—frying in hot oil during Lent, making me scurry down for breakfast. Each doughnut was light and covered with powdered sugar—warm and tasty.

My mother also sewed little lacey dresses, coats, and even pajamas for my doll Cecile, and she spent hours making a light green dress for me when I needed one for a special occasion. She never complained about the little bit of money we had in our family; she took whatever she had to make delicious meals and beautiful clothes. Most of all, everything she made was made with love.

Thank you, God, that love does not mean having a lot of money. Thank you for mothers who give what they can with what they have. Amen.

AUGUST 4   "YOU CAN DO IT"

Be strong, and let your heart take courage. (Psalm 27:14 NRSV)

When I was eight years old, I often rode home from school "double" on a bicycle with my sister. One day on the way home, my heel caught in the bicycle wheel. It was April 1, not exactly a good April Fool's Day. As a result, I was in and out of the hospital and then in bed at home in a knee-high cast for four months.

After I was better, my uncle gave me a new bike. Not exactly what I wanted. To learn to ride it again was a scary thought, but my mother said, "You can do it." She also said this later when I learned to play the piano and organ, and other times, too, when I had doubts about my ability with schoolwork or other endeavors. To this day, when I find something difficult or overwhelming, I still hear the words again: "You can do it."

Thank you, God, for the words of encouragement we received from our mothers and others and now pass on to our children. Amen.

AUGUST 5   A GIFT FROM GOD

Now Sarah said, "God has brought laughter for me; everyone who hears will laugh with me."   *(Genesis 21:6 NRSV)*

We saw him for the first time sitting in a grocery cart wearing a little navy blue snowsuit and a white fuzzy hat. He sat quietly while the social worker shopped. The adoption agency told us to check on him in the store, of all places, and see if we wanted him. He was not yet two years old. We loved him immediately. How could we not want him?

He came to us just before his second birthday, at Christmastime. How shy he was after he had lived in several foster homes. We were told to feed him cookies—the only way he would be quiet. We decided love was needed more, and soon he started to laugh as he said, "Bumpity-bump," and bounced down the stairs in his little pajama outfit with feet. And, yes, even though it was not easy, he did learn to eat healthy food. What a joy this special gift was at Christmas!

Now he is a successful young man with a master's degree, and the father of two dear little girls. His name is Jonathan, which means "Gift of God," and I am happy to be his mother.

Thank you, God, for the gift of children. May we enjoy them each and every one, and give them the best life we can. Amen.

AUGUST 6   OTHER LITTLE ONES

"Let the little children come to me, and do not stop them; for it is to such as these that the kingdom of heaven belongs."
                                            (Matthew 19:14 NRSV)

One year our family had five babies in addition to our own three children—Lee, Lori, and Jonathan. They were foster babies that we had taken home to care for right after they were born. The babies stayed with us until they could sleep through the night, and then they were adopted. Timothy was the first to go. How difficult it was to see him leave. The crib and room were so empty. We all were sad, but we were happy that he had a new home.

Margo, our last foster baby to leave, was happy and plump. But she was also restless. We discovered her mother had been on drugs before her birth, and she was wiggly and unable to sleep easily until the drugs were out of her system. Margo was with us five months before she was adopted. We shed many tears, for she was a part of our family; but we were happy that she was healthy when she left us.

What joy the babies gave us, and we knew good foster homes were so needed then, just as they are today.

Lord, may we reach out in whatever ways we can to help other little ones. Amen.

AUGUST 7   A MOTHER'S PRAYER

"As a mother comforts her child, so I will comfort you."
(Isaiah 66:13 NRSV)

Peace, like a quiet lake, comes with a mother's hug after a bruise
        or fall,
    and lingers at night after the last kiss.
I say a prayer at night for this child, that I may be the best
        mother I can be.
    Thank you God, for peace.
Love is like a running river over stones of troubles and brings calm
        to all
    and lasts the night through.
Love gives a sense of security that all is well until day has come
        once again.
    Thank you, God, for love.
Hope is like a shining ray when sunset comes, and we know that
        no matter what happens
    God is with us in all times.
    Thank you, God, for hope.
Joy is like a bubbling fountain as laughter comes in the midst of
        the difficulties of each day.
    Thank you, God, for joy.
A mother teaches a child right and wrong and bakes birthday
        cakes with love and sprinkles.

Thank you, God, for mothers.
When sadness comes, mothers listen and help their children find
      peace.
Thank you, God, for compassionate hearts and listening ears.

Thank you, God, for love, hope, joy, peace, and compassion. Amen.

AUGUST 8   AN ANNIVERSARY GIFT

And now faith, hope, and love abide, these three; and the greatest of these is love.   **(1 Corinthians 13:13 NRSV)**

Our twenty-fifth anniversary arrived. We had no plans, because we had just celebrated the fiftieth wedding anniversary of my husband's parents. But our children, then ages twelve, ten, and six, had their own ideas. We knew something was about to happen as they whispered and scurried around. That night when we came home, the dining room table was set beautifully, and dinner was ready. To top it off, there was a lovely homemade anniversary cake, and the children sang to us.

Then they said, "We have a gift for you, Mommy and Daddy." They left for a few minutes and came back into the dining room with our anniversary gift. In the arms of one of the children was a little kitten they found in a gutter. It was half-starved and covered with fleas. They said, "We thought this was a perfect anniversary gift for you, and the kitten needed a home."

So she stayed. And we called her Happy Anniversary or Happy Annie, for short. What a gift of love!

What an anniversary!

God, we thank you for our children and their love. Amen.

AUGUST 9   HUGS

[There is] a time to embrace, and a time to refrain from embracing.   **(Ecclesiastes 3:5 NRSV)**

How good a hug feels when we are happy or sad, or when we simply need to feel loved. Sometimes it seems they are God's hugs when we give them to others or receive them ourselves. Often we give hugs to our children when they come home discouraged. These hugs warm their hearts and ours.

Sometimes words are not possible—whether in times of joy or sorrow—and then a hug gives the best message we can give. There is an anonymous saying that goes like this:

> Some people come into our lives and quickly go.
> Some stay for a while and leave footprints on
> our hearts, and we are never the same.

This is so true. Sometimes hugs can leave footprints on our hearts, and "we are never the same." May the memory of hugs—given and received—always be with us.

Lord, thank you for the love and hugs that have helped us through our growing-up years, as well as for the love and hugs we have shared with our children. Amen.

AUGUST 10   A MOTHER-IN-LAW'S LOVE

But Ruth said, . . . "Where you go, I will go; . . . your people shall be my people, and your God my God."   *(Ruth 1:16 NRSV)*

My husband's mother became a special person in my own life as I learned how she faced difficulties and overcame limitations. She adjusted to the role of a farmer's wife after a college education that had prepared her for teaching children. Farm life was demanding as she cared for a large household and extended garden, cooked meals on a coal-burning stove for extra farmhands, washed clothes in the basement and hung them outside to dry, and canned fruits and vegetables.

She made each day special as she cared for four children, cooked delicious meals, and enhanced the farmhouse with flowers from her garden that also adorned the altar at the country church on Sunday mornings—where she also taught children in Sunday school.

In later years, she volunteered at a day-care center for children who would eventually be in special education classes. She loved that role, and the children loved her. My mother-in-law never complained about hard work or lack of conveniences. Her faith was strong. Her love was unending. She was and is an inspiration.

Thank you, God, for the love of our mothers-in-law and the lessons of life they share with us. Amen.

AUGUST 11   REFRESH ME

Those who wait for the LORD shall renew their strength, they shall mount up with wings like eagles.   (Isaiah 40:31 NRSV)

As I awake this morning, bright pink and red begonias, golden mums, and fuchsia geraniums smile brightly in their pots on our balcony and speak of a fresh new day—a day to live in the best way I can.

Today we go to a baseball game with one of our grandchildren. The players are only twelve years old, and they are in the process of learning to bat, pitch, and run. Wow! They really can run!

Their spirit is great. They are not overly concerned about winning; they just want to play the game to the best of their ability. We don't know how it will end, but we enjoy being out in the fresh air, laughing and cheering. We also have a hot dog and warm, large pretzels sprinkled with salt. They help make the day special, too!

Afterward, there are a lot of hugs and love that renew us in our family time. We leave for home refreshed in body and spirit.

May you be refreshed today as you live this brand-new day in fresh and vital ways.

Lord, renew my spirit and my relationships with family members today—whether young or old, near or far away. Amen.

AUGUST 12   CELEBRATING EACH DAY

Let us come into his presence with thanksgiving; let us make a joyful noise to him with songs of praise!   (Psalm 95:2 NRSV)

Tomorrow is our daughter's birthday, and we will celebrate all the days we have had with her from the time she was a tiny baby until now. She is a lovely young woman today, and we have enjoyed celebrating her at every age.

Sometimes we mothers wish our children would stay little forever; but when we see them as productive and creative adults with little ones of their own, we thank God for all the celebrations—little and big—that we've had along the way.

We can find things to celebrate each day—not just on special days. Sunlight and gentle rain, rainbows and snowflakes, whispering soft winds and breezes that seem to blow through our hearts and refresh us—when such moments are shared with our children, they are special, indeed.

Thank you, God, for each day we have to celebrate with our children, and for all you have given us in life. Amen.

AUGUST 13   HOPE

And you will have confidence, because there is hope; you will be protected and take your rest in safety.   **(Job 11:18 NRSV)**

Frost did not deter, kill, hurt, or discourage the purple pansies and bright begonias and miracle mums last night. Neither will pain discourage me, for I know God is present with me as I walk and go from place to place and feel this care and love. Life is fragile. Even cancer will not prevent me from having hope.

Sometimes we protect our little children from hurts or cover tender plants to keep them safe on cold nights. We know that God has a protective blanket around us. Though it is invisible, we are aware of this presence; and it gives us hope.

We can let go of needless worry and concerns and give them to God. For what good is it for us to worry about that which we cannot change? We know there are some areas in our lives that we can change, or some people we can help along the way, including family and friends. May we live this way today: knowing what and how to change, and what to accept that we cannot change. Let us be filled with hope.

O God, thank you for the wisdom you have given us and for hope that is like a shining ray in our lives. Amen.

AUGUST 14   A TIME TO PRAY

And after he had dismissed the crowds, he went up the mountain by himself to pray. When evening came, he was there alone.
(Matthew 14:23 NRSV)

A time to reflect. A time to be silent. A time to pray. A time to be alone with God. We can find a special place in our home—a corner chair by a window, a soft sofa by a lamp, or a comfortable chair in the bedroom—somewhere we can begin each day in quiet. At times this requires that we get up early, but if we take this time as Jesus did—away from the crowds and even away from his disciples—it will help our day. We as mothers need this quiet time.

A quiet time can also take the form of spiritual journaling in a notebook, reading the Bible, or silent meditation as we look at one lit candle or flower to help us be inspired. More important, this is when we can sense God's presence and know what is important in our day, realizing there is not time for everything. Then we can be renewed as we follow Jesus' example. No matter how busy we may be, time apart to pray must be a priority.

Dear God, we pray you will help us realize the importance of time alone with you so that we can live a more abundant life. Amen.

AUGUST 15   A PRAYER SHAWL

Devote yourselves to prayer, keeping alert in it with thanksgiving.   *(Colossians 4:2 NRSV)*

One day a call came from a woman who asked to come and see me. "Of course," I said. A few hours later she arrived at my door with a beautiful light-blue knitted shawl, saying, "This shawl is for you from our Bible study group at church." Then she explained that a prayer shawl was knitted step by step, knit and purl, in the spirit of prayer. Then, when completed, there was a prayer time to sense to whom the shawl would be given. It was decided, to my surprise, that this lovely shawl would be given to me.

Three years ago I was diagnosed with cancer of my bone marrow, but I am still here. Prayers of many people help, and I feel I am doing very well. This prayer shawl means so much to me. I believe I have much to give yet in my life. As I see the prayer shawl draped over a chair, it gives me courage. On a chilly day or night, I wrap it around me, and it gives me comfort.

Prayer is so powerful. May we always be devoted to praying for our children.

Dear God, thank you for the many ways we find a gift, created in prayer, to be a connection between ourselves and you. Amen.

AUGUST 16   DO NOT WORRY

"Do not let your hearts be troubled."   **(John 14:1 NRSV)**

Little petunia leaves crowded the pot, but no purple flowers came as promised. Won't these bloom? What is the trouble? With a little nourishment here and there and persistence, one day there was one little petunia—then another. Now many flowers are overflowing the pot, seeming to say, "See! Aren't you glad you didn't give up?"

Think of a time when you were concerned and worried about a few "trouble spots" regarding your children. Perhaps you've thought, *If only we could have a written guarantee that our child will grow up and get through these problems.* But there are no guarantees. As parents, we do the best we can as we love our children through all times. Most of the time, they do grow up in a fine way, and we look back later and think, *Why did I worry about that?*

Our love and God's love will bring them and us through even the most difficult times.

Dear God, we thank you for your love that is with us each day. May our hearts not be troubled or anxious, but may we give all our cares to you. Amen.

AUGUST 17   ALWAYS ROOM TO LOVE MORE

Whoever does not love does not know God, for God is love.
(1 John 4:8 NRSV)

In the back of a car in England sat a little worn-out, tan dog stitched together—its back and legs and one ear hanging by a few red threads. Its name was Fido. We were on a pastoral exchange at a church near Liverpool. We lived in the manse with our three children, ages two, six, and eight.

Throughout our stay, the chief steward of the church, Doug, took our family to see many scenic areas and historic locations in England, and this little stuffed dog was always in the backseat. Our two-year-old, Jonathan, always held Fido close. He loved this sad-eyed, worn dog with a little ear almost torn off, and he carried him everywhere.

When we were ready to board a train for London on our way back to the United States, Doug handed Fido to Jonathan, who was holding his panda bear he had brought from home. Doug said, "Fido needs you to love him. Everybody needs someone to love some time." And that was how Fido came home with us.

There is always room in our hearts to love more.

Dear Lord, help us know that we can always love more, and that there will always be enough love for everyone. Thank you for your love. Amen.

AUGUST 18   FAITH—A LOVE CONNECTION

***I am reminded of your sincere faith, a faith that lived first in
... your mother Eunice.*** ***(2 Timothy 1:5 NRSV)***

"Mommy, I love you." How wonderful to hear these words from a little child.

As we see projects in a shoe box, hear a book report given in preparation for a class, cheer at a softball game that ends in a tie, listen to a book read or to a piece of music played on the violin, or hold a bouquet of buttercups given by a child—these are the little joys of being a mother—and later, of being a grandmother. Hand-drawn pictures, decorated with crayons or painted in vivid water-colors along with messages that always include the word *love*, are taped on the refrigerator door. Holding a baby or an older child who climbs in your lap or takes your hand on a walk—these are such precious moments.

So, at night I thank God for my children—and my grandchildren—and the happiness they give me; and I pray that I will be a mother—and a grandmother—who always listens and cares through the years, and that God will guide me along the way.

Dear God, thank you for the love of children. May my love always be there for each one in times of happiness and in times of need. Amen.

AUGUST 19   A PILLOW OF LOVE

Let love be genuine.   ***(Romans 12:9 NRSV)***

Our daughter Lori began to teach special education children after her graduation from college. Between planning lessons and grading papers, she took time to cross-stitch a beautiful pillow that is now sitting on an old rocking chair in our home as a reminder of her love. On the pillow are these words written by an anonymous author:

Mother

You filled my days with rainbow lights,
Fairytales and sweet dream nights,
A kiss to wipe away my tears,
Gingerbread to ease my fears.
You gave the gift of life to me,
And then in love, you set me free.
I thank you for your tender care,
For deep warm hugs and being there.
I hope that when you think of me,
A part of you, you'll always see.

We are thankful for the expressions of our children, for little notes and beautiful gifts that help us realize the total relationship that is ours together. Love is the keynote through all the days in all the ways.

We are thankful for our children.

Dear God, help us, we pray, to give good gifts that will be remembered by our children as they grow through the years. Amen.

AUGUST 20   JOY OF THE NOW

I have said these things to you so that my joy may be in you, and that your joy may be complete.   *(John 15:11 NRSV)*

It has been said if we smile when we don't feel like it, often we will end up feeling like smiling. There is so much joy in each moment and each day if we only will recognize it. Sometimes we get so involved in doing rather than being. We need to discover joy on an ordinary day in all that is around us. As mothers, it is important that we also help our children find joy.

There are always hidden joys to be shared. We have only the "now" in life. So let us be happy and at peace and share joy with others with whom we live. Then happiness may be like a stone thrown in a lake that creates concentric circles and reaches out to all others with whom we have contact—under the roofs of our homes and in our churches and communities. Let us spread this joy as far as we can in our world.

Lord, you have promised us joy. May we realize this fully, living each day in a spirit of joy. Amen.

AUGUST 21   HOPE

And hope does not disappoint us, because God's love has been poured into our hearts through the Holy Spirit that has been given to us.   *(Romans 5:5 NRSV)*

Do you ever look at the sun as it sets and see the rays stream through clouds and the atmosphere? At times they seem to be signs of hope for our lives. We need hope when the dark clouds of problems seem to overshadow our lives. Just as the sun's rays cast away the clouds and shine through the darkness, in the same way God gives us hope to face each day, each problem, and each crisis.

One little child asked her mother as she looked at the setting sun, "Mommy, are those steps to heaven?" In a real sense, the sunset rays remind us of the steps of faith, love, and hope. May hope fill our lives and give us peace. What would life be like without hope?

Lord, thank you for the sun, for your son Jesus Christ, and for the hope we can receive as we look to you for help in times of trouble. Amen.

AUGUST 22   A CUP OF WATER

And whoever gives even a cup of cold water to one of these little ones ... will [not] lose their reward.   (Matthew 10:42 NRSV)

We rode in a rickshaw pulled by a bicycle through the busy streets of Agra. We were in India to study missions. One day, in the busy traffic, a car collided with our bicycle, overturned the rickshaw, and threw us into the street. The rider was not hurt and hurriedly pulled us to safety. My husband was safe, too, but I was quite shaken as I sat on a curb with many abrasions, patting my bleeding knees and ankles with a handkerchief.

A little boy noticed me. He ran away and hurried back to give me a tin cup of water. Since I knew it was not safe to drink, I put the cup to my lips and pretended to drink. I felt God's love through his kindness. As he cared, I became calm. We then proceeded to the doctor's office for antibiotics, but the cup of water was the best medicine.

Instead of my giving a cup of water to a little one, a little one had given a cup to me! As I reflect on that time, I wonder if his mother had taught him to be so kind to others. I think so.

Thank you, God, for care and concern from strangers and unexpected kindness. May we be aware of how we can help strangers and others who need our care. Amen.

AUGUST 23   CELEBRATE

This is the day that the LORD has made; let us rejoice and be glad in it.   *(Psalm 118:24 NRSV)*

Each day is a new day, a day to be glad, a new beginning. Old hurts are gone, unfulfilled dreams are put aside, and we rejoice that we can start with new possibilities.

Celebrate a tiny, new, purple petunia as it opens up to daylight. Celebrate lemonade bought on the neighborhood corner, bringing coolness and refreshment on a hot day. Celebrate the warm kisses of your children, hot from playing outside. Celebrate the smiles of your family and friends and the warm love you feel from them. Celebrate soft rain as it refreshes and cleans the earth, brightens grass, and helps the corn grow. Celebrate the little things. Celebrate the big things. Celebrate the day!

As we are open to the potential of God at work within daily life, we find the real rewards of this day—far beyond what might have been expected. At the end of the day, we will realize this is another reason to celebrate.

Dear God, help us be open to each day's celebration and remember to thank you for everything. Amen.

AUGUST 24   THE RAINBOW

I have set my bow in the clouds, and it shall be a sign of the covenant between me and the earth.   *(Genesis 9:13 NRSV)*

Some days the weather prediction is a 90 percent chance of rain. If on target, the rain comes and the winds blow and the earth is refreshed. There are puddles everywhere, and children, if given the chance, like to splash through them. What fun! Suddenly the skies clear and the rain slows to a drip like a bathroom shower that is not quite turned off. Then the sun shines through the entire atmosphere, and a rainbow appears—all colors blending together not only for a beautiful moment but also for a future promise.

To be a mother is to see a rainbow even when it's still raining, because inside your heart you know God will be there in all kinds of weather.

I remember the sparkle in my daughter's eyes at the first sight of a rainbow with all the beautiful colors, and I remember feeling close to God and the covenant the rainbow represents. To share a rainbow with a young child is a special time—a magic moment!

Thank you, God, for rainbows. May your miracle of color always be a reminder of your love shining through any pain and through every dark night of the soul. Amen.

AUGUST 25   A LITTLE ANGEL

Do not neglect to show hospitality to strangers, for by doing that some have entertained angels without knowing it.
(Hebrews 13:2 NRSV)

Several years ago my husband and I were part of a mission trip to the Dominican Republic. Our task was to help build a church in a remote area of the island. The work was heavy, and it was very hot. Several of us planned to teach Bible school to little children while the rest of the team were laying block and sawing lumber.

What a joy to share with those precious wide-eyed children as they learned about God's love, colored pictures, and sang together. One little girl was especially happy to learn about Jesus. She seemed like she was almost my little girl, even though she had a mother and father. After we left we were able to provide for her to go to school and have medical care through a special fund established for children in the Dominican Republic. This arrangement has continued month by month, with letters and photos to and from our home and hers.

What a gift—to help care for this little girl who is part of our family now! Her name is Angelica, an angel.

God of all little children, bless those who live in our homes and those who live far away; in the name of Christ who loved little children. Amen.

AUGUST 26   FORGIVENESS

Anyone whom you forgive, I also forgive.
(2 Corinthians 2:10 NRSV)

At times we think we have forgiven everyone we believe has wronged us. Then something else happens, perhaps minor or more hurtful, and we find that forgiving is not easy—especially if someone we love has been hurt by the offender either physically or emotionally. And yet Jesus has given us this lesson to forgive many times.

We need to accept everyone as a child of God and to love each one as sacred. Each of us is on a journey in life, and mistakes are made. If we do not forgive, it hurts ourselves more than those we do not forgive; we may become bitter or find we cannot live each day fully because of resentment within.

Clara Barton once was asked if she had forgiven someone who had said something hurtful to her. Her reply was, "I distinctly remember forgetting it." So with love and understanding we forgive, and in so doing we have a fuller life.

Lord, help us forgive as you have taught us and to understand and care for each one of your family on this earth. Amen.

AUGUST 27   WORD GAME

See what large letters I make when I am writing in my own hand!   *(Galatians 6:11 NRSV)*

Our family sits on the floor around a "lazy Susan" board game with buttered popcorn in bowls beside us—ready for the word game. We pick up seven letter tiles and wonder, *What word will I be able to make out of these?* Then the game begins.

Sometimes our letters are a mixture of good letters—vowels and consonants—and a word is easy to form. Other times, it is difficult to form any word. We may have the letters "z," "x," or "q," but there is no place to play them.

Life comes in unexpected ways just as the letters on our individual holders. A package comes and surprises us for our birthday, or a telephone call gives us sad news of the death of a dear one. We know that we can make it through all difficulties, just as eventually we pick letters for our game and, finally, are able to play a word. Paul had trouble writing, and we, too, may have various concerns.

We have choices to make in life, just as in our board game. How will we make them?

God, help us make the right choices each day and live in the best way possible. Amen.

AUGUST 28   REACH OUT

And you will be my witnesses in Jerusalem, in all Judea and Samaria, and to the ends of the earth.   (Acts 1:8 NRSV)

At one church my husband served there was a real sense of mission. The mission team served a brunch once a month before and after three church services. On the tables were baskets for donations that helped with the expenses. Parents and children together became aware of sharing in mission near and far.

On one of our mission trips to Jamaica, I visited Saint Ann's hospital. I found that patients could not go home because they had no wheelchairs or crutches, and that the babies I held in the nursery often had no sheets. Many of the mothers could not be at the hospital because they were home taking care of their other children. As I looked at these babies, I was so aware of their needs and lack of nursing care.

When I arrived home, I told about these needs. Sheets, wheelchairs, crutches, and other medical supplies soon filled a whole room. Particularly touching was the response for the children: stuffed toys, dolls, bright clothes, and diapers. My mother's heart was touched by this show of compassion. Later we shipped them to Jamaica. Truly, this was mission!

Lord, help us listen and be aware of how we can draw upon our motherly compassion to serve wherever we are. Amen.

AUGUST 29   BLENDED TOGETHER

How wonderful, how beautiful, when brothers and sisters get along!   *(Psalm 133:1 Message)*

On our little balcony we have a window box attached to the railing that happily grows yellow marigolds, pink begonias, and purple phlox. The colors blend beautifully together. Each seems to have a different personality and way of waving in the breeze, as in a chorus or individual solos. Isn't this like the family of God?

We are all different, yet we can blend together in this world if we have peace within ourselves and live in peace with others, no matter how different.

What about our families? As a mother, do I encourage my children to truly be themselves in their own expressions of goodness and talents that enrich life, though they are quite different from one another?

As we continue this journey of life, we realize that everyone is a part of God's family and therefore we must reach out in love to help the poor, the hungry, the abused, and especially the children.

The flowers in the window box grow together. We, too, can grow together and help others blend together in peace and love.

Lord, help us see one another as children of yours and help us encourage peace with others. Amen.

AUGUST 30   COMFORT

Comfort, O comfort my people, says your God.
                                    (Isaiah 40:1 NRSV)

At times our children have come to us with a bruised knee, a little cut, or hurt feelings. Perhaps we took them on our laps and comforted them so that they could go out and play again, reassured that all is well and they are all right. At times we, too, need someone to put an arm around us when we are in pain, and then we feel better.

Everyone needs comfort at one time or another. Sometimes we may need to call someone because she or he feels sad or is in grief from the loss of a loved one. We also can send notes to those who are suffering physically. After hurricanes or other disasters or tragedies, we can give comfort or a listening ear and provide gifts of food, shelter, clothes, and money to show our care.

As we listen in our quiet times to the voice within, we will feel prompted to reach out in love to comfort those in need. May we be listening, and may we be responsive.

Lord, help us know how to comfort those who need us, and please guide us in this process. Amen.

AUGUST 31   A HOT-AIR BALLOON RIDE

If I take the wings of the morning and settle at the farthest limits of the sea, even there your hand shall lead me.
(Psalm 139:9-10 NRSV)

Several years ago I made a list of seventeen things I still wanted to do in this life. Among them was taking a hot-air balloon ride. My daughter and son-in-law arranged this for Mother's Day one year.

The day came. We drove to Virginia. There we saw this huge multicolored balloon being inflated as seven of us climbed into a rather small basket. My husband said, "I'd rather stay on earth and take pictures!" But he went along after all.

We floated quietly as the sun began to set over the hills with a magnificent view of the countryside. What an adventure—especially when we found out that it was not certain where we would land! After a cell phone call to the ground, a contact finally guided us safely over wires to a nearby field. We came to a stop with a slight bump on the grassy knoll. What an exciting trip! What a wonderful Mother's Day gift.

Life may not always be that exciting, but we can always look for different ways to live each day with enthusiasm—no matter what the day may bring.

Lord, thank you for this beautiful world. Help us see the larger view of your creation and always live with enthusiasm. Amen.

September

Look Beyond

KATHLEEN F. TURNER

SEPTEMBER 1   GOD'S HORIZONS

Jesus said, "You're tied down to the mundane; I'm in touch with what is beyond your horizons. You live in terms of what you see and touch. I'm living on other terms."
(John 8:23 The Message)

Is it impossible to imagine your toddler eating with a spoon? Is it hard to imagine your teen holding a coherent conversation or picking up his clothes? Stages in the lives of our children can seem endless and challenging. I have two daughters—an almost twenty-year-old and a teenager. What helped me during the lingering stages was to acknowledge that my daughters wouldn't be doing "whatever" when they were grown. I looked beyond the present.

It's the same with us. We can get fixated on the mundane of the daily and forget God's panoramic activity. Jesus was not confused in the least about what God was doing for the world through him. He lived here on God's terms.

We moms need to do the same. We live in this world of sight and touch; but through the work of the Spirit of God, we can begin to see what God is doing on a greater scale. And when we can't see, we can believe by faith that God is doing something spectacular.

Let us not miss God in our lives. This month we will intentionally "look beyond" some ordinary, everyday experiences to see what God might have for us.

Dear Father, help me remember that you are constantly work-
ing. Help me always to look beyond what I can see and touch.
Amen.

SEPTEMBER 2   THE MUSTARD YEARS

And this expectation will not disappoint us. For we know how
dearly God loves us.   *(Romans 5:5 NLT)*

What do you get when you put a middle schooler in a lunchroom
with a packet of mustard? A mother who uses stain remover.

Our oldest daughter always had trouble with mustard packets—
pounding, poking, splattering herself and friends. A personal idio-
syncrasy, I reasoned, as I worked at stains. I was wrong. It was a
middle-school illness that our younger daughter contracted, too.
Their classmates seemed equally afflicted. What I loved about my
girls at this stage was that mustard stories were funny. They
laughed; their friends laughed. The globs didn't bother them.

Could I ever be like that about my spiritual life and my relationship with the Lord? Would I ever let God bring me to the point that
I didn't get tripped by the small stuff? Could I ever truly learn not
to grind away on the little things of life? He takes care of the spots
of our lives so we can walk free and tall in his grace. Let us accept
that from him daily so we can live in peace and joy.

Dear God, help me today to revel in your love and forgiveness
so I may have your joy. Amen.

SEPTEMBER 3   BINDING US UP

"Come, let us return to the LORD; for it is he who has torn, and
he will heal us; he has struck down, and he will bind us up."
                                          (Hosea 6:1 NRSV)

Our patience and that of the teacher were wearing thin. Couldn't
chemistry homework simply be done and turned in on time? What
was so complicated about that?

One thing seemed clear: our daughter definitely needed grounding. I firmly insisted on some stiff restrictions. She responded with anger, floods of tears, and stony silence. In her pain, she retreated. I trenched in. I had to be tough.

The next morning she came to me with a coupon I had given her weeks before: "This coupon is good for a Giant Genuine Bear Hug (good for unlimited uses, no expiration date)." We hugged; we cried. Things got better, including the chemistry.

Often we make obedience more complicated than it really is. We tell God our reasons. He still wants obedience. Sometimes he has to "ground" us so we get the point. Yet when we come to him, he welcomes us and brings healing to our relationship with him.

Dear Father, thank you for disciplining me when I am reluctant to obey you and for drawing me close when I do what you ask and return to you. Amen.

SEPTEMBER 4   SUBMERGED CELL

Answer me when I call to you, O my righteous God. Give me relief from my distress; be merciful to me and hear my prayer.... You have filled my heart with greater joy.
(Psalm 4:1, 7 NIV)

She was away at a basketball game, and her cell phone was her lifeline to home. Then she took a bathroom break. Kerplunk! The cell phone took a dive into the toilet, and so did any communication with her via phone that night. We thought the phone was useless after that. To our amazement, when she turned it on several weeks later, it worked! Everything must have dried out.

Do you ever feel that your communication with God has taken a nosedive? You talk and talk, but there seems to be no connection. Our distress seems to short-circuit our connection with God. All David could write about in the first part of Psalm 4 was what was going on around him and how he felt about it.

Then he redirected his gaze to God and what God asked of David. That's when he and God were on the same call. All was well, and David's distress decreased. Nothing and yet everything changed. David was filled with joy.

Loving God, it seems too simple to think about you and see my problems fade, but this is what you promise. Help me believe you. Amen.

SEPTEMBER 5   DO-OVER PARENTING?

They were scared senseless, but he reassured them, "It's me. It's all right. Don't be afraid." So they took [Jesus] on board. In no time they reached land—the exact spot they were headed to.
                                    (John 6:20-21 The Message)

This summer our daughter hits a milestone, and, as a result, my husband and I do, too. She will be twenty, and we will have seen her through the teen years. Then we will have only one teen in our household.

As I reflect on the past seven years, I recall good times—special awards, dress-up moments, breakthroughs in personal and spiritual growth. There also were the dark times—times I'd rather not remember. What if I'd been a better mom? What if we'd done this instead of that in our parenting style?

During those dark times I was scared senseless and didn't know what to do except beg God for help. Often the storm raged longer than I thought I could stand. Gradually the storm subsided. As I look back at where we have sailed, I realize that we now are sailing where we were headed then—except we couldn't see it because of the storm. Christ has been there all the time for us, and he will be there as we continue to sail on.

Gracious God, I need you in the storm of parenting. Help me trust you to land us safely where we need to be. Amen.

SEPTEMBER 6   WHY?

They waffled: "Why don't you give us a clue about who you are, just a hint of what's going on? When we see what's up, we'll commit ourselves. Show us what you can do."
                                    (John 6:30 The Message)

"Why can't I?" Do you ever hear that from your children? "Give me a reason that I can accept, and I'll decide whether to trust you," they seem to say.

Jesus' audience wanted to know what was up first; then they'd commit. "Give me all the info, then I'll decide if it's worth believing." Could that be you and me?

I've been a Christian for a long time, but although I may *believe in Christ* for salvation, do I genuinely *believe Christ*? How much do I truly believe he will use me to advance his Kingdom? How much do I believe he is going to work out personal troubles for my good and his glory? How much do I believe he will give me everything I need to do what he asks of me—including being a great mom? Whenever I doubt, worry, or hold back, I do not believe.

Where are you?

Dear God, show me where I do not believe you; then help me live by the truth of your promises. Amen.

SEPTEMBER 7   NAMING OUR CHILDREN

"To him who overcomes, I [Jesus] will give . . . him a white stone with a new name written on it, known only to him who receives it." ***(Revelation 2:17 NIV)***

We need those nine months of pregnancy to prepare. Picking out a name takes time. I came up with lists of names for each of our children. When I hit upon a name my husband liked, that was it. Even though it was good, I wanted to think about it. But that was it for him. And that's where we stopped—good names from my viewpoint, great names from his.

Jesus Christ has a special name for each one who overcomes this world. What is that name? All we can do is imagine and speculate.

Will the name represent trials we have courageously faced, persistence in prayer, or evangelism? Maybe the name will represent our giving or obedience at great personal cost. Whatever it is, it will be a wonderful name. It will also be a secret name. You won't know mine; I won't know yours. It will be personal, private, between you and God. Think and live today as an overcomer, anticipating your new name.

Dear Father, help me live today with heaven in my heart. Thank you that my relationship with you is personal. Amen.

SEPTEMBER 8   THE TRAVELING LAMB

For he is our God; and we are the people of his pasture, and the sheep of his hand.   *(Psalm 95:7 KJV)*

Plush Lambie has been on my bed for a year and half. He's on loan. I bought Lambie for my mother several years ago after she had surgery. Just before she underwent hours of lifesaving intervention, we gathered around her as she told us about the Shepherd who runs his hand over his sheep every day to check each for any difficulties. She was that sheep, and we entrusted her to the Good Shepherd.

A year and a half ago, when I was diagnosed with cancer, my mother brought Lambie to me with Psalm 95:7 (the passage she had explained before her surgery) ribboned to his hoof. The Good Shepherd was running his hand over me to check for difficulties I was having, and he was working in my life. Lambie's presence comforted me greatly as a visual reminder of my position in Christ.

My flock has grown since then. There are more sheep on my bed and some "grazing" about the house. They remind me of my Savior's constant care and the lifelong impact a mother can have on her children.

Dear Shepherd, thank you for caring for me perfectly, whatever my needs may be. Help me remember that I am the sheep of your hand. Amen.

SEPTEMBER 9   TWO FRIENDS

And this is my prayer: that your love may abound more and more in knowledge and depth of insight, so that you may be able to discern what is best and may be pure and blameless until the day of Christ.   *(Philippians 1:9 NIV)*

Cheryl's mother died suddenly. It was time to clean out a house full of things shrouded in memories. With a van loaded from top to bottom and a Chihuahua between us, Cheryl and I sped from Indiana to New Jersey. We talked, laughed, and ate peeled shrimp and tomatoes.

There was so much to do when we got there—things to toss, things to carefully save. There were things to cry over and things to laugh over. We worked hard, watched chick-flicks until late, ate out, and ate ice cream in.

It was more than a week of cleaning; it was a week of loving and nurturing each other. Cheryl processed the loss of her mother while I processed who I was and wanted to become. I haven't been the same since that trip.

No matter how old we are, we each need support and encouragement along our journey!

Lord, thank you so much for friendships between women. As they have blessed me, let me be a blessing. Amen.

SEPTEMBER 10   MARY ELLEN

Whatever happens, conduct yourselves in a manner worthy of the gospel of Christ.   *(Philippians 1:27 NIV)*

Although she is no longer living, Mary Ellen still inspires me. She loved to write. And though she thought she wasn't very good, she was repeatedly published and even wrote the story of her life, *Survival of the Unfit.*

Mary Ellen also loved the Japanese people and desperately wanted them to know Christ. God called her from a business career and sent her as a missionary to the Land of the Rising Sun.

Even in retirement she was reaching for the Japanese. When my daughter's friend Yuki, a Japanese exchange student, visited Mary Ellen, the veteran missionary chatted in Japanese with her about spiritual matters. Then Mary Ellen relayed Yuki's openness to my daughter, enabling my daughter to share more confidently.

When Mary Ellen was diagnosed with terminal cancer, neither she nor I realized how her example would give me a model for facing a cancer diagnosis myself in a few months. She wasn't super-spiritual about her illness; she wondered why. But until her death she remained a faithful servant.

Loving God, thank you for your faithful servants who leave us an example. Help me follow in the footsteps of the faithful and bring honor to you. Amen.

SEPTEMBER 11   NIGHT-LIGHTS

Jesus once again addressed them: "I am the world's Light. No one who follows me stumbles around in the darkness. I provide plenty of light to live in."   *(John 8:12 The Message)*

While raising our two daughters, we have spent a small fortune on night-lights. Manufacturers designed irresistible lights that looked perfect for the girls' room. At other times we replaced lost lights that later turned up in the toy box, the toolbox, or the laundry room. Sometimes lights broke and needed replacing. But they were necessary. Providing light for children is especially important at night.

Do you feel like a child stumbling around in the dark? Jesus said he has provided a light for you. You don't have to trip in your darkness. Ask him to shine the night-light of truth for you today. What night-light is it? His love for you? Promises of his care? Hope for today? Peace in a crisis?

Wherever we are in our journeys, we may rest assured that Christ has the perfect night-light we need. He provides "plenty of light to live in." Ask him to direct your eyes to the night-light of truth for your life today.

Lord, I will stumble without your light. Cause me to see the light of truth and help me live in it. Amen.

SEPTEMBER 12 COOKED OR RAW BROCCOLI?

"Don't waste your energy striving for perishable food like that. Work for the food that sticks with you, food that nourishes your lasting life, food the Son of Man provides. He and what he does are guaranteed by God the Father to last."
(John 6:27 The Message)

One likes raw broccoli; one likes cooked broccoli. One likes fresh tomatoes; one likes cooked tomatoes. Is your household like this? Is it a challenge to cook for your family?

So much of our time is consumed with food—shopping for it, preparing it, serving it, urging our children to eat it, and cleaning it up. We can get uptight about it.

Are we as concerned about nourishing our children spiritually? Do we take opportunities to offer our children a spiritual snack—a teaching moment during our busy day? How about a spiritual feast—setting aside time to talk about spiritual things before bed? If we were as concerned about our children eating well spiritually as we are about seeing them eat well physically, would they be learning more from us? As we serve stick-to-their-ribs meals, let's plan how to serve spiritual food that nourishes for lasting life.

Dear God, how can I offer my children spiritual nourishment today? Reveal to me what they need and how to serve them from your table. Amen.

SEPTEMBER 13 "MAY I GO TO MEXICO?"

Being confident of this, that he who began a good work in you will carry it on to completion until the day of Christ Jesus.
(Philippians 1:6 NIV)

"May I go to Mexico for ten weeks next summer?" she asked hopefully. Two years ago she had been there for one week with the youth group. The next summer she spent five weeks there on work crew. Now she wanted to be on work crew for the whole summer.

How and when does a parent let a child go? Wouldn't it be great if hospitals gave out individualized child-rearing manuals for each mother? Instead, we study our children and watch what God is doing in their lives.

My daughter loves to serve and has an increasing interest in Hispanic culture. She sees herself in a career helping children, possibly in Mexico. So we have given her more opportunities each summer to explore her talents and capabilities. And, yes, as I write, she is in Mexico for the summer. God is doing something in and through her life because he promised.

What do you see God doing in the life of your child? How are you encouraging and appropriately letting go?

Dear Lord, help me see the unique talents and interests you have given my child. Help me today to encourage and challenge my child. Amen.

SEPTEMBER 14   PRAYERS OF THE MOMS

And when he had taken [the scroll], the four living creatures and the twenty-four elders fell down before the Lamb. Each one had a harp and they were holding golden bowls full of incense, which are the prayers of the saints.   *(Revelation 5:8 NIV)*

Being a mother of teens has challenged me probably more than anything else I've ever done. By nature a worrier, I've tended to get especially upset at night when things are already the "darkest" they can be.

A couple of years ago I purchased a small book that contains scripture prayers to pray for God's will for my daughters. Now when I grow concerned about my girls, I open the volume to the bookmark and continue to pray for my daughters, inserting their names into each prayer. Taking my scripture prayers to God comforts me, for I know God places my prayers in his golden bowls. God doesn't forget what I have asked, and I have confidence because I have asked God to do what he wants to do in their lives.

Is praying scripture for your children a way you could be comforted and be proactive in praying for God's best?

Dear Father, it's not always easy to know how to pray for my children. Help me even in this area to be a godly mother. Amen.

SEPTEMBER 15   SLICKED-BACK HAIR AND A
WRINKLED SHIRT

And such were some of you: but ye are washed, but ye are sanctified, but ye are justified in the name of the Lord Jesus, and by the Spirit of our God.   **(1 Corinthians 6:11 KJV)**

She had so tightly plastered her hair back into a ponytail that I thought, *If older women used the same technique, face-lifts might become obsolete.* Her shirts looked like they came out of the bottom of the laundry basket. Some mornings I barely bit my tongue in time. Now my daughter laughs at her old junior-high look.

Children pass through stages in their spiritual growth, too. Sometimes it's hard to watch them take giant leaps forward only to see them do something completely incomprehensible.

Before we become too exasperated, let's recall where we were before we decided to follow Christ. We were ignorant and made wrong choices; and after becoming followers, we often made poor choices because we were learning and growing in our faith. We are the "such were some of you." In a few years we may look back and be chagrined at the choices we are making right now.

Children need Mom's encouragement to grow spiritually and her gentleness for setbacks. Let's practice both.

God, help me have your patience and gentleness as I teach and challenge my children spiritually. Amen.

SEPTEMBER 16   *"YOU* HAVE ARTHRITIS?"

" 'God, I thank you that I am not like other men—robbers, evil-doers, adulterers—or even like this tax collector. I fast twice a week and give a tenth of all I get.' "   **(Luke 18:11-12 NIV)**

197

She was sympathetic when I was diagnosed with lymphoma, but she didn't say much. One day, months later, I mentioned that my arthritic hip ached. "*You* have arthritis?" she asked, simultaneously shocked and concerned. "That's bad."

Surprised at her intensity, I said, "Cancer is worse."

"No, it's not," she countered, "It doesn't hurt."

My daughter couldn't "see" how much more serious one ailment was than another because her understanding was limited to what normally makes disease evident—pain.

The Pharisees were ignorant of their spiritual disease. They prided themselves on externals—things they had and hadn't done. Inside they rotted away spiritually.

Sometimes we, too, are guilty of focusing on dos and don'ts. That's why we regularly need to ask God to search our hearts for misdirected focus. Do we rest on what we do or say, or on what Christ has done for us? Are we quick to judge externals in other people's lives without bothering to get to know and care about them? Do we need an attitude correction?

Dear Father, please reveal areas of spiritual disease in my life that need your touch. Amen.

SEPTEMBER 17   WHERE WERE THE MUSHROOMS?

I pray also that the eyes of your heart may be enlightened in order that you may know the hope to which he has called you, the riches of his glorious inheritance in the saints, and his incomparably great power for us who believe.
(Ephesians 1:18 NIV)

Our family was hunting for yellow sponge mushrooms. Finding few, we circled back to leave. Then somebody whooped. Gigantic mushrooms grew in the corner of the woods. We couldn't pick them fast enough. Mom couldn't see them, no matter how hard she tried. Even when we showed her one, she couldn't find another. The rest of us found one hundred fifty mushrooms that day. Mom cleaned them for everyone.

Similarly, we can be blind to the great hope and power God offers us. Is it because we only believe God in our heads, not in our hearts?

Sometimes we look at our spiritual lives and ask, "Is this as good as it gets?" Are we actively believing and reaching for what God offers? When do our actions say, "I believe"?

Spiritual eyes see more than physical eyes. Faith propels us to act on our spiritual vision. God wants to do so much in and through us. Will we allow it?

Dear God, open my eyes so I may see what you see and step where you want me to. Amen.

SEPTEMBER 18   "I JUST HAVE TO TELL YOU ..."

"As for us, there's no question—we can't keep quiet about what we've seen and heard."   *(Acts 4:20 The Message)*

It's wonderful to see our children master skills, develop talents, and receive awards as they grow toward maturity. From first words to that college diploma, we moms are often cheerleaders and then megaphones announcing the success of our offspring. We can't help it; we love our children. Not only do we share the successes; we listen to others share the accomplishments of their children. The I-just-have-to-tell-yous flow both ways between moms.

What would that look like if we were the same about what God has accomplished in our lives? "Well, that's different," we may say. But is it? Christians have been forgiven, set on a new journey with their best Friend, given new gifts to use, and assigned worthwhile things to do before leaving to live in a perfect home. What we have is for everyone. What keeps us from saying, "I just have to tell you ..."?

The disciples couldn't be silenced. They believed, so they spoke. If we believe God and what God has done in our lives, how will we live and speak?

Dear God, I want to live out what I believe. I need your help today to do that. Amen.

SEPTEMBER 19   "MANS DON'T WEAR EARRINGS"

His disciples answered, "Where could we get enough bread in this remote place to feed such a crowd?" "How many loaves do you have?" Jesus asked.   *(Matthew 15:33-34 NIV)*

My five-year-old stared at the man ahead of us. She had something on her mind. *What has captured her attention?* I wondered, looking at the man sporting a single earring. After awhile he noticed she was staring at him.

"Mans don't wear earrings," she finally said in a firm voice that he and most people around her could hear. She had stated the facts from her perspective.

The man grinned as I explained that some men, indeed, do wear earrings. My daughter had only her limited experience to determine jewelry trends. My explanation gave her a bigger picture.

The disciples were using their limited experience to determine how to feed the multitude. Jesus wanted to show them something bigger—the power of God. He was kind to them. He could have said how ignorant and shortsighted they were, but instead he asked for a bread count and told the people to sit down. As we learn to see things from God's perspective, we can thank him for his patience.

Lord, I want to see things the way you do. Thank you for your patience as I learn how to do this. Amen.

SEPTEMBER 20   SOMETHING'S OUT THERE!

I will fear no evil, for you are with me.   *(Psalm 23:4b NIV)*

Darkness fell, and lights along the path illumined our walk around the waterfront. Suddenly, my daughter dug her fingers into my arm. The pain demonstrated the intensity of her fear.

"There's a fox out there," she whispered tersely.

"No, there's not," I chuckled.

But she insisted.

"OK, let's go see," I said.

Slowly we walked onto the beach, peered into the darkness, and heard the splash as the "fox"—a small group of Canada geese—left the pier for the lake!

Sometimes I live with a vague, gnawing fear that something terrible is "out there." Do you? We live in unsettling times with enough news to give us ... foxes. How do we banish the foxes out there? We cultivate confidence in the One who exposes the foxes—real or imagined—for what they are. God never meant for us to fear anyone or anything. And when we can't stop our fears, God will meet us where we are and rescue us from the foxes and the grip of fear.

Dear Father, I don't want to live fearfully. Give me your strength today to live fully trusting you ... no foxes, only geese. Amen.

SEPTEMBER 21   CLOTHED

She has no fear for her household; for all of them are clothed in scarlet.   **(Proverbs 31:21 NIV)**

When I was in first grade, my grandmother made me a beautiful dress. It was white with splotches of green and red. Best of all, it had a matching bright red sash that tied into a bow in back. I still remember that dress almost half a century later, and I still love the color red.

The "scarlet" fabric of the Proverbs 31 mother indicates the best fabric or a double thickness, which would have supplied warmth. Every mother can identify with clothing her children well and warmly, even if it's done by way of the mall. But the scarlet we need to be most concerned about is the scarlet of the blood of Christ. We cannot force our children to accept Christ, just as God does not force us. But we can teach them and pray that God's Spirit will draw them so that they are covered perfectly by the blood and clothed in the righteousness of God's Son.

O God, my children need the righteousness that comes by the blood of Christ. Help them come to be washed and clothed in your righteousness. Amen.

SEPTEMBER 22   FAITHFULNESS

Only be careful, and watch yourselves closely so that you do not forget the things your eyes have seen or let them slip from your heart as long as you live. Teach them to your children and to their children after them.   *(Deuteronomy 4:9 NIV)*

Our almost-twenty-year-old and her dad and I sat talking. It was one of those relaxing evenings when we weren't talking about much at all. Then, suddenly, we were talking about important things. My husband and I shared the struggles we had faced in order to grow, and we explained that everyone has some pattern of behavior to overcome. Then we explained how the Holy Spirit helps us by providing an escape and, over time, guides us into new paths of behavior.

Sometimes we don't think what we're teaching our children about God is making an impact. But God may give us a peek of what he's doing in the lives of our children, and we can be encouraged. Whether we see anything or not, we must never give up praying and planting the seeds of faith.

Let's grab those teachable moments and always pray for our children.

Dear Father, help me be a faithful mother who prays for her children and uses special moments to plant seeds of truth. Amen.

SEPTEMBER 23   JUNK FOOD

You show me the path of life. In your presence there is fullness of joy; in your right hand are pleasures forevermore.
                                          (Psalm 16:11 NRSV)

Perhaps it's all the pureed peas and squash we're stuffed with during the toddler years. Or it could be what many articles say: the fat, sugar, and additives create cravings and trick our brains. Whatever the reason, our children enjoy fast food—and truth be told, we do, too. We know it's a poor substitute for what our bodies truly need.

I've watched my teens get hooked on junk food, and now I smile as one chooses fruit, veggies, and glasses of water.

How many times do we get hooked on the "junk food" of the world? For a while it may give us pleasure or distraction. Earthly pursuits aren't necessarily bad; they simply are unable to deeply satisfy us like God's presence. Our innate craving for God can be dulled and our spirits malnourished. Spending time with God feeds our inner being. And our craving for more of God is good because he satisfies with the joy of his presence and pleasures forevermore.

Dear God, show me today where I need to get rid of the "junk food" of the world so I can feast in your presence. Amen.

SEPTEMBER 24   MAY I HAVE THE CAR?

Give all your worries and cares to God, for he cares about what happens to you. **(1 Peter 5:7 NLT)**

I slumped behind the wheel of the family car and dreamed about the day my daughters would drive themselves to the umpteenth event. That was my fantasy until the day my older daughter asked for the car keys. Suddenly I stiffened and devised a thousand reasons why she couldn't go. None of them sounded rational when I said them out loud, so I handed over the keys.

Ever since then I fight the rising fear when my children are out and the wail of a siren pierces the night. I look at the clock a little too much on those evenings and finally sleep deeply when I at last hear the garage door go up.

What are your worries? Can you and I unload them? God says we can. He volunteers to take all of them. Because he loves us, he is ever watching what concerns us. It's such a waste of time for two of us to watch everything, especially when God is on duty. He does know who has the car keys!

Dear God, help me lay all my worries before you and trust you to care for all that concerns me. Amen.

SEPTEMBER 25 THE TALKING BOX

I was too troubled to speak. **(Psalm 77:4 NIV)**

Talking with a teen can be challenging, and neither of my daughters was an exception. My best intentions to have wonderful mother-daughter conversations could deteriorate in no time flat. That's when the talking box came out. I'd write a note requesting a response. Then I'd tuck the note and a piece of chocolate in a pretty little box and set it on my daughter's bed. In a day or so the box came back (minus the chocolate) with a response. That little box helped us communicate when times were tense.

Do times ever get tense with you and God? Do you struggle to talk with God? Does your mind wander when you pray? There are many ways to talk to God.

The psalms are prayers that express the ups and downs of the authors. The writers didn't hide anything from God. A notebook or a journal can be a "talking tool" to help focus thoughts, pour out feelings, examine attitudes, and track God's work in our lives. And we don't even need a bit of chocolate to entice God's response. God hears our written prayers as if we said them out loud.

Gracious God, you speak to me in different ways. Thank you for giving me the freedom to talk to you in different ways, too. Amen.

SEPTEMBER 26 GRANDMOTHER?

"I will be your God throughout your lifetime—until your hair is white with age. I made you, and I will care for you. I will carry you along and save you." **(Isaiah 46:4 NLT)**

Some things happened too late in my life, and some things happened too early. For instance, God brought my husband into my life later than I had planned. And my hair turned silver (not gray, mind you) earlier than I had anticipated.

Most mothers I encountered during my younger daughter's years in elementary school seemed like teenagers. One of my

204

daughter's classmates corrected my thinking one afternoon by innocently asking, "Are you Heather's grandmother?" Ouch.

Although I am glad to see more mothers who are older, our society doesn't look kindly upon the symbols of aging—silver hair, smile lines, or glasses. Somehow women are supposed to be perpetually young and beautiful.

The truth is that God loves us—silver hair, bespectacled eyes, creased faces, and all. God doesn't desert us as we get older but is committed to making us lovely within. It is essential for us to tell ourselves the truth about God's love for us. We are greatly loved by Almighty God.

Lord, when the world tells me I'm not young or beautiful, remind me that you are making me more beautiful in your sight. Amen.

SEPTEMBER 27   FUSSING OVER FUNDS?

"What I'm trying to do here is get you to relax, not be so preoccupied with getting so you can respond to God's giving. People who don't know God and the way he works fuss over these things, but you know both God and how he works."
(Luke 12:29-30 The Message)

Is there ever enough money when you're raising kids? Maybe there is for some people, but my informal surveys indicate that most people struggle with stretching the dollars. Whether parents are buying new shoes for little ones or writing a hefty check for auto insurance for a new teen driver, money sprouts wings and flies away.

Recently a friend came into a significant amount of money. Although I was genuinely happy for her, my mind quickly made comparisons. I slipped into self-pity. "At least *they* wouldn't have to worry about college expenses," I whined.

Then it was as if I snapped to attention spiritually. I didn't have to worry either. For nearly twenty years we have faced multiple financial challenges, yet *never* has God failed to meet our needs. So what was I fussing about?

What is it you're fussing about? Ask God to help you focus on his giving. Remind yourself of how God works.

Dear Father, you have promised to meet all my needs. Help me rest in your promise. Amen.

SEPTEMBER 28   LEAVING A FEW

"I want you to be smart in the same way—but for what is right—using every adversity to stimulate you to creative survival, to concentrate your attention on the bare essentials, so you'll live, really live, and not complacently just get by on good behavior."   *(Luke 16:9 The Message)*

Parenting could easily be called a tightrope act. Balance is critical to success, but finding it can be as difficult as finding the carpet in a teenager's room. Where is the perfect teetering point when your high schooler pours out a painful tale about an injustice at school? It's not easy to know when to race to the phone or hug your daughter and tell her you know she will make a good decision.

Whatever we choose to do, it's important to leave our children with some battles. God does. We are in the great battle of the ages, and there are skirmishes small and large that God allows into our lives daily. Think about your battlegrounds. God allows us to learn much from our difficulties as we strip life down to the barest essentials, the things that truly matter from God's perspective.

Let's pray earnestly to find God's balance.

Dear God, help me know when to intervene and when to step back so you can teach my children what they need to know. Amen.

SEPTEMBER 29   IN THE DETAILS

"Even so, every detail of your body and soul—even the hairs of your head!—is in my care; nothing of you will be lost."
                                    (Luke 21:18 The Message)

We were flying out of New York City after the funeral of my mother-in-law. I was jittery. The whole country was jittery after the events of 9/11.

I matched traveler to suitcase and then breathed a sigh. My nervousness didn't fade. I disliked flying and even more so that day. As I boarded and waited for takeoff, my fear increased. Children at home still needed me. What if . . . ? "God," I breathed, "I'm really afraid." Simply, the Spirit of Christ spoke to me. "Everything is going to be all right."

And it was, not because I was unharmed but because God had every detail of my life in his care. Since that day other things have happened to me, and all has still been well because God is in the details of my life here and forever. The more I believe in God's attention to those details, the more I rest. Are you learning to rest?

Dear God, worrying doesn't change a thing. Please help me let you take care of the details of my life. Amen.

SEPTEMBER 30   GOD'S HIDDEN SERVANTS

Bands . . . had taken captive a young girl from Israel, and she served Naaman's wife. She said to her mistress, "If only my master would see the prophet who is in Samaria! He would cure him of his leprosy." **(2 Kings 5:2 NIV)**

Do you ever feel as though you're hidden away? Are your talents atrophying as you talk baby talk with your little one? Do you pull in a paycheck and pick up a pizza on the way home and wonder if anyone cares? Do you think you're in one of the backwaters of life, forgotten and wasting away?

The Bible is full of people who lived outside the limelight, and it seems as though God takes great delight in shining through those people. Naaman was a very important person, and he was sick. Instead of bemoaning her captivity or retaliating because of her plight, the servant girl of Naaman's wife shared the good news about the prophet in Samaria. As a result of her courage, Naaman was healed. Although nameless, she is memorialized in Scripture.

God never forgets where we are—or the talents he has given us. God glorifies himself through us when we yield to his plans and opportunities. Are you anticipating your next assignment?

Dear Father, sometimes I feel forgotten and useless. Remind me that I am not. I'm ready for duty. Amen.

October

Mothering Ourselves

STEPHANIE THOMPSON

OCTOBER 1 SELF-CARE

Because the Sovereign LORD helps me, I will not be disgraced.
(Isaiah 50:7 NIV)

The month of October marks a transition from summer to fall, a perfect time to slow the pace of life and intentionally turn our attention inward to examine our mental, spiritual, and emotional wellness. By this time of year we have once again settled into a routine that is more or less predictable, so it's time to mother ourselves through reflection, self-renewal, and self-care.

As a mother, I have wrestled with two recurring thoughts. I am not alone. We want to do everything within our power to help our children blossom into confident, capable, compassionate, and contributing members of society. Yet if we are honest, we are continually nagged by thoughts of insufficiency and feelings of inadequacy.

Today and throughout the coming months you are invited to ask these questions of yourself. Is your health and wellness a consideration when weighing competing needs and unending responsibilities? How can we expect to be good caregivers if we don't give care to ourselves? Today, I give you permission to place yourself at the top of your priority list.

Lord, beginning today, I want to begin taking care of myself with the same loving attention as I do my family. Help me. Amen.

OCTOBER 2   LISTENING WITHIN

For you created my inmost being; you knit me together in my mother's womb. I praise you because I am fearfully and wonderfully made.   *(Psalm 139:13-14a NIV)*

I heard a news story about research on the uniqueness of women attributed to the hardwiring of our brains. One of the intriguing findings is that a mother not only can distinguish her infant's cry from that of other infants, but she also can sense, without hearing a sound, when her baby is crying in another room. We women come into the world equipped to listen for and discern even the faintest of sounds from our babies.

So much of our time is spent staying attuned to the needs of our family that we often find ourselves "running on empty." Throughout this month, you are invited to make time to listen to your heart. What "cries" or desires have you sensed but not had time to listen to? What does your heart need in order to continue taking care of you? Listen, and respond with the same degree of love and care as if your baby were crying for you from another room. You deserve to take care of you.

Lord, help me hear the voice of my own heart and help me respond with love, attention, and grace. I want to take care of myself without feeling guilty. Amen.

OCTOBER 3   PLAY DATES

A cheerful heart is good medicine, but a crushed spirit dries up the bones.   *(Proverbs 17:22 NIV)*

There is something almost magical about watching children at play. They run, climb, jump, and laugh with such sweet abandon that it almost makes you envy their freedom. They don't have a care in the world except to have fun and be with their friends. And yet, psychologists note that play is not "just for fun"; it also affords children a venue to work out problems and practice new behaviors.

As adults, we often lose touch with the child within. Life becomes an unending series of responsibilities, obligations, and duties. We forget that life is to be enjoyed. We lose sight of the truth that "playing" not only releases stress but also replenishes our spiritual, mental, and emotional reserves.

What have you done for yourself lately just for fun? I invite you to regularly schedule play dates for yourself. Call a friend and ask if she would like to "play" with you. Do something you haven't done in a long time that makes you feel pure delight.

Lord, thank you for this reminder that I'm never too old to play. With all of my responsibilities, help me make play dates a higher priority. Amen.

OCTOBER 4   FRIENDSHIPS

A friend is always loyal, and a brother is born to help in time of need.   *(Proverbs 17:17 NLT)*

Recently I said to a sister friend, "What would the world be like without friends? I'm so glad you are my friend." This statement was made after a lengthy conversation when I shared several burdens I had been carrying for some time. Our dialogue covered everything from parenting to work to unfulfilled dreams to sick family members and the future. At the end of our discussion, my friend gave me an assignment and a "due date." She is what the book *Vital Friends*, by Tom Rath, describes as a "Navigator friend." Navigator friends are those who listen to your hurts and hopes, hear your dreams, and help you figure out how to "put flesh on them." No woman is an island. If your tendency is to "go it alone," I encourage you to give yourself the gift of nurturing relationships. Reflect on your vital friends. Who do you call when you need direction? Who in your life is an encourager? Prioritize maintaining friendships for your well-being—and theirs.

Lord, thank you for the women you have given me as friends and supporters. It's so good to have someone I can be "real" with. Amen.

OCTOBER 5   GO TO YOUR ROOM

He who dwells in the shelter of the Most High will rest in the shadow of the Almighty. I will say of the Lord, *"He is my refuge and my fortress, my God, in whom I trust." (Psalm 91:1-2 NIV)*

As children, we may have been reprimanded with these words: "Go to your room." Going to our room was experiencing isolation and deprivation from play or connection with friends or siblings.

As adults, we have the power to take ourselves to another kind of room—an interior place of silence and peace where we reconnect with Christ who renews us. When life becomes chaotic or when fear, judgment, regret, frustration, or other draining emotions visit you, mother yourself by going to your room—that secret place within your heart where God is waiting to greet you with love and remind you that you're not alone. Go there now.

Close your eyes and take a long, slow breath in. Imagine God opening the door to your heart and welcoming you to this spiritual time-out. See God smiling at you and nodding in approval. Slowly release your breath and let go of all worry and frustration.

Lord, thank you that I can meet you in the room of my heart whenever I feel overwhelmed, discouraged, or simply exhausted. Amen.

OCTOBER 6   PATIENCE

"My grace is sufficient for you, for my power is made perfect in weakness." Therefore I will boast all the more gladly about my weaknesses, so that Christ's power may rest on me. . . . For when I am weak, then I am strong.   (2 Corinthians 12:9-10 NIV)

It's easy to extend grace to children as they are learning to navigate their world through each developmental stage. They are prone to make mistakes and, as mothers, we readily acknowledge this as part of the maturation process. Yet when it comes to ourselves, we can be very self-critical—not only about our parenting but also about other areas of our life. It seems that once we become mothers, our ability to see ourselves as growing and evolving is eclipsed by our focus on watching our children develop. Intellectually, we know we are still maturing, yet we may feel that "by now, I ought to be done with ..." The truth is, we are still growing up.

Beginning today, become more aware of the times you are being self-critical. In what ways do you feel you are not measuring up? Be patient with yourself. Be gracious toward yourself. You are a masterpiece in process.

Lord, give me eyes to see myself as you see me, and grace to accept myself as I am growing into the fullness of my potential. Amen.

OCTOBER 7   SEEING ANOTHER PERSPECTIVE

"It is more bitter for me than for you, because the LORD's hand has gone out against me!"   ***(Ruth 1:13 NIV)***

There is a saying that goes: "Where you stand determines what you see." In other words, our perspective is influenced not only by what is around us but also by what is inside of us. This is particularly true when it comes to handling difficult situations. Our perspective is colored by every unwelcome experience of the past and the conclusions drawn as a result.

Naomi spoke these honest and devastating words to her daughters-in-law Ruth and Orpah. She had a right to grieve and be angry. What is striking is her apparent inability to recognize the loss experienced by Ruth and Orpah. They lost their husbands and their dreams of growing old together. Naomi only saw her side.

It's easy to get stuck and see situations only from our vantage point. But in order to continue growing spiritually, we must "stand in a different place" and open ourselves to enlarging our perspective.

Practice listening and striving to see another's perspective in your significant relationships.

Lord, thank you for enabling me to demonstrate empathy for others by striving to see their point of view even when I don't agree. Amen.

OCTOBER 8   TAKING CARE OF YOUR BODY

Do you not know that your body is a temple of the Holy Spirit, who is in you? . . . You are not your own; you were bought at a price. Therefore honor God with your body.
(1 Corinthians 6:19-20 NIV)

How do you feel about your body? If you're like me, you probably answered, "I like my body, but . . ." It's the "but" that feeds our generalized sense of body dissatisfaction. We would never tell our children "you're too fat" or "you're too skinny." Yet we think little or nothing about saying these things to ourselves. And with each self put-down, it becomes more difficult to discipline ourselves to treat our bodies with tender care.

What kind of good health habits do you have? Do you exercise regularly and drink plenty of water? When was your last complete physical exam? If it has been over a year, call your doctor now and schedule a visit. Are you eating fresh fruits and vegetables daily?

Pay attention to your body. Get a thorough check-up. Exercise and get enough sleep. "Eat your vegetables," like you tell your children. Drink more water and add a slice of lemon to enhance the taste.

Lord, thank you for my body. I desire to learn how to "eat to live" and not "live to eat." I desire good health and long life. Amen.

OCTOBER 9   WELCOMING NEW EXPERIENCES

"Do you bring in a lamp to put it under a bowl or a bed? Instead, don't you put it on its stand? For whatever is hidden is meant to be disclosed, and whatever is concealed is meant to be brought out into the open."   *(Mark 4:21-22 NIV)*

As toddlers learn to master their environment and themselves, they are fearless and meet life with a sense of adventure and delight. Their "I can do it" attitude fosters developing new skills. They have not become hostages to fear and familiarity. In fact, they fight against limits we force upon them. We can learn a lot about ourselves by watching toddlers.

The older we get, the smaller we seem to create our world. I believe it's because of the enormous responsibilities we carry. The more we have to do, the more we organize life into mundane routines. We don't leave much room for spontaneity. We seek security in the familiar and resist mining our untapped skills, interests, and talents.

Begin to uncover some new skill, talent, or ability within you. In what ways have you placed limits on your creativity? What new hobby, class, or experience have you wanted to undertake but were afraid to try?

Lord, thank you for my life and your love. Please don't allow me to limit you by placing limits on what I think I can do. Amen.

OCTOBER 10   HONORING YOUR EMOTIONS

God, you do what is right. You know our thoughts and feelings.
(Psalm 7:9 NCV)

What makes us so afraid of our emotions? Maybe it is because we are socialized to always be "nice" and, as a result, we fear our strong feelings, failing to understand that they are God's gift. We live in a world that places a higher value on intellect than on emotion, which has caused us to lose awareness of our feelings and emotions as powerful keys to self-knowledge. In his book *Voice of the Heart,* Dr. Chip Dodd reminds us that feelings tell us of our likes, our dislikes, our needs, and our motivations. They warn us of danger and say something about our values and what we are passionate about.

Feeling hurt opens us to healing. Loneliness reminds us of our need for intimate relationships. Anger points to our passion for life. Fear alerts us to danger and increases our discernment.

Today and throughout the coming months, embrace and explore your strong emotions. Discover the hungers that lie beneath them. Prioritize nourishing rather than neglecting them, and you will experience greater abundance.

Lord, thank you for the gifts of my emotions. Amen.

OCTOBER 11   MINDING YOUR MIND

Finally, brothers, whatever is true, whatever is noble, whatever is right, whatever is pure, whatever is lovely, whatever is admirable—if anything is excellent or praiseworthy—think about such things.   *(Philippians 4:8-9 NIV)*

Have you ever been attacked by your mind? These are some signs to look for: seemingly out of nowhere an anxious, fearful, or negative thought pops into your mind. From there, a kind of mental feeding frenzy ensues. You begin to think about worst-case scenarios and begin "mind reading," certain you know what others are thinking.

Maybe it wasn't an intrusive thought but a statement someone said that you can't shake. Again, you start magnifying it until you become mentally exhausted and emotionally drained. In both instances, it was all "in your head."

Whether we recognize it or not, there is always an internal conversation going on in our minds. The woman who "lives upstairs" is constantly talking to us. It is wise for us to become conscious of what she is saying, particularly when we begin sinking into feelings of sadness, fear, or anxiety.

Tune in to "the woman upstairs." When she begins to create a sense of fear or anxiety, read today's scripture for reassurance.

Lord, thank you for the power to control my thoughts. I will meditate on whatever is true, noble, right, lovely, wholesome, praiseworthy, and excellent. Amen.

OCTOBER 12   ACCEPTANCE

"Who of you by worrying can add a single hour to his life? . . . Therefore do not worry about tomorrow, for tomorrow will worry about itself. Each day has enough trouble of its own."
(Matthew 6:27, 34 NIV)

We've all heard that nothing is constant except change. In spite of our careful planning, the unexpected happens. Life shows up and hijacks our peace of mind and sense of control. We quietly lapse into worry about "what might happen" as we try to hold on to hope. Almost daily we are given reminders of how fragile life is—an unwanted diagnosis; an unwelcome rift in relationship; unexplainable mass tragedies. Sometimes it feels as if the world is careening out of control.

Intuitively we know that worrying won't produce any desirable result, but it feels like we're doing something rather than nothing. Accepting that life is fluid, evolving, and continuously changing helps us stay appreciative of each day as an unrepeatable gift. Then few events will knock us off center and steal our peace of mind.

Accept each day as it unfolds. Some days will be "diamond" and some "stone," but all have enough grace and strength to sustain us.

Lord, help me accept the things I cannot change. Give me courage to change the things I can and wisdom to know the difference. Amen.

OCTOBER 13   ASKING FOR HELP

"Ask and it will be given to you; seek and you will find; knock and the door will be opened to you. For everyone who asks receives; he who seeks finds; and to him who knocks, the door will be opened."   (Matthew 7:7-8 NIV)

Years ago I came across a poem titled "The Strong Woman Has Died." The author outlined a number of realities that contributed to the strong woman's premature death—being a single mother rearing children with no support, loving men who didn't love themselves, and the emotional baggage passed down from grandmother to mother to daughter. The poem further asserts that the strong woman died from trying to do too much by herself.

It has taken me the first half of my life to retire my Superwoman cape. I've learned to ask for and receive assistance without feeling guilty or feeling that I'm imposing. To my surprise, I discovered that friends welcome an opportunity to help lighten my load.

Allow others to help you in whatever way feels right for you. When we ask for and give support, everyone benefits. Saying, "I need help," shows strength.

Lord, thank you for my independent spirit. Help me develop interdependency so that I can receive help and give it as I am able. Amen.

OCTOBER 14   MIND CARE

Though it cost all you have, get understanding. Esteem her, and she will exalt you; embrace her, and she will honor you.
(Proverbs 4:7-8 NIV)

At one time it was believed that as we aged we could expect to experience a loss of cognitive functioning. Senility was thought to be a kind of "rite of passage" into the golden years. Now research tells us we not only do not have to lose mental functioning, but we also can strengthen our mind through diet and various exercises and activities. By keeping our mind stimulated and nourished, we can actually increase the health of our mind. That encourages me, especially on those days when it feels like my mind didn't wake up with me.

What do you do to sharpen your mental functioning? What are some of the ways you keep mental health a priority? What good books have you read recently? What foods are good for the brain? Do you enjoy stimulating puzzles or brisk walks around the block? What about artwork—have you created any in recent memory?

Nurture yourself by seeking out knowledge on how to keep your mind healthy and strong.

Lord, thank you for this reminder to prioritize keeping my mind healthy and strong because it honors me and you. Amen.

OCTOBER 15   THE KID IN ME

The heart of the prudent acquires knowledge, And the ear of the wise seeks knowledge.   *(Proverbs 18:15 NKJV)*

I love a good movie, and my favorite ones are those that help illuminate the human struggle toward wholeness. In the Disney film *The Kid*, Bruce Willis portrays an unmarried, highly driven, successful businessman who receives an unexpected visitor. One evening Bruce discovers that a round-faced little kid has taken up residence in his house. As the story unfolds, it becomes clear that the "kid" is the childhood version of Bruce. The kid has come in response to a crisis, and he helps Bruce understand himself by revisiting some painful childhood experiences. Bruce learns why he is so driven, why he's afraid to love, and why he experienced his father as harsh and insensitive. Bruce's character discovers that his father was a grief-stricken man. These insights were gained only as Bruce took time to listen to the child within him.

Are there some qualities or characteristics that you find troubling or undesirable? Listen to your "kid." She will gently bring you to greater understanding and appreciation of the strengths the past has given as gifts.

Lord, thank you for my life and all the experiences that have shaped who I've become. Your grace and love make me whole. Amen.

OCTOBER 16   WHERE IS YOUR REFRIGERATOR?

You, O Lord, keep my lamp burning; my God turns my dark-ness into light. **(Psalm 18:28 NIV)**

I collect inspirational magnets that now cover the door of my refrigerator like multicolor wallpaper. Each one has an insightful, wise, and sometimes humorous thought that stimulates the mind and provides a momentary spiritual breath of fresh air. Whenever my or my daughters' friends visit, they inevitably make their way to the kitchen and read the refrigerator door. Sometimes when I need a quick "lift," I will go and stand before the door and search for just the right one to encourage my heart. If I'm experiencing a particularly challenging time, my eyes may land on "Just when the caterpillar thought the world was over, it became a butterfly," which reminds me that difficulties are birthing something new within me. My perspective enlarges.

Where is your "refrigerator"? Where do you go and what do you do to catch your spiritual breath?

Begin to discover new ways that give your spirit a "breath of fresh air" in moments of stress or tension.

Lord, help me see tough times with new eyes and not resist the growth you are producing within me. I will be all I can be. Amen.

OCTOBER 17   CELEBRATE YOU!

Thank you for making me so wonderfully complex! Your workmanship is marvelous—and how well I know it.
(Psalm 139:14 NLT)

"Celebrate who you are!" is a quotation attributed to Sara Chatwin. Imagine that. Should we actually "celebrate" ourselves? If we believe what the psalmist says, that we are "marvelous" because of the complexities of our physical, emotional, and mental design, we have divine permission to bask in our own wonder. But that's hard for most of us, especially when some of our "wonder" surfaces in the form of strong emotions, thoughts, or responses that shock us. We are quick to condemn ourselves rather than acknowledge these expressions as evidence of our complexity. We can't bear the contradictions living within us. We love, and we loathe. We compliment, and we cut down. We envy, and we become excited at others' good fortune. Life isn't simple. Celebrate who you are and who you are becoming as God's daughter. Most of us don't think highly enough of ourselves.

Celebrate yourself in all of your complexities. Remember that God says you are his wonderfully complex, marvelous masterpiece.

Lord, thank you for making me the way I am! I will not reject what you accept and delight in—me. Amen.

OCTOBER 18   COURAGE TO PERSEVERE

And let us run with endurance the race that God has set before us.
(Hebrews 12:1 NLT)

Each of us is born with a "race" to run, a particular collection of contributions to make over the course of our lifetime. The roads that lead us to accomplishing God's dream, however, are not clearly marked. Often they are fraught with obstacles, detours, and unpaved surfaces. Some days the race feels like an easy walk in the park on a balmy afternoon, and other days like a blazing forest fire with no extinguisher in sight.

When you feel utterly overwhelmed and giving up on your goals becomes increasingly appealing, remember that God has "set" your race. God is for you, not against you. Look for the hidden meanings meant to help you grow. Refuse to give up. It takes courage to stay in your race.

Mary Anne Radmacher put it this way: "Courage does not always roar. Sometimes courage is the quiet voice at the end of the day saying, 'I will try again tomorrow.'" Keep trying.

Nurture your courage by persevering. Don't quit.

Lord, thank you for arming me with strength to overcome the enemies of discouragement, pessimism, and fatalistic thinking. Amen.

OCTOBER 19   THROUGH REMEMBERING

Why are you downcast, O my soul? Why so disturbed within me? Put your hope in God.   *(Psalm 42:11 NIV)*

"They should know better!" This all-too-familiar statement is often uttered in moments when someone has inflicted injury through a careless statement or thoughtless action. We may find ourselves reliving the incident over and over as we try to understand why. We feel hurt because what occurred was so undeserved.

And yet, with younger children especially, who tend to be brutally honest, we would brush off the offense because "they didn't know." In other words, we don't take it personally. We readily recognize the words as coming from someone still in the process of growing up and developing interpersonal skills. Just because someone has grown older does not mean they have matured, grown wiser, or mastered people skills.

Through the practice of remembering, care for the emotional injuries inflicted by others. Remember that whatever is said or done comes from a place that needs God's healing love. Remembering will help remove the sting and free us to go forward without the weight of unforgiveness.

Lord, thank you for the lesson to not take things personally. Even if it is "personal," I will focus on your work within the other person rather than on my wound. Amen.

OCTOBER 20   SACRED PAMPERING

Before a girl's turn came ... she had to complete twelve months of beauty treatments prescribed for the women, six months with oil of myrrh and six with perfumes and cosmetics.
(Esther 2:12 NIV)

It's your turn! Imagine pampering yourself with twelve months of sacred self-care that honors your being. No more waiting for someone to notice how hard you work and deciding to show appreciation. You have been a helper, cheerleader, counselor, doctor, nurturer, problem solver, peace negotiator, and tutor, to name a few things. Mothers are women too! It's your turn to pamper yourself, acknowledge yourself, and renew yourself for the phenomenal job you do taking care of others.

Make yourself your next "project" and try one or all of these: go to a day spa; get a relaxing massage; buy yourself some flowers; have a manicure or pedicure; take a vacation; treat yourself to a professional facial; try a new color of lipstick that makes you think *wow* when applied; take a bubble bath surrounded by candles and soft music; schedule an afternoon for tea and reading a book that makes you think new thoughts; order some special chocolates over the Internet.

Pamper your sacred self. What makes you feel good about you?

Lord, I will honor you by honoring myself through sacred self-care. You desire that I be healthy and whole. Amen.

OCTOBER 21   BE-ING

"Be still, and know that I am God."   *(Psalm 46:10a NIV)*

Not long ago I gave myself the gift of a one-week self-designed retreat. Life had become all work, and I found it a stretch to say what I enjoyed doing outside of working. The answers I sought to the questions my life was asking eluded me. So I took a week to be still. I spent each day in a local park and listened to God through the sunrise, the geese flying in formation and gracefully landing in the pond, mothers strolling their infants, and people walking their dogs. I listened as God spoke through strangers who initiated conversation. I marveled at the reminder that everything in nature and life functions according to design, and that by design, the insight, inspiration, and refreshing we need from God become accessible in the stillness of life.

Discover the art of Be-ing. There is no substitute for stillness. Treat yourself. You will be wonderfully surprised by how God speaks into your being while you are Be-ing.

Lord, I needed this reminder. Before today is over, I will meet with you in the stillness and know you afresh. Thank you. Amen.

OCTOBER 22   SHARING YOUR WISDOM

My mouth will speak words of wisdom; the utterance from my heart will give understanding.   *(Psalm 49:3 NIV)*

You have a story to tell. When you look at your life's journey up to now, with all of its detours and wrong choices, celebrations and disappointments, and periods of grieving the inevitable and unexpected losses of life, you recognize that these experiences have seasoned you and made you a spice for life.

We can sometimes feel a sense of shame over our imperfections and personal history. But telling our story heals us and enables us to be a healing presence for other sisters. There is no greater affirming experience than to talk with a woman, listen as she shares something she has or is "going through," and know in your heart that she is speaking your truth to you. In that moment, you are overwhelmed by God's grace and the awareness that God truly sees you.

Look for an opportunity to authentically share some aspect of your story. You are someone's hope. Another sister can move from despair to determination in hearing her experiences validated through yours.

Lord, you are the author of my life's story. Thank you for courage to be real with other sisters, thereby releasing them and myself. Amen.

OCTOBER 23   FACING YOUR FEARS

I sought the Lord, and he answered me; he delivered me from all my fears. Those who look to him are radiant; their faces are never covered with shame. **(Psalm 34:4-5 NIV)**

In the movie *The Matrix*, the character Neo is on a spiritual quest. Neo has been searching for Morpheus, the leader of the revolution, to awaken people to their life's fullest possibilities.

Neo meets Morpheus and begins his transformation through extensive physical and mental preparation. However, when the time arrives for Neo to use what he has learned, he is overcome with self-doubt and fear. All of his corporeal training did not eliminate his fears. He finds himself running away, again and again, from situations that were designed to increase his self-confidence. It is only when Neo decides to stop running and face what he thought he couldn't conquer that he discovers the power within him is greater than any force outside of him.

Has God been presenting you with "Neo moments," situations

that invite you to face a fear and move through it? How have you limited yourself because of fear?

Recognize when fear is coloring your choices. If you must run, run to God with it.

Lord, I give you my fear of _____ and trust that you will strengthen me and, through it, bring out your radiance in me. Amen.

OCTOBER 24   OWNING YOUR AUTHORITY

Then Jesus came to them and said, "All authority in heaven and on earth has been given to me. Therefore go and make disciples of all nations.... And surely I am with you always, to the very end of the age."   *(Matthew 28:18-20 NIV)*

You are a woman of authority. I'm speaking of authority in its deepest, truest sense—the ability to "author" or create something of enduring significance, something that expresses God's love for this world through you. We do it in rearing our children. But beyond parenting, what do you want to "author"?

Jesus conferred his authority upon the disciples and commanded them to "go and make ..." They "authored" a movement that changed their world and every generation since. They imagined communities where people experienced God's unconditional love, care, and forgiveness through one another for a lifetime.

What has God placed in your heart that you are now ready to "author"? Your life is your message that makes disciples. Own your authority. Make your dreams reality. God is with you.

Listen for what God is asking you to create with your life. Go and make something that will endure.

Lord, thank you for the authority you have given me. My life will speak to others of your love, grace, and power to be agents of change. Amen.

OCTOBER 25   TAKE A LAUGHTER BREAK

The Lord is my strength and my shield; my heart trusts in him, and I am helped. My heart leaps for joy and I will give thanks to him in song.   *(Psalm 28:7 NIV)*

How do you spell relief? In God's dictionary, it's spelled L-A-U-G-H-T-E-R. Nothing lifts the heart and restores sanity like a good laugh. Laughter releases endorphins, the body's "medicine" that naturally elevates our mood and lowers blood pressure. Laughter releases the pressure of stress that can sometimes make us question our sanity.

In some circles, laughter has become a form of group therapy to treat depression. People sit in circles and, at first, force themselves to laugh. Then it becomes contagious and nearly uncontrollable.

When you begin to feel captivated or overwhelmed by your to-do list, take a stress relief break. Think of something humorous you heard or something you remember you or your children did. Begin to laugh. It may feel very unnatural at first, but don't stop. Give yourself permission to feel good for a few moments. Laugh and laugh some more, until it hurts. Then you can say to yourself, "OK, I'm all right now."

Give yourself permission to laugh and feel lighthearted.

Lord, thank you for the gift of laughter. Help me be unselfconscious in using your gift. I am free to laugh, even at myself. Amen.

OCTOBER 26   TODAY IS TOMORROW

This is the day the Lord has made; let us rejoice and be glad in it.   *(Psalm 118:24 NIV)*

Try this fill-in-the blanks exercise: "When _____ happens, then I will _____." Again: "Once _____, then I will _____."

What desires of your heart or promises have you made to yourself that elude you because the "right" time never seems to arrive?

One of my favorite childhood stories about myself relates to the promise of receiving some treat "tomorrow." When tomorrow arrived, I would remind the adult, "Today is tomorrow." In other words, now is the time to fulfill that promise—now is the time to bring delight into my world with a treat. What I love about this story is that it reminds me that we live in a perpetual "now," and that now is all we ever have. We spend so much time living in the future that we miss the moments in our days that enable us to see the beauty, grace, and goodness that surround us.

Be mindful of moments throughout your day. Today is the tomorrow you've been waiting for. Enjoy it!

Lord, help me not take for granted the moments of my life. Life's beauty and goodness is found in those very moments. Amen.

OCTOBER 27   WELCOMING QUESTIONS

Show me your ways, O Lord, teach me your paths; guide me in your truth and teach me, for you are God my Savior, and my hope is in you all day long. **(Psalm 25:4-5 NIV)**

Children are naturally inquisitive—always investigating and inquiring. We take pleasure in their questions because it reminds us of how they are developing—cognitively, spiritually, socially, and emotionally. Questions are keys that unlock the mysteries of life for them. Children are instinctive detectives and relish the hunt to crack open the secrets that confound them.

Then life happens. We become adults, and mysteries are no longer riches to be unearthed but anxiety-producing worries. We don't tolerate the confusion, sense of insecurity, or ambiguity "unknowns" create. We want to know—and preferably ahead of time.

Life is a mystery filled with ambiguity and contradictions. Once we accept this reality, we become open to probing beneath the surface of our experiences. A door closes, a relationship ends, jobs are lost, children disappoint. The list is endless. But if we view each encounter as an invitation to find wisdom embedded in our uncertainty, our angst about the future will be replaced with quiet hope.

Welcome the questions and thank God for the answers.

Lord, show me, teach me, and guide me. My hope is in you, always. Amen.

OCTOBER 28   WELCOMING DARKNESS

And we, who with unveiled faces all reflect the Lord's glory, are being transformed into his likeness with ever-increasing glory, which comes from the Lord, who is the Spirit.
(2 Corinthians 3:18 NIV)

Life in the spirit has been characterized as an exciting adventure. Indeed, growing in closeness with God is indescribably rewarding. But the Christlikeness that is being formed in us does not proceed along a straight, smooth, or pain-free path. We have to struggle to give birth to each level of intimacy with God, which, in turn, changes us from the inside out.

My favorite image of spiritual growth is the butterfly. According to its own rhythms, the caterpillar weaves a cocoon and creates a place where darkness is a divine appointment. The caterpillar is responding to its inner urgings that signal a call to further its development, to become what it was created to be.

Maybe that sense of restlessness you feel in your spirit is your signal. Maybe God is calling you to create a spiritual cocoon, a place within where you can meet God, examine the urgings that are your heart's desires, and recognize what opposes God's best for you.

Seek to discover the message in the darkness. Listen.

Lord, help me unfurl my wings so that I can soar and reveal your glory within me. Amen.

OCTOBER 29   TRUSTING GOD

When I am afraid, I will trust in you. In God, whose word I praise, in God I trust; I will not be afraid. *(Psalm 56:3-4 NIV)*

When my grandson was a toddler, he loved for me to stand at the bottom of the stairs while he walked up three or four steps to jump into my arms. "Do it again," he would say. It did not occur to him that I would not catch him. He was fearless and absolutely trusted my care for him based on our history together.

God's history with us is incomparable, yet we are challenged to trust God, especially for the "big ones" that only omnipotence can handle. Our history with people failing to keep commitments, to honor their word, or to be there when we really need someone colors our expectation of God. Add to that our inability to forgive ourselves for failures and it is no surprise that fear consumes us when we find ourselves in situations that demand we trust God.

Remember your history with God, not people, and recall all the times your greatest level of need was met. Silence fear with the truth of God's faithfulness.

Lord, whenever I'm afraid, I will trust in you. Your history with me proves you can be trusted. Amen.

OCTOBER 30   RECORDING THE VOICE WITHIN

Go now, write it on a tablet ... inscribe it on a scroll, that for the days to come it may be an everlasting witness.
(Isaiah 30:8 NIV)

It's a simple pleasure to sit and go through old photo albums and reminisce about the stories the images convey. Photographs provide a permanent record of the highs and lows that characterize our human experience. They provide an opportunity for us to share with others moments of great significance as well as times of entertainment and recreation.

Journaling is a wonderful discipline to establish on this spiritual journey. It is a practice that invites us to record the private conversations we have with God and ourselves. Journaling gives us a space to reflect on any aspect of our experiences. Journaling enables us to hear our inner voice with greater precision and remove the residue of wounds, past and present. Ultimately, journaling provides us with a permanent (if you choose to maintain them) record of God's activity and faithfulness and our spiritual evolution.

Begin to journal as a way to contemplate, communicate, and cooperate with the unfolding of your life that continues to reveal the magnificence of your Lord and Savior, Jesus.

Lord, starting today I will talk to you with pen and paper. I will not give in to fear that others will read what I write. Amen.

OCTOBER 31   CONTINUE GROWING UP

When I was a child, I spoke and thought and reasoned as a child does. But when I grew up, I put away childish things. "You will know the truth, and the truth will set you free."
(1 Corinthians 13:11 NLT; John 8:32 NIV)

We tend to think of truth as unchanging statements of fact that provide certainty and stability. In our rapidly changing world, we need something to anchor us—something we can hold on to. But truth is not inflexible. It evolves as we grow; and with each new stage comes an invitation to stretch beyond our narrowly defined comfort zones.

When you reflect on the girl you were, the woman you are now, and the woman you are becoming, you see that how you understand yourself, what you've come to know, and what's important to you have continually expanded. The territory of your knowledge, convictions, and the truths you live by has been enlarged. You are a free woman! Use that freedom to continue growing up. There's more to learn about God, yourself, and the ways your life can influence change.

Give yourself permission to reinvent yourself based on the knowledge and truths that define your being.

Lord, thank you for the freedom to be who I am and to embrace who I am becoming. You are my stabilizer and my anchor. Amen.

November

Giving Thanks through the Stages of Mothering

CLARE GOLSON DOYLE

NOVEMBER 1   IN EVERYTHING GIVE
                                      THANKS AND PRAISE

Then we your people, the flock of your pasture, will give thanks to you forever; from generation to generation we will recount your praise. **(Psalm 79:13 NRSV)**

It is November. Many of us turn our attention to Thanksgiving. We decide what we will do for the holidays. But giving thanks is not something that we should celebrate only once a year. Instead, giving thanks should be part of our daily lives; it should be something that we do over and over again.

As mothers, we have so much to be thankful for. We give thanks for the blessings of our children. We are thankful for both the ordinary days and the extraordinary days. We give thanks for strength and endurance when it seems as though we have virtually nothing left to give.

Throughout November we will be exploring all the different stages of motherhood and ways that we can be thankful in the midst of the joys, the heartaches, the stress, the festivities, and the fun.

Dear Lord, today I give you thanks and praise for your most gracious gift of children and for the joys of the challenges of motherhood. Amen.

NOVEMBER 2   WAITING WITH HOPE

For the L*ORD* *will comfort Zion; he will comfort all her waste places, and will make her wilderness like Eden, her desert like the garden of the* L*ORD*; *joy and gladness will be found in her, thanksgiving and the voice of song.*   *(Isaiah 51:3 NRSV)*

W aiting, waiting, waiting, and more waiting. We had been trying for such a long time. I was ready to be a mother. Naively I thought that the moment I wanted it to happen, it would. I had always been able to figure things out and make my plans accordingly. Why should becoming a mother be any different?

Nevertheless, soon I began to wonder if motherhood could even be a possibility for me. Then came doctor appointments, tests, bloodwork, fertility drugs, and of course, more waiting. Month after month we waited. How could I not be a mother? I had been waiting for this all my life. Why weren't things working out as I had planned?

And then it happened. We were expecting! Why did it have to take so long? Why wasn't God's timing my timing? I don't know, but amazingly the timing turned out to be perfect. I was filled with such joy. I wanted to sing and shout. I had so much to be thankful for. I was going to be a mommy.

Dear God, we are often not able to comprehend what we truly need in our lives. Thank you for your timing. Amen.

NOVEMBER 3   NINE MONTHS OF PRAISE

"And now, Our God, we give thanks to you and praise your glorious name."   *(1 Chronicles 29:13 NRSV)*

F rom the moment we got the news that we were expecting, I was ecstatic. I wanted to sing and shout all the time. Yes, even during those queasy days when crackers and ginger ale were a necessity, I was so thankful to God for this blessing.

At the beginning, nine months seemed like a long time. There were plans to be made. Our family and friends showered us with everything we could need and then some. Those days of waiting were full of expectancy. What would our baby look like? What kind of mother would I be?

Some days passed quickly, and others dragged along. There were only a few choice items of clothing left that I could still wear. My body began to wear down, and I was put on bed rest. But the only thing that mattered was that our baby was on the way. It was a glorious time—a time to be thankful, and a time to prepare to be the best mother that I could be.

Dear God, thank you for the days of preparation and for the joyful expectation of becoming a mother. Amen.

NOVEMBER 4   SLEEPING BABIES

Devote yourselves to prayer, keeping alert in it with thanksgiving. *(Colossians 4:2 NRSV)*

When we got home from the hospital with our precious baby, I spent every minute I could with her. I would hold her for hours while nursing, singing, loving, talking to her, and praying for her. I loved watching her, especially when she was sleeping.

But it was hard for me to put her in the crib. After I would finally put her down, certain that she was sleeping soundly, I did not want to leave the nursery. I was afraid that something might happen. I would stand alert even as I experienced extreme exhaustion. Then my wonderful husband reminded me that our precious Elizabeth was God's child, too. God was always watching her and would never leave her. From that moment on, I was able to relax and get the rest I needed. Each time I left my baby, I prayed diligently and placed her in God's hands.

Although I cannot always physically be with my baby, through prayer I am with her. Even more comforting is the assurance that God is always with her.

Dear Lord, thank you for being a most gracious parent, and for being an ever-watchful presence with my baby and with me. Amen.

NOVEMBER 5   EVERYDAY MOTHERING

Sing praises to the LORD, O you his faithful ones, and give thanks to his holy name.   **(Psalm 30:4 NRSV)**

Some days are just monotonous for mothers. The laundry piles and dirty diapers seem to be the center of life. The baby wants Mommy, the toddler wants Mommy, and sometimes there is just not enough of Mommy to go around.

On some of those hard days when everything seemed to get me down, I would load the children into the minivan and head to town. It was a nine-mile drive, and the children soon began to settle down as they rode along. I would sing and talk to the children. We would stop at a large store and go in, not for a specific purchase, but simply to get a glimpse of the outside world. We checked out every aisle, but I never bought much.

On the drive home things looked different. Everything seemed brighter and fresher. A simple change of scenery made all the difference in my perspective. As I walked into my home, I was once again able to give thanks for the children and for all the responsibilities of mothering.

Dear God, thank you for outings that lighten our loads. Help me to once again be thankful for the responsibilities of my daily life. Amen.

NOVEMBER 6   SICK BABIES

Do not worry about anything, but in everything by prayer and supplication with thanksgiving let your requests be made known to God.   **(Philippians 4:6 NRSV)**

Talk about worry. After our second child was born came the sickness. Sick babies are no fun and can cause a mother more than a normal dose of anxiety and stress.

Elizabeth was three and Allen was just a baby when it began. Elizabeth came down with strep throat. She stayed sick constantly. Then, Allen came down with ear infections. He would take maintenance medicine to keep him from getting an infection, and still he would get violently sick. It was horrendous. Both children were miserable and on a lot of medicine. We lived at the pediatrician's office and at the pharmacy. I spent so much time worrying and praying. Finally, the answer came. Both children had to have surgery, and they would do it all on the same day. We had tonsils taken out and ear tubes simultaneously put in. As both of my children rolled into surgery, my prayers went with them. I received a peace that came from knowing that they were in God's hands.

Dear God, thank you for hearing our prayers, being ever present with us, and easing our worries. Amen.

NOVEMBER 7   PICNICS IN THE PARK

Enter his gates with thanksgiving, and his courts with praise. Give thanks to him, bless his name.   *(Psalm 100:4 NRSV)*

When my children were small, I wanted to do so many things with them. Sometimes it was easy to be creative, and sometimes it was really hard. On pleasant days when sunshine cascaded through the window but creativity seemed beyond my reach, we would drive to the park. Before we left, I gathered baby food, bottles, sippy cups, and picnic food. Then we were off to the park. As we drove through the gates, a feeling of peace washed over me. Allen, Elizabeth, and I would picnic and swing and feel the fresh breeze on our faces. The children giggled and squealed with glee. Life was good. I could feel the breath of God, and I was thankful for his love and care, which reminded me that being still in his presence could indeed be creative—it could be time well spent. Indeed, I felt that I was in God's presence and that I could offer him thanksgiving and praise.

Dear God, thank you for your presence in our lives. Help me take time daily to enter into your courts with praise. Amen.

NOVEMBER 8   SETTING THE FOUNDATION

And they sang responsively, praising and giving thanks to the Lord, *"For he is good, for his steadfast love endures forever toward Israel." And all the people responded with a great shout when they praised the* Lord, *because the foundation of the house of the* Lord *was laid.*   *(Ezra 3:11 NRSV)*

When the children were little, we spent a lot of time in the car. Since Daddy is a minister, much of our family time involved traveling to meetings, hospitals, and conference events. It was the best way we could spend time together as a family. The side benefit was that while Daddy was attending to business, we had a lot of bonding time in the car.

We sang songs. We played name games, animal guessing games, name-that-tune games, and number games. We also spent a lot of time praying together. We spent many hours building relationships. Not only did we have family time, but we also built the foundation for spending quality time together. We built a strong foundation by praying together. I give thanks for hours in the car—hours that the world might consider wasted time—as an opportunity for our family to grow closer together.

Dear God, help me build a solid foundation with my children, and I will give you all the thanks and praise. Amen.

NOVEMBER 9   A SWELLING HEAD AND A MIRACLE

"I will comfort you there like a mother comforting her child." When you see this happen, you will celebrate.
                    (Isaiah 66:13-14a CEV)

The vacation was great, except that Allen's head began to swell. We thought it must have been a bump or a bite. As the day progressed, the swelling continued until his eyes were almost swollen shut. Something had to be done. We were headed back to our vacation rental where we thought we would find a convenient-care clinic.

The road signs showed us which way to go. Everyone felt that the signs were wrong, but we followed them because we were unfamiliar with the area. In a very short time, instead of being close to our vacation town, we ended up in a large city with signs pointing to a great university hospital.

By this time Allen's condition was worsening. We pulled right into the emergency room, where he was diagnosed with a severe allergic reaction, treated, and released. The healing was immediate. We were comforted and astonished at the miracle that put us where we needed to be. We were ecstatic and, oh, so thankful for the grace of God that guides us.

Dear God, thank you for your comfort when we are scared. We are blessed by your awesome miracles that bring healing and hope. Amen.

NOVEMBER 10   PNEUMONIA

I will thank you forever, because of what you have done. In the presence of the faithful I will proclaim your name, for it is good.   *(Psalm 52:9 NRSV)*

We thought it was a stomach virus, maybe bronchitis. Elizabeth had been coughing for a while, but it was nothing serious. She had a four-year-old tantrum and fell asleep. When she woke up four hours later, she had a high fever. We got the fever down, and then the horrendous vomiting began.

We were at the doctor's office early the next morning. He examined her, did some bloodwork, and asked if we wanted to cross the street and enter the hospital in town or drive two hours to the closest children's hospital. I was horrified. What was wrong with my baby?

She had a severe case of pneumonia. We called Daddy, who called the grandparents, and within thirty minutes we were across the street with IVs started. The healing process had begun. It was scary, but with great medical care and many prayers, our little one was healed. It was truly a time to rejoice, for God is good.

When our children are healed, we want to thank God forever.

Dear God, thank you for your healing touch. May we always give you thanks and praise. Amen.

NOVEMBER 11   HAPPY BIRTHDAY

I will praise the name of God with a song; I will magnify him with thanksgiving.   *(Psalm 69:30 NRSV)*

"Happy Birthday to you...." We sang the phrase over and over again. It was another birthday party. This time it was for the youngest. Oh, the hours that have gone into birthday parties—the invitations, the treat bags, the games, the activities, and the piñatas. Oh, and how could I forget the cakes that were baked in the wee hours of the morning? There have been teddy bear cakes, Barney cakes, train cakes, football cakes—you name it. Whereas all of these have been time-consuming and stressful at times, they also have been so much fun. I have been making memories for the children—and for us, their parents. The years that the children will desire these types of parties and homemade cakes will soon dissipate. As they grow older, their desires and needs will change. So I want to play fun games as long as I can. And I want to sing "Happy Birthday" loudly and with gusto as I prepare myself to move into the next phases of my children's lives.

Dear God, thank you for birthday parties; they are truly a joyous time of celebration for the children that you have given us. Amen.

NOVEMBER 12   DUST BUNNIES

Surely the righteous shall give thanks to your name; the upright shall live in your presence.   *(Psalm 140:13 NRSV)*

As a mother, I have received a lot of advice from other mothers. Some I have taken, and some I have just given a quick "thank you" as I discarded the advice. One of the most appreciated pieces of advice I received asserted that I could have a spotless house once the children were grown. Now you see, this was something that I worried about. I wanted to have the perfect home, embodied by a sense of order. But this takes time and energy that I would rather give to my children.

I want to enjoy the children now. I want them to remember playing and reading stories together and going to school programs and community events. I don't want them to remember me as the stressed-out woman who always had something to clean. As my children grow older, we work together to take care of things in the house, especially when we are going to have company. Nevertheless, cleaning takes a backseat to our family time, and those dust bunnies will just have to wait until the children are grown.

Dear God, help me spend quality time with my children, today, while they are a daily presence in my life. Amen.

NOVEMBER 13   TRADITIONS

Hezekiah spoke encouragingly to all the Levites who showed good skill in the service of the Lord. So the people ate the food of the festival for seven days, sacrificing offerings of well-being and giving thanks to the Lord the God of their ancestors.
(2 Chronicles 30:22 NRSV)

Traditions are so very important in our lives. That is one reason we have worked so hard to provide traditions for our children. Both my husband and I are PKs—that is, preacher's kids. Our parents often took us to Lake Junaluska, a retreat center and educational training center for our denomination. When our children were born, we began the same tradition.

We have been year after year after year. We talk about what we did there as children. We tell them stories of their grandparents and aunts from years ago. We eat good food at special places, some old and some new. We take pictures of the children by the roses so that we can see how they have changed year to year. It is a special place that they love. It is a tradition that connects us as a family, and that connects us with our ancestors.

Dear God, thank you for traditions that help us be closer to one another and to our ancestors. Amen.

NOVEMBER 14   MUSIC TO MY EARS

Sing to the LORD with thanksgiving; make melody to our God on the lyre.   *(Psalm 147:7 NRSV)*

It began when the children were little bitty, and it continues to grow as they do. "It" is the music and the musical instruments in our house. We started with toy drums and other musical toys, but as Allen and Elizabeth have grown, so has the collection of instruments. We have pianos, drums, chicken shakes, flutes, tambourines, and even a homemade xylophone made lovingly using wood and wrenches. We have it all.

Sometimes the music is loud. Sometimes the music is squeaky, dissonant, and even grating. But it is always melody to my ears. The children are learning skills that will be important to them all their lives. They also are learning wonderful ways of praising God through music. They have used their voices and our many musical instruments as they have grown and offered praise in church. They are truly learning to praise God through song.

Dear God, thank you for children who can make music in whatever form they choose. Amen.

NOVEMBER 15   TRANSITIONS

But thanks be to God, who in Christ always leads us in triumphal procession, and through us spreads in every place the fragrance that comes from knowing him.
                                   (2 Corinthians 2:14 NRSV)

Many families have to move. We have moved a lot because we are a clergy family. Packing up and moving is simply a reality every few years. It is hard to move, and it has become harder as the children have grown up. Now it is more than just Mommy and Daddy who are affected.

Each time we move, we try diligently to prepare the children. We have books that talk about moving and the feelings that go with that. We talk about the process. We prepare for it. We make games out of it. We cry about it. But in all things, we remind the children and ourselves that it is God who guides us and remains present with us. We are following God's triumphal procession, and God will see us through the change. Even as everything else around us changes, God remains the same. God stays right there with us.

Thanks be to God for seeing us through the transitions of life.

Dear God, thank you for being there with us when we move, and for leading us on no matter where life takes us. Amen.

NOVEMBER 16   A HURT NOSE *AND* A MOVE?

With my mouth I will give great thanks to the LORD; I will praise him in the midst of the throng.   *(Psalm 109:30 NRSV)*

It was one of those days. My mother-in-law was hospitalized, and I had my children plus two nieces. I took the children to a photographer for pictures, where only three cooperated.

Later I took the oldest child to school, my husband headed to the hospital, and the rest of us set out to play at the park. Just as we returned home, there was a message from the school. My oldest daughter had been pushed down the slide and had hit her nose very hard, and now she was in need of medical care. I called the pediatrician, gathered the other children, checked Elizabeth out of school, and headed to the doctor's office. Thankfully, there was not a broken bone—only severe bruising.

But the day was not over. During bath time, the phone rang. It was my husband's supervisor, and he was calling to tell us that in two months we would be moving to a new church. What a day!

Sometimes all we can do is give thanks in the midst of the throng of unexpected events.

Dear God, when we are surrounded by the throng, we give you thanks, for we know that you are with us. Amen.

NOVEMBER 17   TIME OF LOSS

But thanks be to God, who gives us the victory through our
Lord Jesus Christ.   *(1 Corinthians 15:57 NRSV)*

It came from nowhere. It was very unexpected. My close friend,
Mary, knew something was going to happen, but she never
expected this. There had been warning signs, but nothing to indicate that the death of her mother was imminent. The loss of a
mother is so very hard, and it is perhaps even harder when it
comes unexpectedly and without warning.

Suddenly mothering took on a whole new perspective. There
was the personal loss of a loved one, and then there was the added
role of caring for those other loved ones who were grieving. As she
remembered her faith and the promises of the scriptures, she realized that there was hope—and there was victory. Mary remembered that death is not the end and that God would give her the
strength to grieve and to care for the other grieving members of
her family.

Dear loving God, thank you for giving us strength in times of
sadness, and thank you for the victory we have in Jesus Christ.
Amen.

NOVEMBER 18   FUSSING AND FIGHTING

We must always give thanks to God for you, brothers and sis-
ters, as is right, because your faith is growing abundantly, and
the love of everyone of you for one another is increasing.
                                   (2 Thessalonians 1:3 NRSV)

The fussing and the fighting seem to be constant between brothers and sisters. Every time we get into the car, one or the other
child starts a fight. Elizabeth will agitate her brother or just out-
right pinch him. Allen will sing at the top of his lungs—and do
anything he knows will annoy his sister. Whether this behavior is
because of boredom or because of an actual desire to fight is
unclear. In any case, it seems to be a regular occurrence in our car.

However, there *are* those rare moments—those times when they get along. They have times of intensely defending each other against outside forces. Then there are those times when they talk together, tell stories, and play games. Those are times for rejoicing and realizing how blessed it is for siblings to grow in love for each other. It is a brief insight into the kingdom of heaven where all of God's children will get along.

Dear God, thank you, thank you, thank you for those times when my children are truly getting along. Amen.

NOVEMBER 19 SPORTS AND OTHER EXCITING ACTIVITIES

I am grateful to Christ Jesus our Lord, who has strengthened me, because he judged me faithful and appointed me to his service.
(1 Timothy 1:12 NRSV)

As a mother, I believe that one of my important tasks is to encourage my children to explore different activities so that they may find things that help them grow, gain self-confidence, and learn new things. We've tried many things that I am absolutely clueless about. We've played soccer, softball, and baseball. We've done reading clubs and gymnastics. We've done drama, music lessons, special church productions, and band.

Even though we have limited each child to a select number of activities at any one time, it seems like all I do is run the family shuttle. At times I feel like there is simply no time and no strength left—that there is not enough of me to go around. Then I turn to prayer, and I remember that this time with my children is a blessing. God has called me to help raise them, and God gives me the strength I need—even on those days when both children are supposed to be in different places at the same time!

Dear God, thank you for this task you have given me, and thank you for the energy needed to be the best mother I can. Amen.

NOVEMBER 20 THE TERRIBLE, HORRIBLE
HAIR DAY

Be filled with the Spirit, ... giving thanks to God the Father at all times and for everything in the name of our Lord Jesus Christ. *(Ephesians 5:18-20 NRSV)*

"My hair is whacked," said Eileen, my friend's fourteen-year-old daughter.

"How would you like it?" her mother asked patiently.

"I don't know!" Eileen screamed. "It's just not right!"

Her mom replied, "I see you are upset, but your hair really looks great to me."

"NO!" hollered the teen.

"Well, what's wrong?" my friend asked.

"It's just not right."

Isn't that the way it is with teens? Some days they are happy about life, and some days they are down over things that seem unimportant to us. And yet those things are very important to our teens.

How do we have the strength and the courage to face the days when our teens are having a hard time? How do we build them up and continue to help them build their self-esteem? We do it by reminding them that they are so very special to us, and that they are beautiful both to us and to God. Even in the trying times we can give thanks to the Father.

Dear God, thank you even for messed-up bad-hair days. Help us love our teens through these hard days. Amen.

NOVEMBER 21 TEENAGE HURT AND PAIN

O give thanks to the LORD, for he is good; for his steadfast love endures forever. *(1 Chronicles 16:34 NRSV)*

Life with teenagers is a new experience for every mother. There are the usual ups and downs, and then there is relationship trauma. Sarah was concerned about her fifteen-year-old. His girlfriend broke up with him, and to make matters worse, she chose his best friend, Carl, as her next beau. It was a tumultuous time in their household. Dealing with teens and their on-again, off-again relationships can be hard.

For mothers, it is not just the early years that are important in our child rearing. Our teens look to us for acceptance and love, especially when it seems like their worlds are falling apart. This can be trying for us moms, because sometimes we are the smartest people on the planet to our children, while other times we aren't even to be seen!

Perhaps we are like our teens, for we draw close to God and then push God away. Thanks be to God that his steadfast love endures forever. I pray that I can show that type of love to my teens.

Dear God, thank you for your goodness and your steadfast love that sees me through each stage of my life as a mother. Amen.

NOVEMBER 22   THE DIRTY JOKE

Entirely out of place is obscene, silly, and vulgar talk; but instead, let there be thanksgiving.   (Ephesians 5:4 NRSV)

Lynn came home from youth group. It had been a very good night, because the others had finally included her in the after-youth silliness and visiting. Lynn came home excited and eager to share everything with her mother, which she did.

It turns out that the big thing that night had been telling dirty jokes, and one had been laughed at a lot. Lynn had not truly understood the joke, so she innocently told the joke as she walked into the house. Mom was horrified, and Lynn immediately saw the look on her mother's face. Mom quickly regained her control and explained the joke, including how ugly it was to her daughter.

We mothers have so many roles. One role is to explain things with grace and compassion so that our teens understand what is acceptable and what is not. We are the models for helping our teens learn that vulgarity and obscenity are not right. And we can teach them how to live lives filled instead with thanksgiving and praise for God.

Dear God, thank you for giving us composure and words of grace in difficult times with our teens. Amen.

NOVEMBER 23   SMOKING, SEX, AND "OH, NO"

"To you, O God of my ancestors, I give thanks and praise, for you have given me wisdom and power."   *(Daniel 2:23a NRSV)*

Mothering is challenging. There are many hard issues that we must cover. I remember my own mother's talks with us as teenagers. Over and over she would say, "Don't smoke," and, "Don't drink," and, "Don't have sex until after marriage." We would politely say, "Yes, ma'am," and if she couldn't see our faces—and sometimes even if she could—we would roll our eyes. How many times did she think she needed to tell us? We'd heard the same thing over and over again.

Of course, I now owe my mother an apology because I understand why she did it—and I understand the impact that it had on my life. She told us over and over because she was doing her best to protect us, her most valuable treasures. She was teaching us to make wise decisions that not only would keep us safe, but also would keep us healthy.

Mothering at this stage is hard, because we think, *No, that can't happen—not to my baby.* But it can and it will unless we as mothers are diligent about talking about the hard issues.

Dear God, give me the wisdom to say the right words to guide my teens in your path. Amen.

NOVEMBER 24   TALKING TEENS

It is good to give thanks to the Lord, to sing praises to your name, O Most High.   *(Psalm 92:1 NRSV)*

Sherry was always going on band trips, school field trips, and youth trips. Wherever her kids were involved, she was, too. She was always careful to be sure they had the space they needed, but she was always close by. As she spent this time with her children and their friends, she discovered that time in the car or at night just before bed was an excellent time for communicating with her teens. She found that they would suddenly open up and ask questions or share parts of their lives with her.

It was a precious time, and it was time that she was very thankful for. Experts seem to agree that times of quiet and semisolitude provide exceptional times for teens to talk with their mothers. In those rare moments, we have a vital role to hear our children, to truly listen to them. We can be there for them and participate in guiding them toward becoming well-rounded, stable, faithful adults.

Dear God, thank you for quiet times when I can be with my child. Amen.

NOVEMBER 25   SANDWICH MOTHERING

He took the seven loaves and the fish; and after giving thanks he broke them and gave them to the disciples, and the disciples gave them to the crowds.   *(Matthew 15:36 NRSV)*

It had been a hard year. Meg's mother had been critically ill, and the family wondered if she would live. Meg's mother-in-law had fallen and broken her arm and collarbone. Meg's own children were ten, twelve, and fourteen, each with at least three special extracurricular activities. Talk about stress.

It can come at any stage in life—this "sandwich mothering." Suddenly we go from just being mothers to our children to also parenting our parents. Sometimes we feel stretched and pulled in so many directions.

Just as the disciples were concerned about feeding the crowd, so also we worry about how we will feed the hungry who count on us. If we can just remember to give thanks and praise, God can and will safistfy the hunger, the need, in our own lives.

Dear God, thank you for supplying our every need, and for giving me what I need to mother both my children and my parents. Amen.

NOVEMBER 26 LETTING GO

Give thanks in all circumstances; for this is the will of God in Christ Jesus for you. *(1 Thessalonians 5:18 NRSV)*

It begins all too soon. It starts with the baby saying, "Me do," and goes on from there. Carol was amazed at how quickly it had gone. It seemed like just yesterday that her baby was going to preschool and then kindergarten, and now she was headed to college. How could this be? It had only been just a few days.

But that is the way it is. From the moment we become mothers, we have to "let go." The older our children become, the more they pull away. It is a natural fact of life. It is the normal progression. It is what we do, what we plan for, what we make preparations for, what we teach them to do. It is the will of God. That's the way God planned it. Sometimes we are accepting of it, and sometimes we just want to pull our "babies" in close to us and never let them go.

Dear God, thank you for my child growing up and becoming more independent, because that is your will and your plan. Amen.

NOVEMBER 27 COMMITMENT AND A
WEDDING DRESS

I bow down toward your holy temple and give thanks to your name for your steadfast love and your faithfulness.
(Psalm 138:2a NRSV)

My mother was not the kind of mother who pushed me toward marriage or who tried to steer me away from marriage. Instead, she taught me about commitment. This was something I realize she actually had been doing since I was a child. I just began to rec-ognize it after I became engaged.

As soon as we announced our engagement and set a wedding date, my mom started encouraging me about starting life on my own. As a mother now myself, I understand a little more about how hard this must have been. She was letting go of me in a very supportive and caring way. She was setting me free, setting me off to begin my own life. And the most unique thing about it was the day we bought my wedding dress, which was six months before the wedding. As we were checking out, Mother looked at me and said, "This is it; there is no backing out."

As mothers, we have to let go, hard as it is. We have to prepare our children to leave the nest.

Dear God, when my children leave home, help me send them out soaring. Amen.

NOVEMBER 28   PULLED THREE WAYS

We always give thanks to God for all of you and mention you in our prayers, constantly.   *(1 Thessalonians 1:2 NRSV)*

Carol was amazing. It was truly incredible how she could be there with her three daughters at whatever stage of life they were in. Then there was the year that they tested her to her limits. One daughter took a new job and moved about five hours from home. She was out on her own for the first time, and her job was in a community where she often was isolated from other people. Both of the older daughters were expecting babies—both with almost identical due dates in two different states.

How could she be everywhere simultaneously? How could she be the mother that each girl needed? All of her daughters needed her, and she couldn't be with them all at the same time. What she did was inspirational. She traveled between the three while holding down a full-time teaching job. What was most important, however, was that she constantly held each girl in prayer. Even though she could not be with each one all the time, she knew that God could, and that God would provide.

Dear God, today and every day I place my children in your care. Amen.

NOVEMBER 29   SICKNESS AND HEALING

O give thanks to the LORD, call on his name, make known his deeds among the peoples. *(1 Chronicles 16:8 NRSV)*

Suzanne's adult son had been through so much. The darkness of his illness had been almost more than she could bear. She had spent many hours in prayer, asking and calling for healing. Some days she had almost given up, and then there was a glimmer of hope. A friend told them about a new medication that just might work. The doctors started it immediately, and though the results did not come right away, small rays of light began to enter into Suzanne's life. Her hope began to be restored.

Then, after years of struggle, the day came: her son was healed. As he drove away in the car toward a restored and renewed life, Suzanne shouted with joy. She wanted the world to know that God had healed her son. She wanted to make known to all who would listen that miracles do happen.

Dear God, restore my hope when all seems lost, and I will give you thanks and praise and spread the word throughout the world. Amen.

NOVEMBER 30   DON'T CALL ME BABY

How can we thank God enough for you in return for all the joy that we feel before our God because of you? *(1 Thessalonians 3:9 NRSV)*

It started when Jack was born. Until he went to school, he thought his name was Baby. As he grew up, he really did not like the fact that his mother continued to call him Baby. But she did. It did not matter how many times he talked to her; she would not stop.

She called him Baby the day he graduated from college. She called him Baby the day he got married. She called him Baby the day he became a daddy. She called him Baby the day he retired. And to the day she died, in her nineties, she called her son Baby. Baby was in his sixties at that time, but to her, he was always her "baby."

It really is true: our babies are always our babies. We may not call them Baby as this mother did, but they are always ours—and they will always be in our hearts.

Dear God, thank you for the joys and blessings of being mothers throughout our children's lives and beyond. Amen.

December

Noticing God's Goodness

LEANNE CIAMPA HADLEY

DECEMBER 1   SNOWFLAKES

When I consider thy heavens, the work of thy fingers, the moon and the stars, which thou hast ordained; what is man, that thou art mindful of him? **(Psalm 8:3-4a KJV)**

A friend of mine told me how to make a snowflake catcher. You cover a small square of cardboard with black felt and then place it in the freezer. When it snows, you can take this little snowflake catcher outside and catch snowflakes. Because the felt is frozen, the snowflakes land on it and will not melt—at least not right way. So, I made one, placed it in the freezer, and waited.

Finally, it snowed, and my friend was correct. The little flakes landed on the felt, and instead of melting away, they sat there—circles of lace, perfectly formed, more beautiful than I could have imagined.

I was overwhelmed with the beauty of these tiny flakes. I began to think of God, who magnificently formed these snowflakes and who gives us so many beautiful gifts each and every day. During this month, as we prepare our hearts and souls for Christmas, may we busy mothers notice even the smallest gifts that God will bring us.

Dear God, may we find the time to notice your goodness during this month as we prepare to celebrate the birth of Jesus. Amen.

DECEMBER 2   CHRISTMAS LIGHTS

The light shines in the darkness, and the darkness did not over-come it.   *(John 1:5 NRSV)*

It is still early December and already some of my neighbors have put out their Christmas lights. During the coming weeks, my entire neighborhood will be ablaze with lights of all shapes, colors, and sizes. Some have those large colored bulbs, and others have small white lights. Some will place candles in each window, and others will hang a lighted wreath on their door. Each night, those lights will shine in the darkness until the light of morning breaks through.

I, like most mothers, worry about the darkness my children might face one day. I worry about wars, terrorism, and whether or not they will be able to reach their dreams. I worry about them driving on busy streets. I worry about so many things.

Looking at these Christmas lights comforts me. They remind me that no matter how dark the world might be for my children, the light of Christ will never fade. They remind me that God's light is more powerful than any hardship my children might face.

Dear God, whatever darkness my children or my family might face, may your light shine as brightly as Christmas lights in the night. Amen.

DECEMBER 3   HOLDING HANDS

I have taken you by the hand and kept you.
                                   (Isaiah 42:6b NRSV)

My oldest son, Julian, is eighteen years old. We were out shopping at the mall tonight trying to get started with gift buying. He reached over and took hold of my hand. It has been a long time since we held hands. He is much too old and "cool" to hold his mother's hand, especially in public! I noticed how large and strong his hands are. It seems like only yesterday I was holding his small hand to keep him from getting lost or running into the street.

As he has grown, he needs me holding his hand less and less. Now holding hands is a rare treat. I may not be holding his hand and guiding him, but God is. What a blessing and comfort to know that God holds the hands of our children, no matter what their age, each and every day.

God, I thank you for holding the hands of your children, including those who are now mothers. Please don't let go. We need you. Amen.

DECEMBER 4   THE ADVENT WREATH

*You shall love the L*ORD *your God with all your heart, and with all your soul, and with all your might.*
(Deuteronomy 6:5 NRSV)

Tonight I got my Advent wreath out so we could start lighting one candle each Sunday until Christmas. On my wreath there are four purple candles symbolizing hope, peace, love, and joy. In the center stands the white Christ candle. I know that hope, love, peace, and joy will be part of my holiday season. I am also aware that many other things will be as well. Shopping, baking, entertaining, decorating, sending cards, visiting relatives, church activities, and children's Christmas programs and parties will also be part of the season.

Christ calls us to love God with our whole heart, soul, and mind. He calls us to place him in the center of our lives each and every day. Just like the candle is in the center of the wreath, I pray that we will be able to keep the light of Christ in the center of our lives.

Dear God, help us during the busyness of this Advent season to keep you in the center of our hearts, minds, and souls. Amen.

DECEMBER 5   CHRISTMAS MEMORIES

"And if I go and prepare a place for you, I will come again and will take you to myself, so that where I am, there you may be also."
(John 14:3 NRSV)

The holidays are such happy times for me, but they are also sad. I am not sure exactly why, but I miss my mom, who died twelve years ago, so much more during Advent. I miss the smell of her homemade fudge. I miss going home and seeing her Christmas tree filled with the ornaments my brothers, sisters, and I made. I miss opening my gift from her, which was always exactly what I didn't need but wanted!

My memories are filled with the joy she brought to Christmas. I remember her making my costume for the Christmas pageant and the little gingerbread houses she made for each member of my class. I remember how she would take me with her to deliver cookies to her friends. I remember loving to hear her sing carols at church.

I miss her so much and find great comfort knowing that she is in heaven and happy. I pray I am bringing my children the same joy my mom brought me.

God, I won't always be with my children. Help me create loving memories and cherish each moment we spend together. Amen.

DECEMBER 6   THE CHRISTMAS PHOTO

[Love] bears all things, believes all things, hopes all things, endures all things. Love never ends.
(1 Corinthians 13:7-8a NRSV)

My niece, Janell, and I are as close as I suppose it is possible for an aunt and a niece to be. She lived with me during her teen years and is like a daughter to me. Each year until she got married and began to share her time with her in-laws, we spent Christmas morning together. Every year on Christmas morning we would sit next to each other, arms around each other, and have our yearly Christmas morning picture taken. So I have all these pictures with the two of us in the same pose. We have, of course, changed. Janell has grown up; I have grown older. Our hair and clothing styles have changed. But our smiles have stayed the same.

In each of these pictures it is obvious how happy we are to be together. Though we have changed over these many years, our love for each other has remained the same! The love I feel for Janell, my two sons, and my husband is constant and unswerving.

God, I know that your love is even deeper than my love. Thank you for love that never fades—your love that never dies. Amen.

DECEMBER 7   A VISIT WITH SANTA

"Let the little children come to me, and do not stop them; for it is to such as these that the kingdom of heaven belongs."
(Matthew 19:14 NRSV)

Last year I volunteered to dress as an elf and assist Santa at a party for children with cancer. There were more than one hundred children and family members there.

Santa arrived, and one by one the children got a turn to sit on his lap. One little boy told Santa of the difficult year he had had with treatments and hospitalizations. Santa listened as if he were the only child at the party. He knew children were lining up; he knew we had a schedule to keep; but for this moment, this child was his only concern. The little boy had come to Santa timid and sick, but he left with a huge smile, believing he was the most special child in the world.

During the business of the holiday season, I get so preoccupied that I often forget to listen to my own children, friends, and family. If I could give them the time Santa gave that little boy, I wonder how much their hurts, pains, and sorrows would be healed.

God, you are always there to listen to us. May we listen to others with the same care and concern you freely give! Amen.

DECEMBER 8   THE PASTOR'S VISIT

"Whoever welcomes one such child in my name welcomes me."
(Matthew 18:5 NRSV)

When I was five years old, I was very ill and had to spend several days before Christmas in the hospital. In those days, my parents were allowed to visit me for only one hour each day. I was sick, I was lonely, I was afraid, and I was scared. I wasn't sure what was wrong with me, but I knew all the adults were worried, so I knew it was bad!

One day, my pastor came to visit. I didn't know pastors visited children. I felt so loved and so cared for! He gave me a little angel Christmas ornament as a gift when he left. I hung it on my hospital bed, and I knew I would be all right because it reminded me that the angels of God were watching over me.

I will never forget what a difference his visit meant to me. And I still have that little angel. Each year I hang it on my Christmas tree.

God, I pray for the children who are ill or hurting. Be near them and send pastors, parents, and angels to comfort them. Amen.

DECEMBER 9   TIME IN THE DESERT

The wilderness and the dry land shall be glad, the desert shall rejoice and blossom; like the crocus it shall blossom abundantly.
(Isaiah 35:1-2a NRSV)

The holidays are not always filled with joy. I call these difficult years "desert times," when life is hard and joy is difficult to find. About ten years ago, I was grieving the deaths of my parents, recovering from a painful divorce, and raising three children as a single parent. It was a desert year!

My friend gave me a blooming Amaryllis. The box had a beautiful picture of a blooming flower on the outside. Inside was a flowerpot filled with a clump of dirt. I laughed when I saw it. It was the perfect symbol for my holidays—a dead clump of dirt. I watered it and set it in the window, and to my surprise, it bloomed. Like flowers in the desert, it bloomed in the middle of winter—four giant red buds. And my soul bloomed with hope and joy along with that flower!

258

If this is a desert holiday season for you, remember my Amaryllis, or plant one of your own. And remember that with God, even deserts can bloom.

God, the holidays can be difficult times. Where there is hope-lessness, pain, or sadness, may you bring joy and peace. May the desert bloom. Amen.

DECEMBER 10   SNOW DAY

"You shall keep the sabbath, because it is holy for you."
(Exodus 31:14 NRSV)

It snowed last night. I got up early, turned on the television, and heard my favorite words: "District 11 schools closed." It is a snow day! I whisper to everyone that they can sleep in. Then I light a fire, make myself a cup of hot tea, and watch the snow fall. As my family starts to wake, I bake my cinnamon rolls that I always keep on hand for days like today. When they finally get out of bed, the house will be warm and smell wonderful.

Our day will be quiet—no schedules to keep and no one rushing off to work or school. I am not sure why, but we all seem to get along better than usual when it is a snow day. We will play games, watch movies, bake cookies, and relax.

This is Sabbath rest. Why, I wonder, does it take a foot of snow to make us stop, relax, and enjoy one another?

God, in the busyness of life, remind us to create Sabbath time. May we stop, rest, and enjoy one another—snow or not. Amen.

DECEMBER 11   FRIENDSHIP

When I remember you in my prayers, I always thank my God.
(Philemon 1:4 NRSV)

Tonight I am addressing the Christmas cards that I will send to my out-of-town friends. As I go through my address book, each name reminds me of a precious memory. Brenda took such good care of me after my parents died. Lynn welcomed me into her kitchen and let me tell her my deepest fears and secrets while our kids were just babies. Wendy always found a positive side to any problem. The list goes on and on, and with each name I give thanks to God that these precious friends have been part of my life. I pray they know how much I love and miss them and how much their support and friendship have meant to me.

Motherhood is such a special time. We need our friends to celebrate it with. It is also a difficult time, and we need our friends for support and encouragement. We all need one another. We are blessed to have one another.

God, I give thanks for my friends who live close by and who live far away. Bless each of them this day and always. Amen.

DECEMBER 12   THE CHRISTMAS TREE

God saw everything that he had made, and indeed, it was very good.   *(Genesis 1:31 NRSV)*

My Christmas tree is so pitiful. It is old, the branches are bent from years of being put in and out of the box, and it leans to one side. Each year when we put it up, we discuss how ugly it is and how we need a new one. We discuss getting a prelit one, taller and with fuller branches. We talk about how much fun it would be to get a live tree instead of this obviously fake one!

And then we start decorating. We put on the lights my dad gave me, then the handmade ornaments my boys proudly brought home year after year from Sunday school. We find the ornaments that Mabel, a close family friend, made each year. We hang the picture ornament of a visit with Santa on the tree. And finally, we place the angel on the top and turn the lights on.

And behold! It is very good. I guess we will get the new tree next year!

God, our tree is beautiful, but the memories it holds and the times we spend together decorating are even more beautiful! Amen.

DECEMBER 13   HOT CHOCOLATE

My soul thirsts for God.   *(Psalm 42:2 NRSV)*

A long time ago, I found the perfect recipe for hot chocolate. It is easy to make and it tastes delicious. You begin with instant hot chocolate mix and pour in hot water. Then add two chocolate candy kisses and one large marshmallow, and stir it with a candy cane.

After we decorate the Christmas tree, we always have this special hot chocolate. I could make this anytime in the winter, but I only make it after we decorate the Christmas tree. You would think that my boys, including my husband, were still five years old if you could see the way they hover around, asking when it will be done.

Then we gather, say a special prayer of thanks that we are a family and that we are together, and we taste the sweetness. Part of the reason it tastes so good is that it is so chocolaty and warm, but the other part is that we are a family who loves one another.

God, our hot chocolate is sweet, warm, and good, but of course it cannot compare to your goodness. May our souls thirst for you! Amen.

DECEMBER 14   CHRISTMAS CAROLS

Make a joyful noise to God, all the earth; sing the glory of his name.   *(Psalm 66:1-2a NRSV)*

Our church had planned to go Christmas caroling. However, when the day arrived, it was snowy and windy, and my teen boys had more homework than they had expected. We debated all morning about whether it was worth it or not.

I, however, had volunteered to bring cookies to eat afterward, and so I talked my children into going with me. They were *not* happy! They complained the entire way to the church, got angry with me because of my choice of music on the car radio, and told me that they would stand there but I couldn't make them sing! I was thinking, *What have I done?*

We arrived at our first home, rang the doorbell, and our group began to sing. My boys refused to even smile at first, but before we had finished the first song, they were smiling, laughing, and singing to the top of their lungs. They sang the entire afternoon. Singing about the birth of Christ melts even the grumpiest of hearts!

God, what a blessing to sing about the birth of your Son. May our hearts continue singing even after the caroling has ended. Amen.

DECEMBER 15   SLOWING DOWN

Let all that you do be done in love. (1 Corinthians 16:14 NRSV)

It is now ten days until Christmas. I had promised myself that this year I would focus on the meaning of the season and not be distracted by other things. That was my intention, and here I am with a million things that need to be done in the next ten days. I have so much to get done, how am I ever going to find time to reflect on the season?

This is when the words of Paul speak clearly to me. Maybe I need to slow down just a bit and remember who I am doing this for. As I wrap each gift, I can pray for the person who will receive it. As I shop for my Christmas dinner, I can pray for those who will not have one this year. As I bake my cookies, I can thank God for my husband and children, for whom I am baking them. Perhaps I can still get to all that needs to be done and, at the same time, do it with great love.

God, help us do all we do during this Advent season with great love, even if it means we don't get everything done perfectly. Amen.

DECEMBER 16   JOSEPH

When Joseph awoke from sleep, he did as the angel of the Lord commanded him; he took her as his wife. (Matthew 1:24 NRSV)

I set out my nativity set today. I love carefully placing each character in his or her proper space. Mary, the three kings, the camel, the tiny sheep, the shepherd, the manger, and the baby all have a special spot. And last but not least, I place Joseph next to Mary.

Mary gets most of the attention at Christmas, since she was the mother of Jesus. But Joseph was also there. And he doesn't always get the credit he deserves for being man enough to take her as his wife and for adopting this child who clearly wasn't his.

As I place Joseph next to Mary, where he will stand caring for her and watching over Jesus, I thank God for all the men who have helped me raise my children: their grandfathers, their father and stepfather, male teachers they have had, and male friends who helped me while I was a single mom. I thank God for these men who cared for, protected, shaped, and molded my children.

God, thank you for men everywhere who hear the call to nurture, care for, and protect children. Amen.

DECEMBER 17   THE CHRISTMAS PAGEANT

And a little child shall lead them.   *(Isaiah 11:6b NRSV)*

I invited my friend to come to the Christmas pageant at church. She told me that since her kids were grown, she no longer found the plays cute. In fact, she found them rather boring. And since her husband had died, she really didn't care for any of the holiday events. She was too sad to enjoy them. But she decided to go anyway, just so we could spend some time together. We sat waiting for the play to start, and she was clearly bored and uninterested.

We watched as each character entered the sanctuary. Mary and Joseph sat next to the manger; shepherds entered and knelt down; and angels sang. I peeked at my friend, and her look of boredom had vanished. She was actually smiling. By the time we all sang "Away in a Manger," she was crying.

She put her arm around me and whispered, "Thank you for inviting me. This is the first time I have felt like celebrating anything in months!" I responded, "Don't thank me; thank these children."

God, thank you for the voices and spirits of children who can bring the joy of Christmas into even the saddest and darkest places! Amen.

DECEMBER 18   THE STORYBOOK

Come, O children, listen to me; I will teach you the fear of the Lord.   *(Psalm 34:11 NRSV)*

Passages like this one that teach our children to "fear the Lord" are often misunderstood. The word for *fear* did not mean to teach them to be frightened of God but, rather, to grasp how wonderful God is.

I found an old Christmas storybook that I must have read to my children a thousand times. It was worn and tattered because it had been read so many times. The pages were dirty from their little fingers pointing at the different pictures of characters in the story. As I opened it, I could still hear the delight with which they pointed, asked questions, and told me what happened on the next page even before I turned. They truly "feared" the Lord! They marveled at the wonder of God sending us Jesus.

My prayer for us this holiday season is that when we hear the stories of Christmas from the Bible, we will be filled with wonder and awe just as children do as they listen to the story time and time again.

God, remind us of your holiness and goodness as we read and hear the sacred words of the Christmas story once again this season. Amen.

DECEMBER 19   CHOSEN BY GOD

The angel said to her, "Do not be afraid, Mary, for you have found favor with God. And now, you will conceive in your womb and bear a son."   *(Luke 1:30-31a NRSV)*

The angel Gabriel appeared to Mary and told her she was chosen by God to give birth to the Son of God, Christ Jesus. The scripture tells us she was "greatly troubled" when she heard the announcement. She was young, a virgin, and pregnant. These were troubling words, to say the least!

The call of God can be greatly troubling! It often comes, like it did for Mary, when we least expect it, and often God calls us to do things we are uncomfortable with or feel unqualified to do.

Mary was troubled, and yet she accepted what God asked of her. If we pause and listen carefully, there is probably something God is calling us to do. It might feel troubling or overwhelming, or it might even seem absurd. If you feel this way, it is probably God. At least it was for Mary.

God, your call is not always easy. In fact, it can be frightening. Help us listen, hear, and respond as Mary did. Amen.

DECEMBER 20   TRUSTED FRIENDS

In those days Mary set out and went with haste to a Judean town in the hill country, where she entered the house of Zechariah and greeted Elizabeth. **(Luke 1:39-40 NRSV)**

After hearing she was pregnant with the Son of God, Mary ran, not to Joseph, not to the rabbi, but to Elizabeth, her trusted cousin. I can just imagine how she ran to Elizabeth's home, looking for support, knowing that she would believe her, and knowing that she would find care there. Mary was in crisis, and she couldn't get to Elizabeth's fast enough!

Mothers are much like Elizabeth for our children. When they are little and fall down and get hurt, they run to us! When they fail their first spelling test, they run home and tell us first. When they get their heart broken for the first time, our hugs comfort them.

What a comfort Elizabeth must have been for Mary. What a comfort you are to your children! What a blessing Elizabeth was to her cousin Mary, and what a blessing you are to those who need you!

God, in time of crisis may we run to your arms and find comfort and acceptance, just as our children do when they run to us. Amen.

DECEMBER 21   THE JOURNEY

Joseph also went from the town of Nazareth in Galilee to Judea, to the city of David called Bethlehem, because he was descended from the house and family of David. He went to be registered with Mary. **(Luke 2:4-5a NRSV)**

Before Jesus was born, Mary traveled to visit Elizabeth back home, and later she traveled to Bethlehem. This was only the beginning of her journey. She and her family would be forced to flee to Egypt shortly after Jesus' birth, journey back to Nazareth and raise him, and eventually she would travel to the place of his death on a cross.

Her journey, like most of our lives, was filled with happiness, sorrow, and unexpected twists and turns. But one thing was certain: wherever she and her family went, God was guiding, supporting, and watching over them.

Wherever you are in your life's journey—whether you are diapering your new baby or babysitting your grandchild, potty training a toddler or teaching a teen to drive, sending a child off to kindergarten or to college—God is with you and with your child.

Like Mary, our families will experience joy and happiness, heartache and difficulties. But through it all, God is there, just as God was with Mary, Joseph, and Jesus.

God, as we journey through life, through good times and those that bring pain, we give thanks that you will always be with us. Amen.

DECEMBER 22   THOSE WHO HAVE NONE

While they were there, the time came for her to deliver her child. And she gave birth to her firstborn son and wrapped him in bands of cloth, and laid him in a manger, because there was no place for them in the inn. **(Luke 2:6-7 NRSV)**

I wonder what Mary had hoped the birth of Jesus might be like. Did she picture having him at home surrounded by relatives? Did she have a special cloth she had hoped to wrap him in? Did she have his little bed prepared at home?

Whatever her dreams were, I doubt they included having the baby in a barn and laying him to rest in a feeding trough for animals. I wonder where she got the cloth to wrap him in. Was it Joseph's cloak? Was it a rag?

All mothers have dreams—not only about where and how their child should be born, but also about how they are going to care for them. Some mothers' dreams come true, but for some, the dream becomes a nightmare. There are mothers who will find themselves homeless this Christmas and without any resources. Perhaps we can donate clothes, toys, and food for their children, because like us, they also have dreams of a perfect Christmas for their children this year.

God, may we reach out with love, generosity, and deep empathy to those mothers who find themselves in need this Christmas season. Amen.

DECEMBER 23   SHEPHERDS

In that region there were shepherds living in the fields, keeping watch over their flock by night. **(Luke 2:8 NRSV)**

As I write this, it is night, my favorite time of the day. As usual, it has been a long, busy day with school, work, errands, housework, cooking, doing dishes, and helping with homework. I have been the coordinator, the schedule keeper, and the chauffeur. I have watched over the safety and well-being of my family. Now I sit quietly, knowing that those I love and care about are safely tucked into bed, resting. The only lights left on in the house are those twinkling lights of my Christmas tree. I sit, I rest, and all is well.

I suppose the shepherds, who were sitting quietly after a long day of tending their sheep, must have felt much like I do right now. It surely had been a busy day for them; they had worked hard watching over their flock and tending to their flock's needs, much as we mothers do for our flocks. The only lights that shone that night were the twinkling stars in the sky. They sat, they rested, and all was well.

God, no matter how dark the night, your light always shines through. All is well. Amen.

DECEMBER 24   PONDERING

But Mary treasured all these words and pondered them in her heart.   (Luke 2:19 NRSV)

What a wondrous night, the night Jesus was born. Angels sang, shepherds visited, and Mary became the mother of Christ. And she *pondered these things.* I suppose she pondered because there are times when words just can't express the emotions of the moment.

I have had pondering moments. How could I ever describe with words the joy at the birth of my children? How can I tell anyone how proud I feel each time my grown sons hug me good-bye? How could I ever describe the love I felt when my niece walked down the wedding aisle? I treasure each of these moments; but there simply are not words to describe the feelings of love and joy I have felt and still feel as I remember them.

On this Christmas Eve, I pray you might find time to be alone, sit quietly, recall all the joyous moments of your life, and simply *ponder.* Hold each of these precious times in your heart and give thanks.

God, for all the good things you have given to us, including your Son, Christ Jesus, we give you thanks. Amen.

DECEMBER 25   SHOWING OFF

So they went with haste and found Mary and Joseph, and the child lying in the manger.   (Luke 2:16 NRSV)

After my sons were born, we had many visitors—as I'm sure you did when your children were born. And it was always the same routine. We would show them the baby, snugly wrapped in a blanket. Then we would lay him down, unwrap the blanket, and proudly show them how long he was, how beautiful his fingers and toes were, and what fat little legs he had. He was a wonder, a miracle, a gift from God. I wanted everyone to see just how precious he was. I never got tired of showing him off.

I can just imagine Mary and Joseph showing Jesus off to shepherds and kings with the same pride and joy that we showed off our babies.

In the midst of the pain and trouble in the world, birth gives us joy and happiness. The baby Jesus brought hope to a dark world; and in the birth of babies, we know that hope is still alive and all things are still possible. As long as babies are born, there is hope.

God, thank you for sending Jesus, the hope of the world. May the hope never die but continue to strengthen with each new birth. Amen.

DECEMBER 26　　　　SEEING AND HEARING

The shepherds returned, glorifying and praising God for all they had heard and seen, as it had been told them. (Luke 2:20 NRSV)

I remember sitting at my granny's kitchen table as a child and listening while my mom and my aunts told stories about becoming mothers. What excitement, joy, and love they felt! I would listen and imagine myself becoming a mother. I would imagine holding my own baby for the first time. I thought I knew what it would be like to have my own children because I had imagined it so clearly.

When the time came that I actually held my own children, I realized that even in my most vivid dreams, I had not come close to understanding the love, joy, and excitement my mom and her sisters had tried to explain. My feelings were much more intense than I had imagined.

The angels told the shepherds what they were going to see: a babe lying in a manger. But I am sure that they never imagined the joy, love, and excitement they would experience when they actually saw the Son of God. No wonder they returned glorifying and praising God!

God, the life experiences you give us are even more precious than we can dream of. Thank you! Amen.

DECEMBER 27   THE BABY'S NAME

He was called Jesus, the name given by the angel before he was
conceived in the womb. **(Luke 2:21 NRSV)**

One of the most exciting things for expectant parents is trying to
find just the right name for the baby—at least it was for my husband and me. I wanted to give my children the perfect names, and
so I looked in books and discussed it for hours. Finally, a name
sounded like just the right one. We had named our baby.

My sons are named Julian and Britton. They sometimes complain about the names we gave them, but I have to tell you, I think
they are beautiful. I always feel a special tug at my heart when I
hear someone call their names.

We can listen to beautiful music, enjoy the sound of birds chirp-
ing, and hear the quiet sound of the ocean in a seashell. These
are all beautiful; but nothing sounds more beautiful to a mother
than her child's name. How beautiful the name Jesus must have
sounded to Mary and Joseph.

Dear God, the names of our children are precious, but nothing is
more precious than the sound of your child's name, Jesus. Amen.

DECEMBER 28   GROWING UP

The child grew and became strong, filled with wisdom; and the
favor of God was upon him. **(Luke 2:40 NRSV)**

Whereas much is written about the birth of Jesus, little is told of
his childhood. What we are told is that he grew, became strong,
and was filled with wisdom. When my children were little, I was
constantly watching them grow. I tracked it on the little growth
chart my doctor gave me, and I marveled as they grew stronger:
first lifting their heads, then rolling over, and eventually sitting
and walking. I would pray that they would grow stronger each day.

Now that my kids are teenagers, I still pray that they grow
stronger each day. I pray that they are strong enough to resist peer
pressure, make it through their first painful breakup, and make

positive choices with their lives. I used to pray for physical strength; now I pray for spiritual strength and wisdom.

May we pray for our children always, each day.

God, may our children grow strong physically and spiritually. May they be wise, and may your favor rest upon them. Amen.

DECEMBER 29   GIVING THANKS

I give you thanks, O LORD, with my whole heart.
(Psalm 138:1 NRSV)

Cleaning up after the holidays is overwhelming. Did you ever notice how much fun it is to get your decorations out, and how tiresome it is to even think of putting everything away? This year, feeling overwhelmed and tired, I started putting things away and suddenly it hit me: cards, ornaments, candles, and nativity sets aren't just things to pack away; they are memories, gifts from my loved ones, and each one has a story to tell. As I pack away each ornament, I remember the person who made it or gave it to me. The little nativity set portrays the story of Jesus year after year and deserves to be packed away with great care. My Advent wreath has been the center of our family devotions for the past eighteen years. I carefully wrap it in bubble wrap.

Suddenly, I am not burdened or overwhelmed by these things, I am filled with thanksgiving for each memory. I pack them away and look forward to getting them back out again next year.

God, we give thanks for all the memories and joy that celebrating the birth of your Son brings us. In his name we pray. Amen.

DECEMBER 30   SEEKING GOD

Seek his presence continually.   *(Psalm 105:4 NRSV)*

I find the holiday season one of the easiest to keep the presence of Christ on my mind. Even with its busyness, there are always carols about Christ being played, cards arriving depicting his message, and decorations that remind us that Christ is part of our lives. Everywhere I go, something about the birth of Christ is displayed. In my home, the tree, the nativity sets, and the Advent wreath all have reminded me that Christ is the center of my life.

Now that my decorations are put away, I will miss these reminders of Jesus' presence; but that doesn't mean I won't be able to keep him in the center of my life. I will just need to be more intentional about including him in my life every day. Without the carols, cards, and decorations, I will need to make time each day to give thanks, read the Bible, reflect, and pray. As the scripture encourages, I will try my best to "seek his presence continually."

God, thank you for the gift of your Son. May we keep him in the center of our hearts, souls, and minds. Amen.

DECEMBER 31   NEW YEAR'S EVE

O Lord, you have searched me and known me.
                                        (Psalm 139:1 NRSV)

It is New Year's Eve. Tonight, by midnight, I need to have formulated my New Year's resolution. Past resolutions have included losing weight (the top choice for several years!), taking more time for my family, spending more time in prayer, being kinder and more patient, and making more time for myself. Of course, I have never done any of these as well as I had planned to when I proudly announced them; I've had good intentions but little follow-through.

This year I want to make a resolution that matters, and I want to follow through with it! I want to make a resolution this year that will truly make the world a better place. And I don't have a clue what to resolve to do. Where do I begin to make a difference? What can I do to make God's presence known in the world? What can I do that will matter? Is there something God wants me to accomplish this year?

God, you know us better than we know ourselves. Help us choose wisely resolutions that will honor you. Amen.